THEORIES OF MACRO ORGANIZATIONAL BEHAVIOR

THEORIES OF MACRO ORGANIZATIONAL BEHAVIOR

A HANDBOOK OF IDEAS AND EXPLANATIONS

CONOR VIBERT

M.E.Sharpe
Armonk, New York
London, England

Library of Congress Cataloging-in-Publication Data

Vibert, Conor, 1962–
    Theories of macro-organizational behavior : a handbook of ideas and explanations /
Conor Vibert.
        p. cm.
Includes bibliographical references and index.
ISBN 0-7656-1294-1 (cloth: alk. paper) – ISBN 0-7656-1295-X (pbk.: alk. paper)
    1. Organizational behavior. 2. Corporations. 3. Complex organizations. 4. Management.
I. Title.

HD58.7.V53 2004
302.3′5—dc22   2003057376

Printed in the United States of America

The paper used in this publication meets the minimum requirements of
American National Standard for Information Sciences
Permanence of Paper for Printed Library Materials,
ANSI Z 39.48-1984.

∞

BM (c)   10   9   8   7   6   5   4   3   2   1
BM (p)   10   9   8   7   6   5   4   3   2   1

Contents

Acknowledgments

At some point, all good things must come to an end. Writing this book was an exciting challenge. I would like to acknowledge a number of individuals who have supported this initiative.

My wife, Sonia, and our children, Colin, Brendan, Jennifer, and Sean (who was just a twinkle in our eye when I published my first book three years ago), are my true inspiration. Sonia's support and understanding, coupled with the children's love, kept this project moving over four years.

I would like to acknowledge the work of two Acadia University students, Brett Eisner and Kevin Miller, for their support early in this project. I would also like to thank Andrew Steeves and Deborah Hurst for their guidance on the organization of this book and editing of early drafts. More recently, I owe a debt of gratitude to Dianne MacPhee, Jonathan Campbell, and Hope Corkum for their editing and support. A special note of thanks is also due to my editor, Eric Valentine, and my publisher, Lynn Taylor, along with her associate Esther Clark.

Also worthy of thanks are my professional colleagues who contributed chapters to this endeavor as well as personal advice. These include Deborah Hurst, Gregory R. Berry, Jean Helms Mills, and Albert J. Mills. Scott Colwell, Edith Callaghan, Roy Soddaby, Janice Thomas, and Alex Kondra were helpful with insight regarding specific challenges. I would also like to thank Bob Hinings, Royston Greenwood, Danny Miller, and Richard Field, whose mentoring earlier on in my career gave me the idea to pursue this endeavor.

Others offered support in far more subtle ways. They include Maurice Tugwell, Doug Mosher, Orlene Bligh-Coldwell, Michael Leiter, Bill McLeod, Stephen Ash, Kelvin Ogilvie, Janice BamBrick, Delores Spencer, Heather Parrish, Joanne Te Bogt, Wanda Demone, Kerry LaFrance, Rosie Hare, Lisa Davidson, Heather Harvey, Joan Masterson, April Samson, Garry McIver, Cathy Carnegie, and finally, to

Darrell Cook, without whose support this project would never have been completed. To these individuals I offer my thanks.

Conor Vibert
Wolfville, Nova Scotia

THEORIES of MACRO ORGANIZATIONAL BEHAVIOR

1

Introduction

Why do large organizations behave as they do? The question is simple and thought provoking. It is also one that is rarely answered or indeed pursued in a comprehensive manner outside of academia. One need simply ponder the activities of firms such as Microsoft, Nike, Calvin Klein, or the International Olympic Committee to appreciate the significance of this query. An investor in the North American stock markets of the late 1990s and early millennium might also understand the importance of not having seriously considered this concern. Indeed, as never before, the fallout from the dot.com era of investing and the questions of legitimacy surrounding investment community–sponsored corporate research suggests a need to revisit our understanding of why corporations act as they do. It also demands that we reconsider how practitioners, investors, academics, and students obtain and process information to make informed decisions. In short, we need to consider alternative means of undertaking business-related analysis.

This book is a response to that concern. Our readers are academics, business analysts, corporate trainers, students, researchers, and the curious. After completion, readers will note an increase in their abilities to understand complex organized behavior occurring in the private and public sectors. It offers a series of different theoretical lenses useful for explaining one event from multiple perspectives or many events from one perspective. *Theories of Macro-Organizational Behavior: A Handbook of Ideas and Explanations* presents a series of well-established theories of organization and economic theories of the firm. For each of these perspectives, a brief overview of the main ideas is provided, along with an example and a concluding critique. To-

---

Author Note: The section of this chapter entitled "How Exposure to the Concepts of Organization Theory Can Benefit Practitioners" is adapted with permission from Conor Vibert, *Competitive Intelligence: A Framework for Web-based Analysis & Decision-Making* (Mason, OH: Thomson South-Western, 2003).

gether, these components allow readers to improve their understanding of why corporations and other large entities act as they do, while introducing them to leading-edge academic thought.

About Organization Theory

Why are corporations such as Wal-Mart, Dell, and IBM so often perceived as top performers? Organization and business strategy theorists address questions of this nature. As scholars, these individuals seek to understand why organizations look and act as they do and why they are effective. Not surprisingly, among academics no school of thought accurately reflects current thinking on these issues (Meyerson and Martin 1988). As a consequence, there now exists a large collection of scholarly insight that suggests many different approaches for explaining and predicting large-scale organized behavior.

Numerous themes connect the different perspectives that make up this body of research and literature known as organization theory. Noteworthy among these themes is the idea that efforts to improve the corporate bottom line do not always drive the behavior of large organizations. Despite popular misconception, profit is not the sole motivator of corporate and organized activity. Indeed, evidence suggests strong roles for reasons other than improvements to the bottom line.

Overview of the Book

The core of this endeavor is a presentation of the theories that fit under the heading of "organization theory." These theories represent a broad overview of this important field of research and include perspectives originating with European, North American, Australian, and Asian thought. Theories covered range from those with strongly critical slants on the one hand to the more mainstream, less critical perspectives on the other hand. The theories covered originate within fields as diverse as economics, management, psychology, sociology, ecology, anthropology, and political science. Profit-driven economic theories of the firm are covered side by side with effectiveness-driven theories of organization. Following the motto "There is no one best way to organize," each chapter suggests to readers a different approach to understanding how organizations should or do behave. For each theoretical perspective, readers are offered a stand-alone modularized write-up.

This book is divided into a number of different parts. To begin, a brief primer is presented to familiarize readers with the topic of organization theory. We then offer a set of perspectives, each categorized under four distinct headings: "Functional Economic Theories of the Firm," "Functional Organization Theories," "Interpretive and Social Constructionist Perspectives," and "Radical Humanist and Structuralist Perspectives." Since most of the past and present of organization theory is located within the functionalist theories tradition, this part of the book is much longer then the other parts. Meanwhile, the third and fourth parts contain more recent theoretical developments. It is also important to note that this book does not intend to replace the more traditional organization theory text. Instead, this book seeks to provide readers with a broad overview of the field, to be used, if chosen, in partnership with lectures, case materials, and other readings that strive to explain large-scale organized behavior. In this book, we address:

- The main issues confronting organizations
- Why it is important to theorize about organizations
- How these theories are constructed
- The main theoretical ideas within the different paradigms
- How learning is enhanced by looking across perspectives.

Part I: Functional Economic Theories of the Firm

Economists have long held an interest in the behavior of for-profit organizations. Much of their insight has been anchored in a long series of research efforts falling under the heading of "theories of the firm." Theories of the firm refer to conceptualizations and models of business organization conduct. Despite the common use of the expression "theory of the firm," no one conceptualization exists to unite those seeking to understand why companies act and organize as they do (Grant 1996). However, a few ideas are accepted by most academics and theorists. Among the most important of these is the idea that observers can explain and predict the structure and behavior of business enterprises.

Furthermore, agreement probably exists that a theory of the firm should represent an "abstraction of a real world business enterprise designed to address a particular set of its characteristics and behaviors" (Machlup 1980). Economic theories of the firm are implicitly managerial in their orientation, while theorists in this tradition "seek to examine regularities and relationships that lead to generalizations" (Gioia and Pitre 1990). Economic theories of the firm are functional and are concerned primarily with predicting the behavior of firms in external markets (Grant 1996). As such, performance ultimately refers to the bottom line in an environment where the firm is considered a singular decision taker.

In this part, as with the others in this book, we deal with how the theories contribute to macro-organization theorizing. Economic theories of the firm discussed include neoclassical, Chicago School, Bain-Mason paradigm, transaction costs, network perspective, agency perspective, stakeholder perspective, resource-based theory, behavioral perspective, game theory, property rights perspective, knowledge perspective, evolutionary theory, and natural environment perspective, which is authored by Gregory R. Berry. These discussions are found in chapters 3 through 16, respectively.

Part II: Functional Organization Theories

A second category hosts those perspectives that are also functional in nature. Implicitly, theories in this group adopt an orientation that takes for granted the role of managers, while theorists in this tradition "seek to examine regularities and relationships that lead to generalizations" (Gioia and Pitre 1990, 590). Five issues differentiate organization theories from economic theories of the firm. First, the objects of analysis are organizations, not just business enterprises. Second, performance or organizational effectiveness is not limited to the corporate bottom line or externally imposed market measures. It may take on many forms, including survival and legitimacy. Third, organizations are not necessarily considered singular decision takers. Fourth, firms or entities under examination are recognized as organizations encompassing multiple individuals. Finally, theorists of this tradition address the structures of internal organization and the relationships between constituent units and departments (Pfeffer 1982).

Under this heading, in chapters 17 through 23, we address organization perspectives that include those of bureaucracy, contingency, strategic choice, resource dependence, population ecology, institutions, and chaos.

Part III: Interpretive and Social Constructionist Perspectives

A third category of theories fits within the paradigm or school of thought known as interpretivism. In contrast to the oversocialized, passive, determined role-taker presented in functionalist theories, interpretive theories provide for an undersocialized, active role-maker. "This perspective is based on the view that people socially and symbolically construct and sustain their own organizational realities" (Gioia and Pitre 1990). Of importance to theorists of this tradition are the descriptions, insights, and explanations of events that reveal the system of interpretations and organizing processes that are associated with modern organizations.

In this part, chapters 24, 25, and 26, respectively, will consider three important interpretive approaches for organization theorizing: symbolic interactionism, dramaturgy, and the use of metaphors. Chapters 27 and 28 address two newer approaches, the sensemaking and organizational rules perspectives. These are authored by Jean Helms Mills and Albert J. Mills, respectively. Chapter 29 offers a discussion on the culture perspective. As with the others in this book, these theories contribute to macro-organization theorizing.

Part IV: Radical Humanist and Structuralist Perspectives

Radical poststructuralism and humanism are rarely associated with managerial theorizing due to their confrontational and oppositional natures. Yet, a close inspection of the ideas found within these schools of thought suggests that organization scholars do indeed make use of these perspectives to understand many phenomena. Unlike the more conservative thrusts of the functionalist and interpretive approaches, theories in the radical structuralist and radical humanist traditions serve to challenge and critique existing taken-for-granted beliefs, assumptions, and institutions. Radical theories add an important perspective to our thinking about organizations, particularly those who are complacent among us.

Radical humanism is a well-established style of theorizing quite common to the discipline of sociology. When applied to modern organizations, theorists in this tradition seek to "free organization members from sources of domination, alienation, exploitation and repression by critiquing existing social structure with the intent of change" (Gioia and Pitre 1990, 588). Theories found under this heading seek radical change by examining the legitimacy of the social consensus on meaning, uncovering communicative distortions, and educating individuals about the ways in which these distortions occur (1990). From a radical humanist approach, we examine organizations from the perspectives of configuration, postmodernism, and critical theory. These write-ups are found in chapters 30, 31, and 32, respectively.

Radical structuralists share an ideology for change-seeking to remove from society, industries, and organizations the sources of domination forced on lower members of the social hierarchy by dominant elites. The normal operation and makeup of modern corporations and organizations are viewed as dysfunctional and capable of transformation only through conflict and revolution. Not surprisingly, theories found under this heading seek to understand, explain, criticize, and illuminate the dysfunctional areas of writing within this paradigm (Gioia and Pitre 1990). Two important areas of writing falling within the structural side of this paradigm, which are discussed in chapters 33 and 34, respectively, are the Marxist and poststructuralist feminism perspectives, with Deborah Hurst authoring the latter chapter.

How Exposure to the Concepts of Organization Theory Can Benefit Practitioners

Does academic thought matter? Why should professional analysts, business researchers, management writers, and consultants pay attention to the ideas found in this book? Aside from the simple response of "they can improve analysis," a number of reasons can be offered:

- The ideas of this book are the result of observation, data collection, and data analysis. They exist and are referenced because evidence exists to support them. This evidence and the core ideas that they support have passed critical review and are accepted among scholars.
- For practitioners, knowledge of these ideas can lead to a career-related competitive advantage over one's peers by differentiating and enhancing his or her own analysis.
- These theories can help analysts and consultants improve de-

cision making by enhancing the credibility and acceptance of their own arguments by incorporating these ideas into discussions, interactions, and presentations to decision makers and colleagues.

- Relativism suggests that knowledge of any particular event or activity is not objective and universally accepted, nor does it have definite foundations. Picture one company or its actions analyzed through dozens of different lenses. The concepts outlined in this book are these lenses.
- Use of these concepts can also help overcome a researcher's bias toward the use of online information sources. Windle (2003) suggests that many professionals may rely too heavily on online information sources for intelligence needs. Exposure to new management concepts offers researchers and professional analysts a portfolio of mental frameworks with which to position different information strands.
- Fleisher and Bensoussan (2003, 114) suggest many corporate researchers and consultants suffer from tool rut or the overuse of the same analytical tools that in part stems from instruction from accountants and finance professors. The set of theoretical frameworks presented in this book offer analysts ideas to overcome these shortcomings.
- Finally, the breadth of explanations found in this book can also help nascent professionals establish their credibility. Fleisher (2003, 86) suggests that specialized knowledge of other related fields is one prerequisite for a profession. For burgeoning fields of practice, organizational theory can be thought of as a related field (Vibert 2003).

2

A Primer on Organization Theory

Deborah Hurst and Conor Vibert

Picture yourself getting ready to take a Ph.D. comprehensive exam on organizational analysis. The process is probably familiar to anyone who has written an exam to enter a profession such as law, accounting, or medicine. You have been studying for this test in a small room for four months. Yet, six hours from now, you will hopefully be over a major hurdle in your program and all will be well. You will have completed the exam and with any luck you will move on to the next stage in your pursuit of academic or professional accreditation.

In this case, however, before that happens you have a number of questions to answer, one of which is, what is organization theory? Your hard work begins to pay off as a number of ideas jump into your mind. One approach is to simply answer the question directly by providing details in a manner that is comprehensive and concise—a daunting task. With this strategy, the idea would be to clearly demonstrate knowledge of the theories housed within the discipline and to do so in a manner that illustrates the breadth and depth of your competence.

A second alternative might be to approach the task by shifting the focus to the underlying reason why scholars study organizations (Hayagreeva Rao and Pasmore 1989). What may or may not be surprising is that not all authors agree that the purpose of studying organizations is to help increase profitability or effectiveness. You recall the thoughts of one set of authors (Hayagreeva Rao and Pasmore 1989) who suggest four distinct ways to characterize the study of organizations.

1. Organization studies falls under the category of "Social Innovation." The purpose of studying organizations is to improve organizational design and effectiveness. Research is useful and researchers are experts.

2. Organization studies may be seen as a "Critique." Effectiveness is an ideological goal and serves as the aim of dominant corporate and class groupings. Improvements in effectiveness originate in the oppression and legitimization of the status quo. Research is an unceasing critique of power and ideology.
3. Organization studies may fall under the heading of "Hermeneutics." It is nothing more than a discussion of the moral future of organizational research. Researchers are not experts but citizens involved in a dialogue with their fellow citizens. It is neither a vocation nor a critique; rather, it is an interaction.
4. Organization studies may also be viewed as a "Language Game." From this perspective, the study of organizations is a conversation between members of a specialized interpretive community. Scholars are contestants in the game of defining truth and research is a form of play. Knowledge consists of competitive production and justification of claims.

Another approach soon pops into your mind. As opposed to mapping the field of theories, an alternative approach can answer the question, what is organization theory, by mapping the field of research perspectives (Hayagreeva Rao and Pasmore 1989). Researchers are either trusting or suspicious. Knowledge is either an instrument for accomplishing an objective or something we talk about.

Now you begin to gain confidence and with this arises a fourth approach to constructing an effective argument. Your thoughts turn to answering the question by mapping the field in terms of how the theories are built. What are the underlying assumptions that may serve to tie together the seemingly disparate views? You recall that Gioia and Pitre (1990) make use of ideas from Burrell and Morgan (1979) to build such a case. Organization theories can be conceived of fitting within one of four paradigms that are in turn based on different metatheoretical assumptions. Each paradigm generates distinctive analyses that are fundamentally opposite to the other paradigms. When we examine organization theories in this way, we come face to face with the underlying theoretical assumptions.

Unfortunately, an approach of this nature demands a bit of clarification. In particular, the definition of the term "paradigm" is somewhat cloudy. A paradigm, as defined by Kuhn (1962), is difficult to characterize. To understand a paradigm, we need to distinguish what a paradigm *is* versus what it *does*. A paradigm is a significant scientific achievement recognized by a particular community of scientists that provides a model from which springs a coherent tradition of research and general way of looking at the world. Principle functions of paradigms include determining problems appropriate for study, specifying acceptable ways to study problems, and delimiting acceptable types of theories and explanations.

Well-developed paradigms may contain a number of theories that are metatheoretical and that also involve statements about the nature of acceptable theory. Kuhn (1962) uses the following concepts: normal science, anomaly, crisis, revolution, paradigm shift, and incommensurability. Generally, a paradigm is that which precedes theory (or what lies behind propositions), functions as a research program, and implies that theory is not static but is continuously modified by new findings.

With this clarified, it becomes apparent that the ideas of Burrell and Morgan (1979) and Gioia and Pitre (1990) are quite intriguing. They assume that most theories are either subjective or objective in nature. Most theories also explain efforts to regulate behavior or radically change it. Within these parameters, organization theories can be pigeonholed into four categories: radical humanist, radical structuralist, interpretive, and functionalist. It is the underlying assumptions of each of the four paradigms that clearly differentiate alternative theories. These assumptions are as follows:

Functional theories of organization seek to search for regularities and attempt to test for the existence of such regularities in order to predict and control organizational behavior. Theory is developed within this perspective by refinement through causal analysis. New theories are rarely built. Instead, existing theories are improved through hypothesis testing and efforts to falsify them.

Radical structural theories attempt to identify sources of domination and push for large-scale change through persuasion. The way to build a better organizational life is through a revision of existing structures. If a motto applies to this school of thought, it is liberation through structural analysis. Existing institutions and structures are oppressive, and the key to overcoming such oppression is collective resistance.

Radical humanist theories attempt to describe and critique organizations so that change may occur. From this perspective, the key to effective change is to alter the overall consciousness of employees and stakeholders. Researchers within this perspective strive for disclosure through critical analysis. Radical humanists would rarely make use of established scientific procedures such as hypothesis testing and literature reviews. Instead, they would focus on understanding why a particular social reality is constructed and maintained and whose interests are served.

Finally, theorists working under the umbrella of an interpretive perspective seek to describe organizations and explain organizational life in order to diagnose and understand. Within this school of thought, theories are built through code analysis. Efforts are focused on discovering how social reality is constructed and maintained.

With this approach in mind, it becomes apparent that much of organization theory is located within a relatively narrow range of theoretical possibilities defining one paradigm: functionalism. However, not all of organization theory is located here. Increasingly, scholars are challenging paradigmatic boundaries with organizational theorizing.

As you mull over these ideas, you realize that you are able to develop a powerful response to the challenge confronting you. It is now time to roll up the sleeves and demonstrate competence.

We present a number of theories in this volume to whet your analytical appetite. Please note that we in no way intend to be fully comprehensive in representing the different theories. Rather, we provide informative exemplars of different paradigms in an effort to demonstrate the diversity of possibility within organizational theorizing. An undergraduate student interested in more comprehensive coverage should consider volumes that deal more specifically with the topic of organizational design.

Part I

Functional Economic Theories of the Firm

Economists have long held an interest in the behavior of for-profit organizations. Much of their insight has been anchored in a series of research efforts falling under the heading "Theories of the Firm." Theories of the firm refers to conceptualizations and models of business organization conduct. Despite the common use of the expression "theories of the firm," no one conceptualization exists to unite those seeking to understand why companies act and organize as they do (Grant 1996, 109). However, a few ideas are accepted by most academics and theorists. Among the most important of these is the idea that observers can explain and predict the structure and behavior of business enterprises.

Furthermore, agreement probably exists that a theory of the firm should represent an "abstraction of a real world business enterprise designed to address a particular set of its characteristics and behaviors" (Machlup 1980, 25). In other words, they are concerned primarily with predicting the behavior of firms in external markets (Grant 1996, 109). As such, performance normally relates to the bottom line in an environment where the firm is considered a singular decision taker.

Economic theories of the firm exist within the functional paradigm—the lower right-hand quadrant of Burrell and Morgan's (1979) work that is noted in chapter 2. Functional theories are implicitly managerial in their orientation, while theorists in this tradition "seek to examine regularities and relationships that lead to generalizations" (Gioia and Pitre 1990, 590).

The research literature related to economic theories of the firm is extensive and increasingly well developed. Boatright (1996) suggests that the different perspectives that form its core may be characterized under the headings of neoclassical, behavioral, or managerial thought.

The theory of the firm has a long and tangled history. In economics, neoclassical marginal analysis regards the firm as a profit-maximizing unit in order to explain various economic phenomena. For the purposes of such inquiry, marginalists see no need to inquire into the inner workings of actual corporations. Beginning in the 1950s the marginalist theory of the firm has been challenged by behavioral and managerial theories that draw on empirical investigations of corporate decision making. Behavioral theorists (Cyert and March 1963) find that objectives other than profits are pursued by managers; that firms aim at internal efficiency as well as external, market maximal returns; and that even the pursuit of profits is tempered by a willingness to settle for satisfactory rather than maximal returns. Managerial theories contend that non-competitive markets allow managers wide discretion in determining corporate objectives and that some managerial behavior, such as the preferences for growth and risk avoidance, benefits managers to the detriment of shareholder interests. Although these theories are intended to be descriptive, they have normative implication that firms ought to be profit maximizing, even if other factors, lead in practice to other results. (2)

To this may be added perspectives that concern themselves with real-world corporate behavior such as game theory (Axelrod 1980) or those that are influenced by behavioral thought but bear resemblance to Darwinian thought: evolutionary theory (Nelson and Winter 1982). Most economic theories of the firm reject two of the major assumptions that are central to the neoclassical perspective: decisions are made under conditions of perfect knowledge and the objective of the firm is solely to maximize profits (Grant 1996). Like the evolutionary perspective, many theories of the firm, such as the resource-based theory of the firm (Shoemaker 1990), are influenced by ideas originating with neoclassical, behavioral, or managerial thinking. Indeed, the Chicago School theory (Stigler 1968) of the firm and the Bain-Mason paradigm (Bain 1968) exist to counter other economic perspectives (Conner 1991).

Among the most important of the theories of the firm that reject these two assumptions is a group that originates with the work of Coase (1937):

From a Coasean view, the firm is a market writ small in which parties with economic assets contract with the firm to deploy these assets in productive activity. The reason for deploying assets in a firm instead of the market is to realize the benefits of team production through the reduction of transaction costs; but insofar as assets are firm-specific, their holders will demand certain conditions for their participation. (Boatright 1996, 2)

Termed the "modern theory of the firm," this perspective portrays the corporation as a nexus of contracts where firms are more efficient alternatives to market transactions. It also lays the foundations for three different hybrid perspectives: agency theory (Jensen and Meckling 1976), transaction cost economics (Williamson 1976), and property rights theory of the firm (Hart and Moore 1990). Finally, included in this part is a chapter on the network perspective, one that suggests organizations should be thought of as neither markets nor hierarchies.

In this part, as with the others in this book, we deal with how the theories contribute to macro-organizational theorizing.

3

Neoclassical Economics Perspective

Do the terms "supply" and "demand" sound familiar? How about "equilibrium point"? Or "perfect competition"? They probably do and they fit within a school of economics termed "neoclassical" that originated in the late nineteenth century and is probably what most of us think of before we take our first course in economics. Neoclassical theorists focus on marginal analysis of output, that is, the costs and benefits associated with production on a per unit basis.

A neoclassical economy consists of consumers and resource suppliers (Rutherford 1992). Within this context, organizations exist to satisfy the needs and desires of these parties (Conner 1991). Organizations involved in production purchase supplies from consumers and create products. Products refer to the outputs achieved by the many inputs (supplies, labor, technology, and so on) working together. Not surprisingly, from this perspective firms own or have the right to (through contracts) the productive services of these inputs.

Within the neoclassical perspective fits the theory of perfect competition, which is based on the following assumptions:

- An optimal input mix can be determined.
- The marginal contribution (contribution per unit) of each input is easily calculated.
- All parties involved (i.e., suppliers, firms, and consumers) have perfect and complete information and understand this information.
- Resources are completely mobile and perfectly divisible; thus, they are able to be used in the process that will yield the highest value.
- Supply is equal to demand; thus, prices are determined by the market at this equilibrium point. (Milgrom and Roberts 1992)

What many people are unaware of is that there also exists a neo-classical theory of the firm. Demsetz summarizes this style of thinking as follows:

> Neo-classical theory's objective is to understand price guided, not management guided resource allocation. The firm does not play a central role in the theory. It is a well known "black box" into which resources go and out of which comes goods, with little attention paid to how the transformation is accomplished. In the theory's core model, perfect competition, the transformation accords with the dictates of known technology and prices. Management has no real influence. Nonetheless, the firm in this theory and the household too, serve an important objective, that of conceptualizing an economy in which there is extreme dependency. Production takes place in firm. Consumption and resource supply take place in households. People must depend on each other, and self-sufficiency is thus barred. Multi-persons firms are not needed to play this role. A farm is a firm whether owned and worked by a single person or by many, if its crop is produced for the market rather than for those who have produced it. (1997, 1)

According to this perspective, all industry participants are identical because of perfect information and perfect allocation of resources (Conner 1991). Stated a different way, every firm has equal access to the same productive technology, information, and resources that are perfectly mobile and divisible. This ensures that each firm in an industry will be able to obtain exactly the right inputs to produce the desired outputs.

If each individual firm is able is to maximize its profits, and all firms are identical, a market equilibrium of zero economic profit results for each firm in the industry (Milgrom and Roberts 1992). Economic profit is different from accounting profit in that it indicates above normal returns for a firm in an industry. This, again, is because all firms are equally able to team the proper inputs, and therefore there is no competitive advantage for any one firm.

The size of the firm is bounded by the assumption of diminishing marginal returns (Conner 1991). That is, at some point it becomes more costly (on a per unit basis) to produce one more unit of a good. At this point, the firm has achieved its most efficient level of production. In perfect competition, this level of production is very small relative to the size of the market; thus, many firms can (and must) successfully produce to meet the demands of the market.

Of course, it is almost impossible to find firms whose behavior conforms to the neoclassical model. And why is this? Well, first, in most industries there exist firms with market power that set prices that other firms follow. This contradicts the assumption that the market sets the price at the equilibrium of supply and demand. Second, economies of scale play a role. In real-life cases, an increase in inputs of X percent yields a return for the firm greater than X percent. This contradicts the theory of diminishing marginal returns, which states that firms would be bounded to a certain level of output (Conner 1991). Third, externalities may play a role. Externalities are events that affect parties other than those involved in the market of certain firms. An example is environmental damage by a firm involved in production. When externalities exist, there is some cost or benefit involved that is not accounted for. This leads to misrepresentation of the actual equilibrium point of an economy. Finally, a fourth reason is that most firms encounter searching, matching, and coordination costs. These are costs associated with finding the right product, person, or price in an economy. In the perfect competition model, these costs would be nonexistent as all parties have full information on all the players in an economy (Milgrom and Roberts 1992).

Other more abstract and advanced discrepancies exist; however, these examples demonstrate some of the fundamental reasons for the failure of the neoclassical system. Other critics claim that a system of perfect competition does not necessarily lead to an efficient system. Indeed, adherents of the Chicago School perspective might suggest that a state of efficiency can exist under imperfect competition. Furthermore, "neoclassical theory has no serious treatment of business ownership" (Demsetz 1997, 3) and it offers no productive role for management. In other words, it does not explain economic organization and it lacks realism (Williamson and Winter 1993, 183).

To conclude, there is one powerful reason why readers should pay attention to the insights of neoclassical economics. Most economic theories of the firm respond to this model either explicitly or implicitly. It is this and other views of organized behavior that they wish to displace.

4

Chicago School Perspective

Do the names Frederick Hayek or Milton Friedman sound familiar? Some of you may recognize them as influential figures in the world of economics and public policy. They are also among a group of economists whose insights have helped to put the University of Chicago's School of Economics on the map as perhaps the most influential in the world in recent years. Just count the number of Nobel laureates on staff and you will see why.

Work originating with the Chicago School emerged to blunt public policy initiatives arising from Bain-Mason type of industrial organization economics. Work in this latter area had emphasized, among other things, the role of barriers to entry as a means to suppress competition within industries. It suggested that the key to long-term profitability and growth was participation in an industry, not necessarily competitive behavior (Barney 1986). This thinking had guided public policy in many areas of the United States in the years following the Great Depression. Unfortunately, in many industries the result was a dominance by a group of large corporations that were neither very innovative nor very well managed.

Theorists of the Chicago School wanted to get back to the basics and talk about the effects of the market and prices on future corporate and industry success. They wanted to understand and encourage competition—not block it—because they believed that competition based on price and market dynamics was healthier for the economy in the long run than the protectionist slant of the Bain-Mason type of industrial organization paradigm. If a goal existed, it was to help profit-maximizing firms overcome certain kinds of cost impediments. In order to build a case for themselves, they developed an alternative explanation of why companies grow—one that is now the predominant viewpoint in the field of economics.

Much of the seminal work of the Chicago School perspective, as it relates to a theory of the firm, can be credited to Stigler (1957, 1961) and, as Conner (1991) suggests, some key points are implicitly suggested as opposed to explicitly stated. From this perspective, firms exist to enhance efficiency in production and distribution (1991). In a perfect world, it is in the best interests of industry players to collude in order to grow their profits. Indeed, when allowed to do so the combined profits of all firms in an industry will be maximized. In other words, as opposed to battling among themselves it really is in the best interest of the industry leaders to work together and act as one big monopoly.

Unfortunately, because of a historical lack of trust, pulling off something like this is quite costly. Actually, it is too costly. Most firms will try to take advantage of any loopholes in their agreement to further their own best interests, or they will simply work to the letter of their agreements and no more. Thus, any gains made by working together will be offset by the costs of monitoring each other and enforcing previously agreed on behavior. As a result of these high costs, effective collusion is not likely to persist.

If this is true, then how do companies attain above-average profits? Chicago theorists suggest that it is because some firms are more efficient in their means of production and distribution than their rivals or competitors. The size and scope of a firm is determined by its efficiency. Accordingly, if a firm can make efficiency gains, it will grow; if not, it will shrink as competitors erode its source of competitive advantage (Conner 1991). This is the major implication of this perspective.

Underlying this view is an awareness that each company uses a different set of inputs that it uses to produce a different set of outputs. Furthermore, different competitive forces act in different ways on each firm to make the acquisition and transformation of the inputs a nontrivial matter. This view also suggests that the key role played by new entrants to an industry is that of imposing the need for efficiency on established firms. An important underlying assumption is that the possession of specific information matters. Those that have pertinent information are able to accomplish tasks that those without are not able to do. There are advantages in knowing how to become more efficient and this knowledge gives some firms power. New entrants typically possess such knowledge and it is they, through their drives for efficiency, that dictate which firms will prosper. Those that do not become efficient with their means of production and distribution will earn lower long-run profits than those that do.

One last point is also quite important. The Chicago School emphasizes the importance of the natural movement of firms toward equilibrium. In other words, although a new entrant might have an initial advantage in terms of efficiency, many of its competitors will imitate it over time. Soon, they will become just as efficient and with that the playing field will return to normal (Conner 1991). Furthermore, none of the firms in the industry will enjoy above-average profits until a new entrant again sets a new benchmark for efficiency.

One application of this idea falls under the concept of breakpoint analysis. An industry breakpoint is

> a new offering to the market that is so superior in terms of customer value and delivered cost that it disrupts the rules of the competitive: a new business system is required to deliver it. The new offering typically causes a sharp shift in the industry's growth rate while the competitive response to the new business system results in a dramatic realignment of market shares. (Strebel 1992, 543)

Identifying product offerings ahead of time that may prove to underpin a breakpoint is a difficult task. Organization analysts will often seek to simplify this challenge by looking for common indicators that signal the coming onset of an industry transformation. Of use are signals that an industry's products or services are either diverging away from a dominant offering or converging toward a common denominator (Strebel 1992). A classic example of a divergent breakpoint product offering is the Netscape Navigator browser. A product that emerged from a period of convergence was the IBM personal computer.

To suggest that thinkers from the Chicago School have been influential would be an understatement. That their ideas have been of benefit to all is somewhat debatable. The ideas of this perspective are worthy of criticism. Three in particular are important to note. First, underlying this perspective is the notion of the market and its forces as dominant. Unfortunately, recent events suggest that this may not be the case. The dot.com meltdown, Wall Street brokerage scandals, Enron, and the events of September 11, 2001, suggest a powerful role for governments and political events:

> The new reality is most broadly manifested in the stock market. . . .
> Try as you might to predict the future with discounted-cash-flow mod-

els or technical charts or quantitative analysis, it is no use. A single bomb detonated by a lunatic in a city thousands of miles away makes all of your calculations redundant. You can't predict political events, and such events are dominant. (Den Tandt 2002, B9)

Second, the efficiency to which it speaks is unquestioned and narrow in scope. Inefficiency is associated with waste and the forces of the market are assumed to be the instruments for removing such waste. "Unfortunately the marketplace also creates waste through its notoriously short memory, difficulty thinking through more than a few months ahead and a chronic weakness for fashion which like the shapes of shoe-heels can come and go abruptly" (Saul 1994, 173). From this perspective, it is private organizations that champion efficient operations. "Yet it would be hard to imagine operations more efficient than most state-owned utilities. They deliver water and energy, collect sewage and garbage, maintain transportation infrastructure and generally make the lives of tens of millions of people possible in a relatively smooth and invisible manner" (172).

Third, within the broader context of research falling under the umbrella of the Chicago School, there is surprisingly little work on the topic of a theory of the firm. As Conner (1991) notes in her interpretation of Stigler's (1961) work, many of the ideas presented are implicitly assumed as opposed to explicitly stated. Finally, social and cultural factors are mostly ignored as are the roles of actors operating within organizations. As never before, the Chicago School has pushed many to ask: Should efficiency be used as it is now in many cases, as the paramount criteria for decision making? The Chicago School is somewhat silent in this regard. Unfortunately, what is forgotten by many individuals is that much of the work of this esteemed institution is just that—*theory*.

5

Bain-Mason Perspective

Toyota, Nissan, Hyundai, and Honda. The names are familiar and so are the cars. However, they and their predecessors were not always so. Indeed, only a few decades ago, rare was the appearance of an Asian-built car on the roads of North America. Surely it was a quality issue. Or, maybe manufacturers like Ford, General Motors, Chrysler, and American Motors simply priced their products more attractively. If not, then obviously these latter auto producers were more effective advertisers. Of course, the real story is somewhat different. The theory behind the behavior of the old auto industry and others like it is the topic of this chapter.

Does the term "industrial organization economics" ring a bell? It should, as the logic behind this thinking was among the most influential in the Western business world over the last five decades. Researchers in this tradition concern themselves with "how productive activities are brought into harmony with society's demands for goods and services in an organizing mechanism such as the free market and how variations and imperfections in the organizing mechanism affect the degree of success achieved by producers in satisfying society's wants" (Scherer 1980, 25).

The industrial organization model was originally developed to assist government policy makers in formulating economic policy, beginning as a response to the catastrophic effects of the Great Depression of the 1930s. Within this context, economic theorists had sought to develop models to assist firms in obtaining greater than normal economic returns on their business investments. What is now a vast body of intellectual insight was not originally an overly complicated theory. It became known as the structure-conduct-performance model.

> Industry structure determined the behavior of firms whose joint conduct then determined the collective performance of the firms in the marketplace (Bain 1968; Mason 1957). Performance was broadly defined and in the economist's sense of social performance, encompassed dimen-

sions of such as allocative efficiency (profit), technical efficiency (cost minimization), and innovativeness. Conduct was the firm's choice of key decision variables such as price, advertising, capacity, and quality. Thus in policy terms, conduct could be viewed as the economic dimension of firm strategy. Finally, industry structure was defined as the relatively stable economic and technical dimensions of an industry that provided the context in which competition occurred (Bain 1972). . . . A final crucial aspect of the Bain-Mason paradigm was the view that because structure determined conduct (strategy), which in turn determined performance, we could ignore conduct and look directly at industry structure in trying to explain performance. (Porter 1981, 611)

Among the major findings of scholarly research in this area was that industries with large barriers to entry, with a small number of firms, with a large degree of product differentiation, or with low demand elasticity are characterized by firms earning higher returns than firms in industries without these attributes (Scherer 1980).

The implications suggested by theorists of this tradition were fairly simple (Barney 1986). Firms seeking to obtain high returns should focus on creating and/or modifying the structural characteristics of their industry to favor high returns. Firms seeking high performance would be rewarded for their participation in the right industry. If industry profits were high, all would benefit. Thus, any attempts to alter industry structure should be blocked. Blocking adversaries or protecting high-industry profits meant creating high barriers to entry, reducing the number of firms in the industry, increasing product differentiation, or reducing demand elasticity. In a nutshell, the aim of organized behavior from this perspective was to shield the firm to the maximum extent legally possible from competitive forces (Porter 1980).

Reading between the lines, this style of business operation was, if anything, anticompetitive (Teece 1984). Profits and revenues could be grown by blocking new firms or by lobbying the government to keep out new adversaries. Actually developing new and innovative products and services was not necessary as long as each firm kept to its own turf. While highly effective in the protected competitive environments of the 1950s and 1960s, the societal changes of 1980s and 1990s pushed this style of thinking into obsolescence. Why did new schools of thought replace the Bain-Mason paradigm or at least arise to offer alternative lenses for understanding how corporations should compete and why they behave as they do? Why did many corporate and academic adherents of this powerful theory look for different explanatory frameworks to guide their thought processes? One need simply return to the example of the North American auto industry and the seemingly endless erosion of market share of U.S. car manufacturers to grasp the cost that is still being paid for previously protected operating environments.

The advent of the Internet, the impact of technology, the increase in the speed of communication and product innovation, the loosening of national borders to increased trade, the economic success of foreign countries such as Japan and Korea, and a growing acceptance of globalization and freer trade among nations have all served to push economists to build new theories to help us understand our complicated world.

Despite its position as one of the dominant paradigms of recent history, industrial organization economics, in its original forms, has many defects (Teece 1984). Research in this tradition has been fairly static and mathematical and has offered few insights into the important area of change management and how organizations adapt. It has also been silent in regard to the effects of bureaucracy on success and failure. Indeed, the internal workings of contemporary organizations have been treated, for the most part, as black boxes. The Bain-Mason paradigm also "assumes a one-way causal relationships from the market structure to the performance variable," yet "the causal relationship may just as well go the other way—from profitability to market structure" (Tsoukas and Knudsen 2002, 420).

Porter (1981, 612) suggests other shortcomings. Theorists of this tradition conceive of the industry as the unit of analysis and of firms as identical. The firm in question is freestanding, thus ignoring the multidivisional features of many large entities. The structure of the industry in question is stable and it determines the performance of the corporation in question. Firms are not assumed to be capable of altering the outlook of their competitive environment. Also taken for granted is the view of a firm as a unitary decision-making unit, ignoring the internal struggles that characterize most organizations. In other words, for the most part it ignores the influence of individual insight and interpretation on competitive and environmental forces.

6

Transaction Cost Perspective

Cool summer evenings are a good time to think and stargaze. On such occasions, one often ponders life's anomalies such as why military hammers can cost as much as $400 to build or why air force toilet seats can put tax payers back a cool $3,500. For those engineers among us, the Big Dipper may induce queries such as: Which firms can truly build or at least manage the construction of a modern nuclear-powered aircraft carrier or attack submarine? Pentagon planners and an economic theorist or two were also interested in such oddities just a few years ago and set out to explain their occurrence. This subject is the topic of this chapter.

Since the writings of Adam Smith, an assumption among many economists has been the primacy of market forces or the "invisible hand" for managing the conduct of business between the major institutions of capitalism. Left to its own devices, the free market would serve to effectively organize transactions among firms in the most efficient manner. Unfortunately, real-world dynamics proved that even when left to their own devices, some markets do indeed fail.

Not surprisingly, as with any powerful theory, a number of thinkers have come to criticize this approach as incomplete. John Maynard Keynes is perhaps the most famous of such doubters. The founder of what is known as Keynesian economics, this scholar suggested that the forces of the market should not be left to their own devices and that government had an effective role to play in economic life.

Others took a different track in their efforts to solve the puzzle of market failure. Market failure refers to a situation where transaction costs become excessive. The result of market failure is that too few companies or individuals participate in the market (Geroski 1997). The U.S. government and its major defense contractors faced such a situation beginning in the late 1960s as they began to observe a decrease in the number of corporations that could seriously bid on major contracts. They discovered that as each generation of tank or airplane was developed, fewer and fewer players stayed in the game. Furthermore, as the products and services increased in complexity, contractors found themselves dealing with cost overruns that were difficult to control as well as with technologies that they did not necessarily understand.

Williamson (1975) responded to concerns such as this by building an economic theory that seeks to guide managers in their efforts to organize in an optimal manner. He suggests that one means to address market failure is for managers to choose between the internal organizing features of a bureaucracy or those of the market when attempting to control important economic transactions. His logic provides a framework for outsourcing and vertical integration decisions. Its implication for managers and theorists is blunt. An organization will change its structure in response to a problem. Recognize the problem and one might be able to predict an outcome.

Williamson (1976) defines transaction costs as the costs of operating the economic system or the costs of consumption over and above the purchase price of a product or service (Geroski 1997). Transaction costs arise principally when it is difficult to determine the value of the goods or service being produced or provided. They can arise either because the nature of the good or service is complex or because the exchange partner—the other firm—is untrustworthy. Williamson summarizes his theory as follows:

> Markets and firms are alternative instruments for completing a related set of transactions. Whether a set of transactions ought to be executed across markets or within a firm depends upon the relative efficiency of each mode. The costs of writing and executing complex contracts across a market vary with the characteristics of the human decision makers who are involved with the transaction on the one hand and the objective properties of the market on the other. Although the human and environmental factors that impede exchanges between firms (across a market) manifest themselves somewhat differently within the firm, the same factors apply to both. (1985, 41)

Central to this explanation is the difficulty of writing and enforcing contracts under uncertainty. Transaction cost theory is based on two behavioral assumptions. First, actors are boundedly rational, that is, intentionally rational, but only in a limited sense. Second, actors are opportunistic—they pursue self-interest with guile.

In addition to these assumptions, three conditions must be present before a firm will prefer internalizing a transaction over contracting for the transaction: a high level of uncertainty must surround the transaction, assets involved in the transaction must be highly specialized to the transaction, and the transaction must occur frequently (Williamson 1975).

The logic of transaction cost economics can be summarized as follows. A high level of uncertainty regarding future outcomes makes it extremely costly, if not impossible, to write and enforce a contract that specifies all possible future conditions. Designing a complete contract is further hampered by the bounded rationality of the actors involved, but with an incomplete contract the actors in the contract cannot be trusted to remain true to their originally declared intent; instead, they will act opportunistically and exploit any gaps in the contract. If the contract involves a high level of assets specialized to the contractual relationship, the difference between the value of these assets, when employed in their present activities and their value in the next best use, represents a sunk cost if the other firm walks away from the contract. The first firm, therefore, becomes locked in and bears the transaction costs resulting from its partner's opportunistic behavior. These costs will be greater when the transaction is frequent. When a transaction involves high levels of specialized assets, is highly uncertain, and is frequent, the transaction costs associated with contracting will be high enough to dictate internalization. On the other hand, when transactions occur infrequently, involve highly certain outcomes, and do not involve specialized assets, the market will be a more efficient means of lowering transaction costs.

As noted earlier, transaction costs are often significant and can vary in dollar value because of opportunistic behavior. Opportunistic firms either shirk or adopt holdup behavior (Williamson 1985). Shirking behavior occurs when the seller of a product or service has more information about it than does the buyer and may opportunistically misrepresent its value either in terms of quality or the amount of labor needed. Actions necessary to reduce shirking incur search costs, negotiation costs, monitoring costs, enforcement costs, and a residual loss. Holdup is another concern and refers to just that—conscientious attempts to hold up work. This leads to one of two results: investments in production or service development may simply be decreased, or expensive investments may be made toward efforts to prevent holdup. These solutions include making credible commitments, "exchanging hostages," and negotiating, monitoring, and enforcing contracts.

Criticisms of transaction cost economics are numerous. First, the theory is pessimistic in regard to managers and their behavior (Donaldson 1990; Moran and Ghoshal 1996). Indeed, managers are not considered trustworthy. Sadly, this ignores the idea that these individuals may indeed act in the best interests of their employer. Second, an assumption that may be incorrect is the role of the market as the natural medium of the transaction (Donaldson 1995). Third, transaction cost theorists may oversimplify the challenges facing organizations (Donaldson 1995). Indeed, in a knowledge-based economy, one might ask how important transaction costs are for corporate prosperity. Fourth, the theoretical foundation of this perspective ignores much of the previous theorizing and research on the topic of management and organizations (Donaldson 1995, 178). Fifth, the theory is ill equipped to deal with a major corporate concern of the new millennium: a corporate desire for ongoing employee learning or continuous improvement. Indeed, what a contract's perspective fails to address is the question of how one contracts for learning. Sixth, this perspective suggests that organizations are formed in response to a problem (Tsoukas and Knudsen 2002). This thinking ignores the role of historical development or ongoing actions by the corporation and its managers to prosper and grow.

Finally, along with other economic theories of the firm, transaction cost economics may be irrelevant in the eyes of practitioners.

> We believe that major source of the growing gulf between theory and practice lies in the lack of realism and balance in most theories. . . . [F]or any theory to be useful, the theory's "use in practice" must be considered but this is rarely done. . . . [M]anagement scholars have increasingly turned a blind eye to the extreme stylization and sweeping assumptions in the ideas that they have borrowed from different disciplines to analyze managerial and organizational issues. It is not just that the ideas we have borrowed are ideal; they are also biased. . . . [T]heories of today are dominated by a profoundly pessimistic view of organizations, concerned far more about unintended consequences of organizing than about organizing for their intended purpose, and by an even more skeptical view of individual-organization interactions grounded in an assumption that the human role in organization is largely passive and frequently pathological. (Moran and Ghoshal 1996, 70)

7

Network Perspective

It was a beautiful beach day on the south coast of Nova Scotia as Jill Hiscock sat watching the waves and pondering the events of the past decade. Now a successful exporter of apple products, Hiscock realized that she could never have done it without the help of friends, family, and a few timely introductions. In the early 1990s, she was looking for a career and wondered if she could take advantage of the agricultural opportunities surrounding her home in one of Canada's three fruit growing regions, the Annapolis Valley. Having lived previously in the western Canadian city of Calgary, she was amazed that many of the tasty food products sold at local farm markets and taken for granted by many Nova Scotians were not available throughout North America. With no dependents at the time, she set out on an entrepreneurial odyssey hoping to make a living as an exporter.

Her first challenge was to find exportable products. This she accomplished by visiting the local farm markets and talking to the farmers who in turn put her into contact with local small producers. With a portfolio of interested producers, she then set out to learn about running a business. Her initial steps were suggested by a neighbor who knew that the local university offered a small business counseling center. A visit to the center opened the door to a number of other critical connections. Registering as a company was suggested. A second neighbor, an accountant by training, suggested the sole proprietor route. Writing a business plan was also suggested. A visit to the four local banks provided her with the forms and instructions to write the plan. Despite a rejection from all four banks for a loan, a cousin was impressed enough by the plan to provide start-up funding.

Having no experience in the export market, Hiscock faced two other major challenges. How to identify an initial target market was dealt with in the business plan. The university counseling center suggested the services of the MBA student consulting center of another regional university. With the help of the students at the center, she had the market targeted within a month. With a business plan, suppliers, and initial funding in place, a business professor acquaintance suggested a next step of addressing the specific mechanics of exporting products to the United States. He pointed her to an export trade commissioner employed in the regional office of the Canadian government. Six months later, the first of her products were for sale on shelves throughout the southern United States.

Aside from telling the story of a successful but fictitious small exporter, this vignette emphasizes the role of networks in helping many organizations and businesses to succeed. The study of organizational networks has attracted the attention of analysts, practitioners, and observers of corporate behavior for a number of reasons (Nohria 1992). First, technological advances in manufacturing and communications, most notably the Internet, have increased the complexity of corporate relationships. This has drawn the attention of researchers to the ideas of network analysis as a means of making sense of these complexities. Second, the tools and processes of the network approach have become both fashionable and accepted in academic circles. Third, the nature of competition has changed in the last decade or so. Competitors in many industries can now be found throughout the world and are often located in geographic clusters such as the North Carolina Research Triangle. They can take many different forms including alliances and joint ventures, and can be of different sizes ranging from subsidiaries of multinationals to entrepreneurial start-ups. Indeed, one need simply ponder the players found in a typical industry and consider the firms and organizations that participate as suppliers, customers, distributors, competitors, regulators, auditors, marketers, and advertisers. Then consider the decision makers in each of the major players. Individually, they have their own set of personal relationships that include coworkers, friends, professional contacts, alumni colleagues, and so on. Together, these individuals and organizations comprise a social context, one that is increasingly difficult to ignore when considering how and why corporations, small businesses, and institutional players act and behave as they do.

This leads to a general statement that underlies much of recent work on the network perspective, at least as it relates to an organization's position among others. "Network perspectives build on the general notion that economic actions are influenced by the social context in which they are embedded and that actions can be influenced by the position of actors in social networks" (Gulati 1998, 295). In other words, work-related transactions tend to overlap with patterns of social relations (Granovetter 1985). For example, an owner of a horse ranch that boards thoroughbred race horses may choose to hire stable hands through references of friends and business associates rather than through the open market.

That corporations and other organizations are embedded in a social context is among the most important building block of insight related to the network perspective. Underlying research on this topic is the notion that networks arise when individuals, whether organizations or humans, interact (Tolbert et al. 1995, 343). Why might they arise? One reason is that they "have stronger incentives and adaptive capabilities than hierarchies while offering more administrative control than markets" (Williamson 1991, 281). Furthermore, "they are particularly apt for circumstances in which there is a need for efficient, reliable information. Indeed, the most useful information is rarely that which flows down the formal chain of command in an organization or that which can be inferred from shifting price signals. Rather it is obtained from someone whom you have dealt with in the past and found to be reliable" (Powell 1990, 304).

Researchers seeking to study the relationship of networks with organizations have at their disposal an increasingly well-developed set of social network analytical tools and concepts. Tolbert et al. (1995) summarize some of the common theoretical concepts used by network analysts. Readers should consider individuals to be interchangeable with organizations. "Centrality" is the word that analysts use when seeking to measure who reaches the most other individuals. The extent to which every individual can be reached by every other individual is referred to as "connectivity." The number of individuals who are reached by any individual on average is termed "network size." "Clique" refers to whether some individuals interact with only one another. "Structural equivalence" is a term that refers to whether some individuals interact with the same set of other individuals. A "block" is the descriptor of whether some sets of individuals interact only with some other sets of individuals.

As noted earlier, "embeddedness" refers to "the process by which social relations shape economic actions in ways that some mainstream economic schemes overlook or misspecify when they assume that social ties affect economic behaviour only minimally" (Uzzi 1996, 674). A structural hole is a "relationship of non-redundancy between two contacts. . . . As a result of the hole between them, the two contacts provide network benefits that are in some degree additive rather than overlapping" (Burt 1992, 65). Nonredundant contacts have no direct contact with one another or have contacts that exclude others. Finally, the following is the concept of weak ties (Granovetter 1973):

> People live in clusters of others with whom they have strong relations. Information circulates at a high velocity within these clusters. Each person tends to know what the other people know. Therefore, . . . the spread of information on new ideas and opportunities must come through the weak ties that connect people in separate clusters. The weak ties so often ignored by social scientists are in fact a critical element of social structure. Hence, the strength of weak ties. Weak ties are essential to the flow of information that integrates otherwise disconnected social clusters into broader society. (Burt 1992, 72)

The use of social network analysis tools and concepts by researchers has enhanced our understanding of the behavior of alliances (Gulati 1995) and organizations in networks. For instance, Tolbert et al. summarize recent research findings as follows:

> Firms cluster because of their involvements on each other's boards, . . . such clusters relate to community influence, to corporate giving, to the adoption of defenses against corporate takeovers, or to the prices firms pay when acquiring other firms. We also know that network positions are related to power and that the structure of resource dependence relations shadows how firms conform to the demands of other firms or how they extract profits from one another. (1995, 343)

Network analyses processes and concepts have enabled a number of important questions to be answered. One will note the obvious implications for managers and practitioners. For instance, in organizational terms is there an optimal means of connecting to network partners? Uzzi (1996) suggests that firms that connect to their networks by embedded ties have greater chances of survival than do firms that connect to their networks via arms-length ties.

Is there an optimal network position? Burt (1992) argues yes and suggests that it is those that provide the most access to information or resources, offer the least constraints, and take the least effort to maintain.

Is there an optimal form of network that organizations may wish to join? Uzzi's response is that "optimal networks are not composed of either all embedded ties or all arm's length ties, but an integration of the two. A crucial implication is that embedded networks offer a competitive form of organizing but possess their own pitfalls. . . . Thus a firm's structural location, although not fully constraining can significantly blind it to the important effects of larger network structure, namely its contacts contacts" (1996, 694).

What good comes from participation in a network? One set of writers suggests that "strategic networks potentially provide a firm with access to information, resources, markets, and technologies; with advantages from learning, scale, and scope economies; and allow firms to achieve strategic objectives such as sharing risks and outsourcing value chain stages and organizational functions" (Gulati, Nohria, and Zaheer 2000, 203).

Another trio of theorists argue that "networks are also adept at risk spreading and resource sharing to avoid costly duplication of independent effort; offer enhanced flexibility compared to other forms of integration such as take-over or merger; and provide increased access to know how and information through collaborative relations before the formal knowledge stage" (Clegg, Hardy, and Nord 1996, 2).

Summarized, these benefits can take two forms. Membership in a network can improve the information that an organization has access to and it can enhance its control over its destiny. Theoretical explanations of informational benefits arise from research on the topic of embeddedness. "Relational embeddedness suggests that actors who are strongly tied to each other are likely to develop a shared understanding of the utility of certain behaviour" (Gulati 1998, 297) because of their extensive social relations. "Structural embeddedness refers to the informational role of the position an organization occupies in the overall structure of the network" (297). Companies participating in networks can obtain a control advantage by being located between two other companies. This middle position can prove beneficial when the other two firms are seeking a relationship with the firm in question or are in conflict with each other (Gulati 1998; Burt 1992).

Why might networks or interactions not arise? One group of scholars answer this by suggesting when "the advantages for interacting are absent for one or another party or some institutional constraints inhibit interacting" (Tolbert et al. 1995, 344). This builds on the idea that "networks also have a potential dark side and may lock firms into unproductive relationships or preclude partnering with other viable firms" (Gulati, Nohria, and Zaheer 2000, 203).

While much of the previous discussion addresses the role of an organization as part of a network, another research stream portrays the organization as a network. Indeed, the network organization has caught the attention of many a writer and scholar. It has been described as the prototypical organization for the future and is what many think of when one associates the word "network" with "corporation," "firm," or "company." It is also an idea that although conceptually attractive, means different things to different people. For instance, one description notes the role of communications technologies:

> It is decentralized, and consists of an internal network where activities which are distributed around an internal network of divisions or units, linked through electronic forms of communication in very communication-intensive organizations by modern information technology. Hierarchies become one means among many to coordinate and control actions across people, knowledge, time and space. . . . Decisions are based on expertise, openly solicited and listened to in the organization. (Clegg, Hardy, and Nord 1996, 11)

A second description suggests a very human influence:

> Organizations consist of multiple, overlapping networks with permeable boundaries. Members are interlocked in a variety of relationships that "transcend office walls" through community projects, childcare concerns, informal friendships, neighbourhood activities, and company socials. Since communication serves as a building block that connects individuals, groups, and inter-organizational levels, organizations are clusters of task activities, social interactions, innovations and a variety of organizational processes. (Putnam, Phillips, and Chapman 1996, 384)

A third description points to some of the hoped for and desirable attributes of a network organization. "Although the precise definition of the so-called 'network organization' varies from person to person, in general it is regarded has having many properties—flexibility, responsiveness, adaptability, extensive cross-functional collaboration, rapid and effective decision making, highly committed employees, and so on not found to the same degree in alternative organizational forms" (Moss Kanter and Eccles 1992, 525).

Along with descriptions such as these, research on the topic of networks within organizations or "personal interaction patterns" has provided insights associated with power (Krackhardt and Hanson 1993), turnover, organizational culture (Kilduff and Corley 2000), information flows (Stevenson and Gilly 1991), attitudes, promotion opportunities, income (Carroll and Teo 1996), the role of coalitions (Stevenson, Pearce, and Porter 1985; Stevenson, 1990), and social support (Tolbert et al. 1995, 344).

Unfortunately, despite this growing body of literature, answers to these questions, and insight into organizations in networks and organizations as networks, our understanding of the behavior of these entities is far from complete. An important reason for this shortcoming is simply the nature of a business network—which can be described as an entity that is not structured as a market nor as a hierarchy and one where efficiency may not be the most important determinant of its form.

> Networks are "lighter on their feet" than hierarchies. In network modes of resource allocation, transactions occur neither through discrete transactions nor by administrative fiat, but through networks of individuals engaged in reciprocal, preferential mutually supportive actions. Networks can be complex. They involve neither the explicit criteria of the market nor the familiar paternalism of the hierarchy. The basic assumption of a network relationship is that one party is dependent on resources controlled by another and that there are gains to be had by the pooling of resources. In essence, the parties to a network agree to forego the right to pursue their own interests at the expense of others. Individual units exist not by themselves but in relation to other units. These relationships take considerable effort to establish and sustain thus they constrain both partners ability to adapt to changing circumstances. As they evolve it becomes more economically sensible to exercise voice than exit. Benefits and burdens come to be shared. Expectations are not frozen but change as circumstances dictate. . . . [T]he entangling strings of reputation, friendship, interdependence and altruism become integral parts of the relationship. (Powell 1990, 303)

Despite the important insights that have arisen from this perspective, there are a number of shortcomings associated with this body of insight. Unclear is the answer to the question: Are network organizations discrete mechanisms or do they consist of a continuum of forms ranging from pure market to pure hierarchy (Barney and Hesterley 1996, 122)? Some theorists argue that the primary tool of this style of research, social network analysis, has been used mainly as "a tool for analyzing data about organizations rather than for understanding organizations per se" (Tolbert et al. 1995, 344). These same scholars also suggest that many of the insights obtained from this stream of research could also have been obtained using other perspectives such as resource dependence. Furthermore, most research of this tradition does not take into more than one network (Gulati 1998).

Moss Kanter and Eccles (1992) add a few other criticisms. Most current methodologies used by researchers to collect data are fairly time consuming and represent a noticeable intervention in the organization in which data are collected. User-friendly software that enables managers to assess the characteristics of networks of which they are members is still fairly rare. Furthermore, the issue of relevance arises from time to time. Indeed, it is not always clear what managers want to know about networks. Also, there is still little attention paid to how networks are constructed by their members and how the members are using them.

Finally, some theorists argue that the network perspective is not really a cohesive theoretical perspective, but rather that it resembles a catchall heading for a broad array of research interests. One need simply to examine the indexes of Pettigrew, Thomas, and Whittington's *Handbook of Strategy and Management* (2002) and Hitt, Freeman, and Harrison's *The Blackwell Handbook of Strategic Management* (2001) to understand why this might be the case. Networks are tied to research on organizational change, multinational corporations, the entrepreneurial process, globalization, governance, strategic alliances, and decision making. If we also examine the index of Clegg, Hardy, and Nord's *Handbook of Organization Studies* (1996), one notes a connection of the network perspective with organizational culture, postmodern theory, structuration theory, transaction cost theory, and metaphorical theory. One last example suggests the use of a network perspective can help researchers understand firm conduct and performance in five important areas of strategy research: "industry structure, positioning within an industry, inimitable firm resources and capabilities, contracting and coordinating costs and dynamic and path dependent constraints and benefits" (Gulati, Nohria, and Zaheer 2000, 205).

8

Agency Theory Perspective

Imagine this: You are forty-two years old. You have just been named CEO of a Fortune 1000 company. Five thousand employees now refer to you as "Boss." Fifty thousand individuals and entities own stock in your corporation. Thousands of analysts, academics, journalists, and market watchers now care about what you say. Suddenly, into your mind pops a number of questions. To whom do you really report? How will your performance be judged? What rules or regulations should guide your behavior? What does success mean in your case? These are issues directly or indirectly addressed by agency theory, the topic for this chapter.

Using the metaphor of the contract, agency theory addresses the agency issue in which one party (the principal) delegates work to another (the agent) who performs that work. Agency theory is concerned with resolving two problems that can occur in agency relationships (Eisenhardt 1989). The first is the agency problem that arises when the desires or goals of the principal and the agent conflict and when it is difficult or expensive for the principal to verify what the agent is actually doing. The problem here is that the principal cannot verify that the agent has behaved appropriately. The second is the problem of risk sharing that arises when the principal and the agent may prefer different actions because of the different risk preferences. In the corporate world, an agency relationship exists between a firm's outside stockholders and its managers to the extent that stockholders delegate the day-to-day management of their investment to those managers (Jensen and Meckling 1976).

Agency theory comprises two complementary streams of thinking. Positivist agency theorists attempt to identify various contract alternatives by addressing situations of conflicting goals between agents and principals and by seeking to describe governance mechanisms that limit an agent's self-serving behavior. According to Eisenhardt (1989), the agency problem is solved through the use of outcome-based contracts and information monitoring systems.

Principal-agent theory seeks to determine the optimal or most efficient contract under varying levels of outcome uncertainty, risk aversion, information, and other variables. Essentially, the question asked is whether behavior-oriented contracts (e.g., hierarchical governance) are more efficient than outcome-oriented contracts (e.g., transfer of property rights or market governance). Under the principal-agent theory, principals have either complete or incomplete information regarding agents.

When information is complete, principals will make use of behavioral contracts to monitor agents. When information is incomplete, principals must deal with the agency problem because of the fear of opportunistic behavior in the form of moral hazard (lack of effort) or adverse selection (misrepresentation of ability) on the part of the agents (Eisenhardt 1989). In this situation, principals are theorized to have the options of monitoring agents through hierarchy-related investments in information systems (such as budgeting systems), reporting procedures, boards of directors, separate layers of management (Barney 1996), or market-related contracts based on the outcomes of agent's behavior. This latter option in turn serves to transfer risk to the agent.

The agency relationship between managers and shareholders can be effective as long as managers make investment decisions in ways that are consistent with stockholders' interests. Thus, if stockholders are interested in maximizing the rate of return on their investment in a firm, and if managers make their investment decisions with the objective of maximizing the rate of return of those investments, then stockholders will have few concerns about delegating the day-to-day management of their investments to managers.

Unfortunately, in numerous situations the interests of the firm's outside stockholders and its managers do not coincide. From a financial perspective, there are two primary sources of agency costs (Jensen and Meckling 1976). A first is when managers decide to take some of a firm's capital and invest it in perquisites that do not add economic value to the firm but do directly benefit those managers. A second source of agency costs is the risk profile of the managers. According to this line of thinking, stockholders lose out when managers are more risk averse in their decision making than stockholders would prefer them to be.

From an organizational view, agents might not adequately pursue the interests of principals for two reasons: moral hazard and adverse selection (Jensen and Meckling 1976). Moral hazard refers to a lack of effort on the part of managers. Adverse selection means that agents misrepresented their abilities when hired. The use of moral hazard and adverse selection as concepts suggest an important implication of agency theory for readers and managers. Executives are not to be trusted. Shareholders need to diligently protect their interests from these individuals.

Criticisms of agency theory are numerous. First, most of the research has been written from the perspective of principals and not agents, thus it has an inherent investor focus (Barney 1996). It offers little in the way of advice for agents. Second, agents are viewed in a somewhat negative, untrustworthy light. Indeed, it tends to overestimate their willingness to shirk or cheat (Rousseau and Parks 1993). Many individuals have no choice but to work and cannot afford risk-taking behavior. Third, its views of humans and organizations are unrealistic in another sense. It portrays humans as being motivated primarily by financial gain (Barney 1996). Fourth, it is also primarily a theory of short-term contracting and perhaps oversimplifies its view of organizations as a nexus of contracts (Rousseau and Parks 1993). Indeed, little attention is paid to internal sources of control such as social relationships and corporate culture. Fifth, a deeper philosophical concern is the view of the organization as a problem to be solved (Pfeffer 1997). The problem is, of course, how might principals protect themselves from agents. Sixth, implicitly organizations or firms are also conceived as autonomous and unaffected by the environments within which they operate. As a result, little insight is offered regarding interorganizational cooperation or the changing nature of employment relations. In an era when work is being outsourced as opposed to being internalized, agency theory assumes away many of the issues important to managers such as worker loyalty and commitment. Indeed, when faced with empirical research results that suggest change, theorists of this tradition appear unable to offer creative or unique interpretations (Pfeffer 1997, 51). Research in this area has also led to a "neglect of information problems that do not involve agency relationships. These are associated with planning in a world in which the future is highly uncertain, and they include problems of product choice, investment and marketing policies, and scope of operations" (Demsetz 1997, 3).

To conclude this discussion of agency theory, it is interesting to note the comments of Lubatkin, Lane, and Schulze (2001). Agency theory

> has become a widely used theoretical lens with applications intended to inform research about corporate governance, CEO compensation, firm performance, firm risk, and strategic decisions such as diversification, and mergers. Despite its frequent use, the theory's relevance . . . continues to be debated. (229)

9

Stakeholder Perspective

Picture this: You have just completed an MBA and are hired by a major oil company. You have spent considerable time and energy over the past year chasing this opportunity and feel that success is at hand. Informal comments from your new colleagues suggest that you are being sized up for a new position: assistant vice-president for special projects. For the time being, however, your relationship is one of a three-month probationary contract. In this capacity, you have been asked to tackle one project: to identify the major threats facing your company in the next three months and produce a plan of action for addressing each one. You soon come to the conclusion that a period of reflection might be of use prior to commencing work.

After deciding that twenty-four hours of visible inactivity might be the maximum acceptable to those watching your progress, you also come to the conclusion that numerous analytical frameworks are available to you. But where should you start? One template in particular sticks in your mind and that is a stakeholder perspective. This approach addresses the concern head on by identifying a stakeholder as any group or individual who can affect or is affected by the achievement of an organization's purpose. Put another way, stakeholders are defined by their legitimate interests in the corporation, not by the corporation's interest in them.

Stakeholder theory attempts to explain and guide the operation of the going corporate concern, viewing it as an entity through which multiple and not necessarily overlapping purposes are pursued. As with other theories, the stakeholder perspective has numerous versions credited to it (Donaldson and Preston 1995). It may be used to describe specific organizational characteristics. It can also help identify the links between stakeholder management and the attainment of traditional corporate objectives such as growth or profit. Stakeholder theory can also be given a moral foundation, in many cases being used to interpret the function of an organization along ethical lines.

Stakeholders can take many forms, ranging from employees, to shareholders, to religious groups. Table 9.1 lists a number of potential stakeholders for a typical large organization.

A stakeholder perspective is of use in many instances, two of which are noteworthy. Specific issues may arise that demand a well thought out corporate response. A product may be tampered with, as was the case with Tylenol, or a special interest group might target a company, as Greenpeace did with Royal Dutch Shell. As each issue arises, important stakeholders should be identified, the anticipated impact of the issue on each noted, and the expected reaction of each documented. An understanding of stakeholder concerns can also be useful for planning purposes. Important stakeholders can be identified, and for each, a list of potentially worrisome issues developed, an impact assessment undertaken, and expected reactions noted (Freeman 1984).

Clearly, it should not be surprising to learn that many stakeholders have different and often contradictory interests. One important contemporary challenge for managers is to achieve organizational goals while at the same time meaningfully addressing the concerns of their stakeholders and maintaining an advantage over competitors (Donaldson and Preston 1995). At a theoretical level, this alone is a monumental task. In practical terms, the range of options can be bewildering. Once identified, should managers attempt to address specific stakeholder concerns on a case-by-case basis as illustrated earlier or should a universal code of behavior be put in place (Jones 1995)? The former solution is time consuming and costly for big corporations if those concerns are large in number and may be impossible to carry out if some stakeholders' concerns clearly run counter to those of others. On the other hand, the latter approach is manageable if one focuses on the links that bind stakeholders to the corporation as opposed to their concerns.

Not surprisingly, theorists have developed more than one explanation for how organizations manage stakeholders. One approach is as follows:

> In such a view a firm consists of multiple constituencies, each with different interests and values. Organizational actors act in their self-interest and in doing so may be in opposition to one another. An organized entity it is not necessarily a unitary actor with a unified purpose. Instead it consists of many actors with different value systems

Table 9.1

Who Are Stakeholders?

Owners and stockholders	Suppliers
Creditors	Competitors
Customers and clients	Corporate management
Employees	Public interest groups
Labor unions	Persons in the media
Labor communities	Persons in education
Local government	Persons in the arts
State or provincial government	Military personnel
Federal government	Religious groups
Scientific labs	Sources of new technology
University research and faculty	

and preferences who act in their best self-interest. From this perspective, a firm is a forum for facilitating processes that generate superordinate goals from the meaningful representation of different stakeholders. However, such synthesis is not always assured. Sometimes one group may gather sufficient power to suppress and prevent the mobilization of opposition groups. Those in authority and power can address conflict in two ways. First, they can use the hierarchy to address conflicts at one level through command and control exercised at a higher level. Or, they can use time to address conflicts through sequential attention to goals. (Garud and Van de Ven 2001, 215)

A second useful approach is to visualize each stakeholder as being bound to the corporation through a contract, be it a legal document as in the case of many suppliers or purchaser agreements, or through a moral obligation, as in the case where a potentially pollution-spewing manufacturing plant situates itself in proximity to an established and vibrant neighborhood. As Jones (1995) notes, in all cases, despite differing contractual forms, it may be in the best interest of corporations to manage these contracts on a consistent, ethical basis.

The *contract* is an appropriate metaphor for the relationships between the firm and its stakeholders. Ample precedence exists for a broad definition of contract. Contracts can take the form of exchanges, transactions, or the delegation of decision making authority, as well as formal legal documents. . . . The firm can thus be seen as a *nexus of contracts* between itself and its stakeholders.

Top corporate managers, because they contract with all other stakeholders either directly or indirectly through their agents and have *strategic positions* regarding key decisions of the firm, can be considered the contracting agents for the firm. The firm is thus recast as a nexus of contracts between its top managers and its stakeholders.

Firms exist in markets in which competitive pressures do influence behavior but do not necessarily penalize moderately inefficient behavior. Given that the contracting process gives rise to agency problems, transaction cost problems and team production problems, in general, commitment problems, efficient contracting will be profoundly affected by the costs of solving these commitment problems. Because these commitment problems abound, firms that solve commitment problems will have a competitive advantage over those that do not. Further, because ethical solutions to commitment problems are more efficient than mechanisms designed to curb opportunism, it follows that *firms that contract through their managers with their stakeholders on the basis of mutual trust and cooperation will have a competitive advantage over firms that do not.* (420)

A specific example of how this approach may benefit a company is in the area of new business development. A common challenge for many Western corporations has been the management of business operations in countries where the use of bribes is not uncommon. Clearly, corporations can address this issue on a country-by-country basis and download responsibility to specific individuals in cases where inappropriate behavior is discovered. Or, as many companies have done, a blanket corporate-wide policy can be set that prohibits employees from accepting or making use of bribes. By asking each and every employee to sign a contract committing him- or herself to this code of behavior, corporations are legally able to protect themselves from deviant behavior.

This source of competitive advantage does not, of course, mean that firms employing ethical contracting frameworks will always outperform firms in which contracting mechanisms are based on the assumption of opportunism. However, all else being equal, firms in the former group will have an advantage over firms in the latter group. They should experience reduced agency costs, lower transactions costs, and fewer costs associated with team production (Donaldson and Preston 1995). More specifically, monitoring costs, bonding costs, search costs, warranty costs, and residual losses will be reduced. The resources saved can benefit not only the firm employing ethical contracting, but also the stakeholders with whom it contracts (Jones 1995).

The stakeholder model represents an interesting ideal. Treat stakeholders fairly and with respect. Trust them and cooperate with them and the benefits will accrue. In many instances, this model should hold. However, the world of commerce is too fluid and complex to place much money on such a bet. Despite the best of efforts to prove or suggest otherwise, corporations are autonomous entities, each with its own unique internal political dynamics and externally driven demands. Sometimes, good friends are sacrificed for the long-run bottom line. In other cases, people change jobs and leave companies. Furthermore, powerful buyers or suppliers often behave in a manner that runs counter to the best interests of other stakeholders. For many, perhaps the greatest appeal of this perspective is an underlying rejection of the notion that corporate management exists to serve the interests of shareholders. Of course, this perspective is just an ideal, but it is also probably worth pursuing.

What are some of the criticisms of the stakeholder perspective? Freeman and McVea (2001, 203) offer a few. First, its origins are with practitioners. Some observers suggest a need for academics to focus their efforts on detailed studies of concrete business situations in order to strengthen the applicability of this perspective. Second, among academics the stakeholder perspective is often viewed as a theory of business ethics as opposed to a theory business strategy. As a result, it has not drawn the research attention that it deserves. Third, it may be too accommodating as an overarching framework. Although research in this tradition encompasses ideas from ethics, agency theory, resource-based theory, and transaction cost economics, few are integrated in a meaningful manner.

10

Resource-Based Theory Perspective

How will the major institutions of our time prosper and survive in the coming years? Answers to questions such as this used to be quite simple. On the surface, the following answer is also quite simple. Scholars, managers, and consultants alike are coming to the conclusion that the future success potential of large for-profit institutions must come from within. In most industries, gone are the days when large corporations were able to protect themselves behind walls of government regulation or artificial industry entry barriers. Indeed, the disappearance of stable industry definitions has led to a state of fear and anxiety about the future among many executives. Faced with these pressures, corporate managers are being told to look inward and consider what they do best, both now and in the future, as opposed to trying to do everything for their current customers.

This style of thinking falls under the heading of the resource-based theory of the firm. Its basic argument is that no two firms are the same, and each may possess resources or capabilities that allow it to succeed. Success for a firm is defined as average profits obtained through a sustained competitive advantage over its competitors (Porter 1980). A firm can obtain a sustained competitive advantage using strategies that exploit rare, valuable, nonsubstitutable, and difficult-to-imitate resources and capabilities. In more detail, the theory can be summarized as follows:

> The firm must be concerned not only with profitability in the present and growth in the medium term but also with its future position and source of competitive advantage. Firms must think about how they will compete when their current strategies are copied or made obsolete. . . . Competitive advantage can be sustained only if capabilities creating the advantage are supported by resources that are not easily duplicated by competitors. . . .
>
> Resources must be valuable (rent producing) and non-substitutable. In other words they must contribute to a firm capability that has com-

petitive significance and is not easily accomplished through alternative means. . . . Strategically important resources must be rare and/or specific to the firm. They must not be widely distributed within an industry and/or must be closely identified with a given organization. Although physical and financial resources may produce a temporary advantage for a firm, they often can be readily acquired by competitors. On the other hand, a unique path through history may enable a firm to obtain unusual and valuable resources that cannot be easily acquired by competitors. (Hart 1995, 998)

Researchers working within this school of thought suggest that competitive advantage depends on the match between distinctive internal or organizational capabilities and changing external or environmental circumstances (Coase 1937; Penrose 1959). Mahoney summarizes the views of others by suggesting that a firm is

both an administrative organization and a pool of productive (interdependent) resources. Productive resources may take the form of human capital, physical capital, legal capital and intangible capital. These resources supply the genetics of firm heterogeneity. The heterogeneity of resources suggests the uniqueness of a firm. . . . A firm may achieve rents not because it has better resources but rather it makes better use of its resources. The firm may make better ruse of human capital by assigning workers correctly to where they have higher productivity in the organization and the firm may make better allocation of financial capital toward high yield uses. Top management resources may be an important source of rent generation. (1992, 126)

Accordingly, strategy is a definition of a firm not in terms of what needs it satisfies, but in terms of what it is capable of. The primary issue addressed, then, is what a corporation can do better than its competitors (Barney 1996). As noted earlier, the possession of specific resources represents the basis of these capabilities. For instance, in order to pioneer state-of-the-art communication technologies, firms such as Nortel Networks and Cisco Systems need to employ groups of highly trained scientists, engineers, and project managers; own or have access to advanced laboratories; and possess deep cash reserves in order to finance long-term research efforts. In turn, profits are ultimately the result of owning and having control of such capabilities. Efforts to develop capabilities thus have one major competitive goal: to prevent imitation by rivals.

The implication for analysts and readers is a conceptually appealing framework for identifying an entity's key strengths, although the task of doing so is normally a nontrivial undertaking. While its aim is to explain long-term corporate success, it doubles as an effective model for understanding organizational failure. For example, why do many pizzerias fail? In the light of this perspective, the answer is quite obvious. If we examine the case of a typical restaurant, its resource-enhanced capabilities may allow it to obtain profits that initially are greater than zero and perhaps greater than the industry average. However, depending on a host of factors, such as location, low barriers to entry, or the existing number of competitors, its offerings may not necessarily be rare in its operating environment. Although perhaps excellent, it most likely does not provide customers an eating environment or food that is nonsubstitutable from their viewpoint. Indeed, if they want to, most potential customers may choose to eat at home, at other restaurants, or simply spend their money in a different manner. Finally, despite the best of intentions, most great pizza recipes or restaurant environments can be copied or approximated. Thus, while many restaurants are profitable and do thrive over time, few are able to suggest that their resources allow the development of capabilities that are rare, difficult to copy, and nonsubstitutable.

The resource-based theory of the firm represents a powerful explanatory tool. However, it does have a few shortcomings. Specifically, identifying important capabilities and resources is often difficult. By definition, many of these same important resources are supposedly tacit and socially complex. Other definitional problems abound. Barney (1996) makes a compelling case for the role of luck when explaining how some firms come to build capabilities that are difficult to copy. Yet, is luck a recurring feature or a one-shot advantage offered a company in a specific context?

Another concern left unanswered by existing research is "how do firms acquire the right resources" (Cool, Costa, and Dierickx 2001, 66)? These authors also suggest that little is known regarding the implications of different resource positions under different competitive situations. Barney and Arikan (2001, 174) suggest four different concerns. The theory offers little insight into how strategies might be implemented once key resources are identified. It fails to address the issue of multiple potential strategies arising from the possession of individual resources. It fails to offer meaningful advice as to how stakeholders might appropriate rents from successful strategies. Finally, the resource-based theory of the firm is still young and the evidence to support it is not yet plentiful. Indeed, few empirical studies have been undertaken that might support or refute its main ideas (Barney 1996; Barney and Arikan 2001; Cool, Costa, and Dierickx 2001).

11

Behavioral Perspective

"A federation of hundreds or thousands of entrepreneurs." This phrase has been used to describe modern universities and colleges. Although similar in many ways to corporations or government organizations, universities are distinct in their acceptance of tenure as a tool for ensuring that professors can create knowledge, free of the fear of job loss, in an environment where diversity of opinion and ideas are valued. The impact of tenure, budget constraints, and a host of interested and active stakeholders creates an environment where the practice of management and decision making is not what it appears to be from the outside. "Organized anarchy" is a term that has been used to describe universities and the challenges faced by administrators. Ideas originating from the study of this form of organization have led to the development of a body of intriguing insight known as the behavioral theory of the firm (Cyert and March 1963). Over time, the insights from this body of research have helped scholars and practitioners understand the behavior of many different types of large corporations and have influenced the development of numerous other theories of the firm, including agency theory, transaction cost economics, game theory, and evolutionary economics.

The fundamental premise on which the behavioral world is built is the premise that individuals have bounded rationality (Simon 1947). "Bounded rationality assumes that individuals satisfice; that is they select the first alternative that is good enough because the costs of optimizing in terms of time and effort are too great" (Ackoff 1981, 22). In other words, there are limits on how rational an individual can actually be. "A theory of bounded rationality also assumes that individuals develop shortcuts, rules of thumb, or heuristics, to make decisions in order to save mental activity" (Nelson and Quick 2000, 314). The implication for organized behavior is as follows:

> Given the limitation and systematic biases of the individual, those operating from a behavioral perspective tend to view the organization

as a more efficient information processor than any individual. The firm is considered to be an institutional response to uncertainty and bounded rationality at the individual level. (Mahoney 1992, 107; Simon 1947)

In other words, faced with ongoing constraints, firms will also focus their energies on making satisfactory as opposed to optimal decisions. From this perspective, a firm is conceived as a coalition of various constituencies (Cyert and March 1963), where ambiguity and uncertainty characterize almost all areas of business or organized activity. Administrators face a challenge of constantly having to balance competing and divergent interests. Fortunately, behavioralists believe that managers can be effective in their balancing act. Indeed, meeting the needs of "stakeholders (shareholders, customers, employees, unions, managers) is possible if managers make decisions to integrate and mediate the interests of shareholders, employees and customers" (Mahoney 1992, 108; Aoki 1984).

Yet, from time to time the challenge can be overwhelming given that the goals of the ruling coalitions constantly shift as do the makeup of the coalitions themselves. The result is an internal decision-making process characterized by negotiation and bargaining where decisions are made incrementally and quite often in a disjointed manner.

Cyert and March (1963) suggest that unique features characterize business decision making. They are: quasi resolution of conflict, uncertainty avoidance, problemistic search, and organizational learning.

> Most organizations, most of the time exist and thrive with considerable conflict of goals. Except at the level of non-operational objectives, there is no internal consensus. Conflict is resolved by constructing acceptable-level decision rules, sequential attention to goals and by having individual subunits deal with a limited set of problems and a limited set of goals. . . . Organizations avoid uncertainty . . . by solving pressing problems rather than developing long run strategies and . . . they negotiate the environment. They impose plans, standard operating procedures, industry tradition and uncertainty absorbing contracts on the environment. . . . Search is stimulated by a problem and is directed toward finding a solution to that problem. . . . Organizations adapt over time. . . . When an organization discovers a solution to a problem by searching in a particular way, it will be more likely to search in that way in future problems of the same type. When an organization fails to find a solution by searching in a particular way, it will be less likely to search in that way in future problems of the same type. (116–124)

How is order maintained in what appears to be a somewhat disorganized environment? Three properties normally hold:

> First, since preferences are unclear, the organization discovers its goals from what it is doing rather than by defining them clearly in advance. Second, since it has "unclear technology" its own processes are not understood by its members, and it works by trial and error more than knowing what it is doing. Third since there is fluid participation, the organization is involved in what is constantly changing. (Pugh and Hickson 1989, 142)

These ideas present a "picture of the firm . . . as . . . a searching information processing, satisficing, allocating institution" (Mahoney 1992, 101). These same characteristics also suggest an alternative means to test the validity of the behavioral perspective. For instance, what would a behavioral theory of organization look like if a computer simulation developed the logic and parameters? Cohen, March, and Olsen (1972) set out to find the answer. Programming their simulation model to view organizations as a series of decisions to be made, they construct what is termed the "Garbage Can Model of Organization Decision Making." Guess what? It appears to be somewhat valid. Building on the ideas of the behavioral perspective, they understand that in environments characterized by ambiguity, a decision maker may not know all the available alternatives or the results of each alternative. He or she may also not have a clear set of rules to guide choices from the alternatives.

Thus, decision making is conceived as a time-sensitive process of four almost independent streams or flows that include problem streams, solutions streams, participant streams, and choice opportunity streams. These streams are constantly moving through an organization. The confluence of the streams at some point results in a decision.

Problem streams are the issues or problems facing the organization or part of it at a particular time. Solutions streams are the solutions available to a decision maker that may have no direct connection to the problems that may need solutions. Participant streams are the decision makers and others who are available to decide. Choice opportunity streams are the chances to decide (Cohen, March, and Olsen 1972).

The garbage can metaphor was chosen deliberately. The contents of a real garbage can consist of whatever people have tossed into the can. A decision-making garbage can is much the same. The four streams flow toward the garbage can and whatever is in the can when a decision is needed contributes to that decision. On the surface, decision making is portrayed as chaotic, but this form of chaos is explainable. Solutions look for problems to solve, and decision makers make choices based on the arbitrary mix of the four streams in the garbage can.

How realistic is this model? Observers of universities and colleges might respond that it is very realistic. Picture the world of a major scholarly institution where the collegial style of governance combined with professorial tenure often leads to continued course offerings of little interest to anyone but academics. Picture in this same environment presidents with no real authority beyond that of moral persuasion. Furthermore, think of an environment where it is possible to justify the hiring of biologists in response to job advertisements seeking physicists. Now think of an organization employing thousands of individuals, almost all of whom think of themselves as independent entrepreneurs tied together in many cases by nothing more than an institutional name and a series of concrete buildings. These all fit within the same type of organization that, in many cases, first sets budgets and then searches for ways to spend the money.

A number of criticisms are leveled at the garbage can theory of the firm. First, its genesis is a computer simulation model. Second, as noted by the theory's authors, its strongest applicability is to special types of organizations such as colleges or universities that are not always subject to the discipline of the market. Third, it is not a particularly simple model of organization. But then, to be fair, it may mirror the complexity of some of our major organizations.

Likewise, the behavioral perspective is also imperfect. Although sound in its descriptive ability, the behavioral perspective portrays all organizations as similar. Yet, it contributes little to our understanding of the impact of environmental forces and ignores the potential role of environmental determinism. Furthermore,

> it is firmly rooted in a model of individual decision-making, . . . it is not clear that it can be extrapolated to the group and organizational levels. . . . Procedural rationality may not always be descriptive of how individuals take action. There is no obvious place for emotion in a (boundedly) rational process. . . . By abandoning optimality and settling for satisfying, boundedly—rational models have difficulty explaining

how innovative entrepreneurial strategies come about; how organizations discover and learn new logics. Finally, decisions need not be the precursor to all organizational actions. (Chakravarthy and White 2001, 189)

The behavioral perspective may also overestimate the ability of internal coalitions to guide, if even haphazardly, the direction of an organization. Put another way, "it is a theory of search that does not predict the kinds of strategies that firms will adopt" (Bromiley, Miller, and Rau 2001, 270). At the same time, for some organizations it may underemphasize the influence of powerful management teams or individuals to reduce internal ambiguity. Finally, it is silent in regard to more recent advances in theorizing such as the role of capabilities or the connection of knowledge and intellectual capital to the overall success of an entity.

12

Game Theory Perspective

The shifting dynamics of the new millennium marketplace have offered corporate managers a challenge: make sense of the great uncertainty facing your organization and do so while continually growing your firm's profits within an organization that is flexible enough to turn on a dime. Managers have long been aware of the need to grow their profits, but increased uncertainty and need for flexibility have introduced an added complication. In many cases, the best way to remain flexible and protect one's long-term interests is to work with one's previous enemies. Unfortunately, in an age where old enemies are now occasionally thought of as friends, it is not apparent to many managers when it is in their best interest to compete and when to cooperate. One theoretical perspective termed "game theory" addresses this important concern.

To understand organized behavior in the following terms, think of a company that is facing a dilemma and is aware that its action will affect a competitor:

> The essential elements of the game are players, actions, information, strategies, payoffs, outcomes, and equilibria. At a minimum the game's description must include the players, strategies, and payoffs, for which the actions and information are building blocks. The players, actions, and outcomes are collectively referred to as the rules of the game and the modeller's objective is to determine the equilibrium. . . . Players are the individuals or entities that make decisions. Each player's objective is to maximize equilibria. . . . Nature is a non-player that takes random actions as specified points in the game with specified probabilities. . . . An action is a choice that [a player] makes. Information is the knowledge at a specific time of the values of different variables. . . . A player's strategy is a rule that tells him which action to choose at each instant of the game given his information. . . . A player's payoff is either the utility received after all players and Nature have picked their strategies and the game has been played out or the expected utility received as a function of the strategies for chosen by himself and the other

players. . . . The outcome of the game is a set of interesting elements that the modeller picks from the values of actions, payoffs, and other variables after the game is played out. . . . Equilibrium is a strategy combination consisting of the best strategy for each of the players in the game. (Aoki 1984, 21–27)

Game theory is an overarching term that encompasses many different mathematical games including Battle of the Sexes, Prisoner's Dilemma, Boxed Pigs, and Pure Coordination. As the Prisoner's Dilemma is most often associated with this style of theorizing, it will be used to illustrate the potential importance of game theory for contemporary management.

In its simplest form, the Prisoner's Dilemma involves two participants. For illustrative purposes, the example used is that of two consulting engineering firms working in a project-based alliance relationship. Electric Company (EC) is an electrical engineering firm that, for new client development purposes, is bidding with its main competitor, Electrical Engineering Associated (EEA), for the first time on a major hospital project. Numerous bids are expected, of which the EC-EEA alliance is but one. Although this bid is considered the strongest, there are no guarantees that they will be awarded the contract. Furthermore, it is not uncommon for bidding relationships in this industry to break up when one partner perceives its interests to be best served through participation in another relationship.

Within this context, EC and EEA can either cooperate or not cooperate. In other words, they can either work together to win the bidding process or they can refuse to cooperate and proceed to work with other partners. Table 12.1 shows their payoffs depending on their choice of action. If EEA and EC cooperate with each other, they have a greater payoff than if neither cooperates. Their combined chances of winning the contract are quite good, and if they do, they simply split the proceeds equally. However, if EEA cooperates and EC does not (or vice versa), then EC receives the highest possible payoff while EEA loses out. In this case, EC can abandon EEA and join another winning team. EEA, unaware of EC's duplicity, continues to cooperate and receives only compensation for its bid-related expenses. Both firms benefit equally when neither cooperates, but with a much lower payoff than when both cooperate. In this case, both firms are compensated for their bid-related expenses and both have an equal chance

Table 12.1
Game Theory—Prisoner's Dilemma Example

		Electric Company	
		Cooperate	Do Not Cooperate
Electrical Engineering Associated	Cooperate	7:7	3:9
	Do Not Cooperate	9:3	5:5

of joining the winning bid team. However, that team's chances of success are lower than that of an EEA-EC bid.

This logic offers an explanation for high alliance failure rates. In its pure form, a firm's total payoff is always higher if it does not cooperate despite the existence of an alternative that is better for each bidding partner (the 7:7 payoff that results when both partners cooperate).

Interestingly, despite the logic of the Prisoner's Dilemma, there are reasons to suspect that a strategy of noncooperation is not necessarily the best one. Axelrod (1980), a political science professor at the University of Michigan, was also curious about this issue. In 1979, he organized and ran a tournament for computer programs constructed to address the Prisoner's Dilemma. The algorithm that won consistently was quite simple: Cooperate on the first move and thereafter do exactly what the opposing player does. In other words, winners do best by sharing and never attempting to put one over on an opponent.

Game theories are normally grouped under one of two headings: "Dominant Strategy Equilibrium" or "Nash Equilibrium" (Rapoport 1960). Games that allow one firm to be clearly dominant refer to the possibility of a response that is better than *any* strategy a competitor might use. The results of Axelrod's tournament suggest a Dominant Strategy Equilibrium. If a firm's response is simply better than another firm's equilibrium strategy, then it is categorized under the heading Nash Equilibrium.

Gulati, Khanna, and Nohria (1994) suggest a second alternative to the "do not cooperate" advice of the pure Prisoner's Dilemma game: Make a visible irreversible commitment up front. Partners will then fall in line.

> As opposed to acting to alter the potential payoffs, one company can irreversibly commit itself to one of the choices already available to it.

Then the other firm takes this into account in making its decisions . . . thus the commitment that a less desirable outcome emerges can be sufficient to ensure that this outcome does not emerge in the first place. (65)

An irreversible commitment can take many forms. In the case of a bidding relationship, an example might be an offer by EEA to pick up the transaction costs of EC if the bid fails. A second example would be an offer by EC to let EEA pick EC's representatives for the project should the bid be successful.

The conclusions of both of these research efforts suggest one very important implication of an applied game theory: Corporate executives are conscious that the actions of their firms affect each other. Game theory is not an effective tool for explaining competitive behavior when corporate decision makers ignore the reactions of other firms. Indeed, game theory is most useful when executives put themselves in the shoes of others. An example of this is a city capable of supporting only two television stations. Executives of each station clearly understand that the rates that each charges for television ads impact the other. However, air-time buyers and viewers of one station do not necessarily share a concern for the welfare of the other station. The game is between the television station executives, not buyers of air-time or television viewers.

The use of game theory is not limited to bidding alliances or television station advertising. Some other examples when it might be used are as follows:

> *The professional baseball team owners choosing new franchises.* All the owners know that each new franchise potentially takes away market share from one or more of their members but each new team increases the revenue pool available to all.
> *The Shell Oil Company contracting for engineering services with Bechtel.* Each company understands that the extent of services provided affects the price. Shell would prefer a low price while Bechtel would prefer a high price.
> *A professional sports team executive setting up a performance-based compensation plan for a star player.* The team executive chooses a plan that anticipates the effect on the player.

Game theory offers a number of lessons for managers. Under the right scenario, collaboration can pay off. Despite the logic of much of contemporary economic thought, game theory research demonstrates that corporate competitive behavior does not necessarily operate in a winner-take-all environment (Hofstadter 1983). There are situations when rules reign.

Game theory also has numerous drawbacks. In its present form, it is not a tool that lends itself to easy use by the typical manager. In many instances, effective use is time consuming and involves a nontrivial understanding of math. It also imputes a high level of rationality and information processing capability to executives, thus leading many researchers to question the usefulness of game theory for management decisions (Bowman, Singh, and Thomas 2002, 43). Its strength as a framework for assessing competitive interactions is also a limitation. Indeed, only a limited number of issues of interest to contemporary managers can be formulated in this manner and even fewer in a simple scenario such as that of the Prisoner's Dilemma. Furthermore, in terms of modeling interactions, it appears biased in favor of taking into account expected future behavior:

> Indeed, it seems to be a general principle . . . that what constitutes a rational choice is never allowed to depend on what happened earlier. In defining rational behavior, only future states matter. This implies that we overlook, by definition, the path-dependency of our decisions since each new decision is assumed to be taken de novo. All decisions are fully reversible and there are no historical constraints. (Tsoukas and Knudsen 2002, 422)

Game theory also contributes little in terms of our understanding of how entities are organized. "For the most part, game theorists have adopted a black box view of the firm. . . . [I]t treats all firms in an industry as fundamentally uniform" (Tsoukas and Knudsen 2002, 422).

13

Property Rights Perspective

How does one motivate an employee? For decades, organizational behaviorists and industrial psychologists have struggled to answer this question. To most nonacademics, money immediately comes to mind as one possible response. Challenging and rewarding job tasks, attractive physical work places, and collegial operating environments would also probably find places on most personal lists. On paper, answers such as these appear fairly obvious. Unfortunately, the Internet economy and the inherent opportunities for dramatic personal wealth creation have placed in question the effectiveness of many traditional managerial solutions. Never before has the function of attracting, motivating, and retaining talented individuals taken on such prominence. Luckily, academics continue to tackle this issue through diverse lenses. One important school of thought contends that a reasonable response may be tied to an understanding of the nature of the firm itself and its boundaries. Theorists working in this paradigm suggest that a sound understanding and prudent use of property rights by managers and directors hold the key to the resolution of this and other important organizational challenges.

The idea of a property right is not new. Indeed, economists have been working with this concept for almost eighty years. A classical definition suggests that "[a] property right is the liberty or permit to enjoy benefits of wealth while assuming the costs which those benefits entail. . . . [P]roperty rights are not physical things or events, but are abstract social relations. A property right is not a thing" (Fisher 1923, 27).

How are property rights associated with our contemporary for-profit institutions? To begin, the definition of a firm is somewhat different.

The private corporation is simply one form of legal fiction that serves as a nexus for contracting relationships, and which is also characterized by divisible residual claims on the assets and cash flows which can generally be sold without permission of the other contracting individuals. . . . The firm is not an individual. It . . . serves as a focus for a complex process in which the conflicts of individuals (some of who may represent other organizations) and organizations are brought into equilibrium within a framework of contractual relations. (Jensen 1998, 56)

Furthermore, consider that the organization of a firm revolves around two aspects of ownership: residual control and residual returns (Milgrom and Roberts 1992, 23). Owning an asset means having the residual rights of control, that is, the right to make any decisions concerning the asset's use that are not explicitly controlled by law or assigned to another by contract. Residual returns refer to the rights of the owner to whatever remains after all revenues have been collected and all debts, expenses, and other contractual obligations paid (Grossman and Hart 1986).

The determination of residual control and returns are important matters because of the inability to write and enforce complete contracts—ones that specify what everyone is to do in every eventuality at every future date and how the resulting income in each such event should be divided (Milgrom and Roberts 1992, 293). It is the distinction between rights of residual control and rights to residual returns that sets the boundaries of the organization. Were an owner of assets to simply desire the rights to residual returns of his or her assets, then he or she has the option of contracting with another organization allowing it to undertake the actual operating function necessary to achieve a profit. On the other hand, possession of the rights of residual control of assets allows owners to integrate the resources necessary to produce goods and offer services on a for-profit basis (Hart and Moore 1990, 1121).

How can a group of individuals be organized to produce products or services over time? What appears to be a fairly simple question actually leads to fairly complex responses when one considers that the output of this form of endeavor may be the joint product of several workers' contributions with outputs attributable to any individual that are difficult to define and hard to observe (Alchian and Demsetz 1972). This creates an incentive problem of shirking that, were individual output observable, could be easily overcome by giving each worker title to what he or she produces (Milgrom and Roberts 1992). A solution in this case is for one member of the team to undertake a specialized function—to monitor the other workers and to have the authority to expel members of the team who perform unsatisfactorily and replace them with new members. But who will monitor the monitors? The solution is for the monitor to receive the residual returns (Alchian and Demsetz 1972). This is the classical firm where the boss hires, fires, and directs workers who are paid a fixed wage.

Of course, the role of property rights in organizations can be addressed from the point of view of recipients. For instance, one might ponder human behavior, as many economists do, as a process of maximizing utility or satisfaction. Most of us live under conditions of scarcity and cannot fully possess everything that would ensure maximization of our utilities. Thus, we choose the best from the choices available to us. In many instances, this condition of scarcity leads us to exchange our ownership rights with others if they increase, or have the potential to increase, our own personal utility. In turn, our employers (unless we are self-employed) have the ability to increase their own utilities by distributing ownership or property rights to us in exchange for services that matter to them (Barzel 1989). Thought of in these terms, property rights are "the rights that an organisation gives to its members to receive and use organisational resources" (Alchian and Demsetz 1972, 781). Managers can improve organizational outcomes by distributing ownership of property rights to employees or stakeholders who are most inclined to positively alter the bottom line.

An important implication of this perspective is that success depends on how property rights are distributed to employees, owners, and other stakeholders. Not surprisingly, property rights offered to individuals employed at different organizational levels are not always similar. Rights common to members of the general workforce include notification of layoffs, severance payments (in some cases), lifetime employment, long-term employment, pensions and benefits, stock ownership plans, and various degrees of participation in decision making. For those at the executive levels, property rights are normally stronger and the means to motivate such individuals may include golden parachutes, stock options, large salaries, mandated control over the distribution of scarce resources, and clear authority for decision making (Jones 1998, 192). Another group of individuals with strong property rights are shareholders whose claims of ownership allow them to share in the profits and success of the corporation.

Why are property rights important? In one sense, when well defined, property rights establish the boundaries for employee conduct. To some extent, they also determine the amount of flexibility that any one individual has when acting on behalf of an employer. As an example, consider how a multinational consulting engineering (MCE) firm might motivate a lone sales manager in a far-flung corner of the world to operate prudently and in its best interest. At issue is the perceived necessity in certain parts of the globe to offer bribes and favors in order to acquire new business contracts. It is in the best interest of the MCE to acquire new contracts, but not in a manner that is unethical or illegitimate. Bestowing property rights such as stock options to the sales manager is one means to ensure that his or her behavior will remain consistent with accepted Western business practices.

Property rights can also take other forms. For example, a consumer electronics company sells its products through its own retail outlets staffed by a sales force in its employ and through an independent chain of retail outlets. In the former case, where a sales force is used, the list of individuals who have previously purchased products from the consumer electronics company is its property right. An example of how the consumer electronics company might increase the motivations of individuals employed by the independent retail chain is to make use of a system termed "back-loaded" to reward (Jones 1998, 192). Back-loading works as follows: an individual receives an initial commission somewhat lower than the acquisition cost of a client but gets renewal commissions that are in excess of the agent's serving costs associated with obtaining the renewal. The goal of this system is to increase repeat purchases or purchases of more than one of the consumer electronics company's products. It works well regardless of who owns the property rights of the list of the previous product purchasers.

A number of criticisms have been directed toward this perspective. The first is an understanding of the firm as a nexus of contracts. This contractual dimension allows little room for explanations of organizational goals, motivations, intentions, or socially responsible behavior (Jensen 1998, 57). It denies a role for managers and the function of decision making. It also suggests ambiguity in terms of the boundaries of the firm. According to Jensen, "viewed this way, it makes little or no sense to try to distinguish those things that are 'inside' the firm from those that are 'outside' of it" (1998, 56).

Second, it suggests that organizations are formed in response to a problem. As a result, they are predominantly inertial (Moran and Ghoshal 1996) and do not adapt to internal or external changes over time. Third, the theory may be irrelevant to practitioners as it denies a role for humans and is overly simplistic in its description (1996). Fourth, there is an overly pessimistic view of organizations and an unwarranted bias in favor of shirking and opportunism in much of the writing on this topic (1996).

The use of property rights as a strategy for increasing employee motivation may also have a number of major drawbacks. Two or more employees may have the property rights to use the same assets. When this occurs, one or more of these individuals may be careless and blame others if damages occur (Milgrom and Roberts 1992). Free rider issues may arise when one individual benefits more from the use of the resource of the organization in question than the organization itself. In this instance, those offering the property rights may be faced with the problem of having too few property rights to give to those in need of motivation. Finally, not all organizations are able to offer property rights of equal perceived value (1992).

To conclude, property rights give owners control of residual returns, while stakeholders, executives, and workers are offered access to organizational resources. While these rights are granted by the organization, senior managers are normally offered stronger property rights as well as the authority to set the rights of stakeholders and employees.

14

Knowledge Perspective

Why do firms succeed? Responses to this question are normally quite complex as simplistic answers rarely do justice to the topic. They may also differ by company and industry. To understand why, visit the nearest pharmaceutical manufacturing facility. Ask for a plant tour. If time permits, you may be given an opportunity to see how this operation works. Don't be surprised if included in the tour is a demonstration of how ingredients are mixed, pills are bottled, and packaging is undertaken. You may also be told specifically which ingredients are mixed to form a particular medication and in what quantities. However, if you ask to meet the researchers and scientists who develop these drugs, don't be surprised to learn that they are unavailable as are their phone numbers and e-mail addresses. The point of this tale is that pharmaceutical companies understand that knowledge is ultimately their only source of sustained competitive advantage. They will protect what is important to them by different means—in this case by patenting medications and processes and by striving to ensure that the brains behind the patents are not tempted to leave their employ.

Firms are institutions for the production of goods and services (Grant 1996). If this idea is taken as a starting point, then

> The essence of an organization is its ability to integrate individual specialized knowledge and apply it to new products and services. These capabilities are structured hierarchically according to the scope of knowledge that they integrate. The key integration mechanisms are direction and routines. The central organizational problem is coordination. (Eisenhardt and Santos 2002, 144)

Thus, the basis of any existing or potentially sustained competitive advantage is the knowledge possessed by its employees. Knowledge takes on many different meanings. It may refer to information, processes, designs, ideas, the abilities that reside in employees, and so on. It may be tacit or explicit (Kogut and Zander 1992). Whatever its manifestation, knowledge ultimately sustains the firm financially (Grant 1996).

Successful organizations recognize knowledge as an asset and will strive to acquire, develop, and protect it. This theory of the firm describes how organizations manage knowledge and suggests that for protection, successful entities will use the tools of the legal system as well as proactively develop specific internal mechanisms and structures (Spender and Grant 1996).

For the purpose of this discussion, assume that knowledge assets take two forms: intangible and tangible (Liebeskind 1996; Kogut and Zander 1992). Intangible assets reside in the minds of individuals. Tangible knowledge assets are the ideas, processes, formulas, lists, plans, designs, and innovations that are protected by legal means such as copyrights, patents, trademarks, and trade secrets.

Laws governing trade secrets offer owners of commercial information that provides a competitive advantage the right to keep others from using such information if the information was improperly disclosed or acquired by a competitor and the owner of the information took reasonable precautions to protect it. To be considered a trade secret, information must have a commercial value and clear efforts must be made to keep it confidential (Trade Secret Law: Overview 2000).

Laws governing copyrights protect the literal form of creative expression such as those produced by authors, composers, artists, designers, programmers, and webpage designers. They do not protect the ideas or concepts underlying an expressive work. To be eligible for copyright, a creative work must be original, fixed in a tangible medium of expression, and be produced by an exercise of human intellect (Copyright Law: Overview 2000).

Laws governing trademarks protect the distinctive (unique, creative, or well known through use) names, designs, logos, slogans, symbols, colors, packaging, containers, and so on that are used to identify the source of their goods and services and distinguish them in the marketplace (Trade Mark Law: Overview 2000).

Finally, a patent is a document that grants a monopoly for a limited period of time on the manufacture, use, and sale of an invention. Laws governing patents give the inventor of a new and nonobvious invention the right to exclusive use of that invention for a limited term (Patent Law: Overview 2000).

Unfortunately, these legal protective tools are incomplete in their coverage. Despite the best of efforts to limit its use and awareness, the inherent knowledge is mobile, residing in the heads of individuals, and in many instances is a public good (Grant 1996) that is usable by many people. Thus, it is easy to imitate and its illegal use can be very difficult and costly to detect. "The protective mechanisms are also narrowly defined under the law, costly to write, and limited in their effectiveness when knowledge is only partially original and long lived. However, despite being incomplete, they are important and their value increases dramatically when used and combined with individual and organizational knowledge" (Spender and Grant 1996, 7). These latter forms of intangible knowledge are also considered assets but are even harder to recognize, quantify, and protect. As a result, organizational features such as employment contracts and structural organizational features are among the primary vehicles used for protection (Liebeskind 1996).

An employment contract contains rules that pertain to the duties to be performed by the individual, the employers' reporting hierarchy, incentives, and other items. Conduct rules reduce the mobility of employees and often the mobility of the knowledge they possess. For example, a firm can legally monitor its employees' telephone conversations, e-mail communications, and mail. Some corporations forbid their employees to discuss business in public places where they may be overheard, while others forbid their middle-level managers from holding memberships in industry associations. Stock options, bonuses, and benefits can be offered or withheld and geared to long-term productivity or profit. In terms of organization structure, design teams can be structured to limit their dependence on any one individual. The performance of key design and development tasks can be hierarchically and geographically dispersed. Combined employment contracts and structural arrangements are potent tools for preserving corporate knowledge (Liebeskind 1996).

A knowledge perspective offers an explanatory framework for firms seeking to foster innovation and achieve long-term success. Yet, it does have its shortcomings. Research suggests that knowledge related to organizations can take many forms, perhaps too many. For example, Choo (1997) lumps knowledge into three categories: tacit, rule-based, and background. Knowledge can also be thought of as residing in the individual as the sum total of individual competencies, information, and knowledge, while collective knowledge consists of organizational principles, routines, and practices that are held in common by a large number of organizational members (Zander and Kogut 1995; Matuzik and Hill 1998, 683). Other examples include explicit, tacit, private, and public knowledge. Aside from academic efforts to define the term and form useful constructs and variables, "knowledge" is increasingly becoming a popular and fashionable concept plagued by ambiguity that serves as an umbrella for numerous disparate and unconnected theorizing and research efforts. Sadly, many of these initiatives appear to be based on anecdotal and secondhand information.

Efforts to measure knowledge are still in their infancy. Performance and assessment instruments are at best incomplete and many build on existing financial measurement tools (Bontis et al. 1999).

Of all the critiques, Eisenhardt and Santos (2002, 158) is the most thorough. They suggest a number of flaws. Mainstream research in this area may be nothing more than a special case of the resource-based view of the firm. A key underlying assumption of this perspective—that knowledge is the most important resource of the organization—may simply be incorrect and is certainly not supported empirically. Consensus is lacking among scholars. Indeed, there exists more than one version of a knowledge-based theory of the firm. Furthermore, many of the assertions of this perspective—such as whether the effective management of knowledge offers firms a sustained or temporary competitive advantage or whether the sources of such advantage lie in the knowledge itself or knowledge processes—are not yet supported empirically. Finally, these shortcomings, and others, lead them to suggest that this perspective should not yet be considered a theory of organization of strategy.

To conclude, unfortunately, as with most theories, the knowledge perspective can offer its adherents no guarantees that success will necessarily accrue to those organizations effective at creating or protecting knowledge.

15

Evolutionary Perspective

Why do some companies change to such an extent that if two snap-shots were taken five years apart, one would barely recognize the resemblance? Why do some organizations begin their lives as manu-facturers of cans and then evolve into financial services conglomer-ates? Why are some of the world's largest accounting firms also among the world's largest purveyors of information technology solu-tions? According to the evolutionary perspective, the answers lie in a complex mixture of market pressures and organizational responses.

The key intellectual problem addressed by an evolutionary theory of the firm is "understanding the ongoing interrelated processes of change in technology and organization" (Winter 1993, 187). Change in this instance refers to a "dynamic process by which firm behavior patterns and market outcomes are jointly determined over time" (Nel-son and Winter 1982, 18). The implication for managers and readers of this notion is that organizations and their strategy may not easily be copied. They may be more secure than is apparent.

> In the evolutionary view the question of how the boundaries of a firm are determined is akin to the question of how the boundaries of a tropical rain forest are determined. The thing (metaphorically speaking) knows how to reproduce itself. It must reproduce itself through time to continue to exist and the processes that are involved in reproduction through time are the basis of growth in spatial and other dimensions. Give it the appropriate environment and it will grow. Encroach upon it by some method, it will tend to grow back. The rain forest metaphor is particularly appropriate because the "competencies" of the forest are diverse; it can exploit many differentiated environments in differentiated in different ways—but as a whole it is a collection of competencies quite different from those exhibited by a deciduous forest of the tem-perate zone. (Winter 1993, 190)

How are firms conceived?

> Firms are modeled as having certain capabilities and decision rules (genes) that, over time, are modified by both deliberate problem-solving (search) efforts, entrepreneurial discovery and random events (mutations). Decision rules are the generators and selection is the test. The higher order decision rules of the firm may be interpreted as their strategies. Natural and human selection winnow out firms with comparatively poor decision rules and capabilities. (Mahoney 1992, 131)

Three concepts are unique to this perspective: routines, search, and selection environment. "At any time, organizations have built into them a set of ways of doing things and ways of determining what to do." These are termed "routines" (Nelson and Winter 1982, 400). Routines or "predictable behavioral patterns" can take many forms, including technical procedures, rules for hiring and firing, investment or advertising policies, and strategies for mergers and acquisitions. There also exist three classes of routines. They may govern short-term corporate behavior. They may determine the growth or decline over time of a firm's capital stock. They may also serve to change, over time, the operating characteristics, or operating rules, of the firm. These latter types of routines involve employees scrutinizing the organization's activities as well as the reasons for why it acts as it does. In some companies, these employees may be organized as market analysis departments or research and development laboratories (1982).

> The term *search* denotes all those organizational activities which are associated with the evaluation of current routines and which may lead to their modification, to more drastic change or their replacement. The *selection environment* of an organization is the ensemble of considerations which affects its well-being and hence the extent to which it contracts or expands. (400)

In Nelson and Winter's own words, an evolutionary theory of the firm may be summarized as follows:

> At each point of time, the current operating characteristics of firms, and the magnitudes of their capital stocks and other state variables, determine input and output levels. Together with market supply and demand conditions that are exogenous to the firms in question, these firm decisions determine market prices of inputs and outputs. The profitability of each individual firm is thus determined. Profitability oper-

ates, through firm investment rules, as one major determinant of rates of expansion and contraction of individual firms. With firm sizes thus altered, the same operating characteristics would yield different input levels, hence different prices, and profitability signals, and so on. By this selection process, clearly, aggregate input and output and price levels for the industry would undergo dynamic change even if individual firm operating characteristics were constant. But operating characteristics, too, are subject to change through the workings of the search rules of firms. Search and selection are simultaneous, interacting aspects of the evolutionary process: the same prices that provide selection feedback also influence the directions of the search. Through the joint action of search and selection, the firms evolve over time, with the condition of the industry in each period bearing the seeds of its condition in the following period. (1982, 18)

Consistent throughout this perspective is the flavor of evolutionary thinking. An organization is thought of as a "a state of affairs where some antecedent condition existed and the state of affairs now observed reflects the cumulative effect of the laws of change operating on that antecedent condition" (Winter 1993, 187). Unfortunately, the problem for the evolutionary strategist is just that. How does he or she infer from observation the evolutionary problems that must have existed to produce the firm behavior that we observe today (Mahoney 1992, 133)?

The evolutionary perspective has other shortcomings. One in particular is an underlying assumption of relatively complete information by a firm about the future of its competitive environment. Unfortunately, this position is normally unrealistic. Strategic management efforts can reduce competitive uncertainty but not completely. Thus, luck plays a role in reducing uncertainty to a point where a state of relatively complete information exists (Barney 1986, 796). Second, although evolutionary theory seeks to explain the growth and survival of capitalist corporations, it ignores the role of their capital structure in this process (Mirowski 1988, 165). Third, to some extent the firm is a black box with no stable characteristics over time (166). Fourth, in this approach organizations are formed as a result of a series of historical occurrences or decisions. This ignores the idea that an organization may be formed in response to a problem, as suggested by transaction cost theorists (Tsoukas and Knudsen 2002). In conclusion,

Moran and Ghoshal (1996, 71) add to these criticisms by suggesting that theories of economic organization may lack relevance to managers, may be incomplete due to only a partial borrowing of ideas from base disciplines, and may not be realistic in their portrayal of organized behavior.

16

Natural Environment Perspective

Gregory R. Berry

Ecomanagement, "eco" meaning ecological and not economic, means more than saving the whales. The argument is often made that protecting the natural environment is not in the best economic interests of the firm, and there is minor validity to this perspective as economic growth and environmental protection are still perceived as separate agendas. Most contemporary managers have moved beyond this restrictive and "old" paradigm framework though, believing that there is no greater overall threat to business and society than the continuous exploitation and pollution of the natural environment. There are global problems harming the biosphere and human life in alarming ways that may be irreversible (Schmidheiney 1992), and business and industry create at least some of these problems.

The ecological or natural environmental perspective on managing the firm is part of the broader perspectives of ethics and corporate social responsibility. Ethical and social responsibility issues involve all aspects of organizations, the behaviors of their members, and their impact on society. These perspectives argue that because business is the dominant institution on the planet and also the institution most responsive to change, business has the responsibility of leading the way toward a nonpolluting and sustainable ecological future. Unfortunately, business has a weak tradition of taking responsibility for the environmental consequences of industrial practice.

"Corporate environmentalism" has been historically defined through the laws and regulations created to protect the environment and the public. The U.S. Environmental Protection Agency was created in 1970 to monitor the environmental performance of business and industry (Piasecki, Fletcher, and Mendelson 1999), and we now live in the age of environmental compliance and its complex demands. Public outrage and government regulation have accelerated awareness of social expectations on business, if not an increasing acceptance of ethical and social responsibility by the business community. Public awareness of the consequences of unsafe business practice was dramatically brought home with the Union Carbide Chemical facility explosion in Bhopal, India, in 1984 that killed over 6,000 people. The first international acknowledgment that local pollution was affecting the planet as a whole was the Montreal Protocol in 1987, with thirty-five nations signing an agreement for ozone layer protection.

North American society does not want polluted air, water, or soil. The ecomanagement perspective of the firm broadens the firms' concern from stockholders to stakeholders (Freeman 1984), and thus broadens the basis of firm decision making beyond the purely firm-specific economic benefit to concern for the benefit of the community and society, as well as the firm (Friedman 1993).

The cost of compliance and regulation is estimated at $300 billion per year in the United States alone (Piasecki, Fletcher, and Mendelson 1999). This cost results in some industries, such as the steel industry, becoming increasingly noncompetitive in the global marketplace, especially given that many foreign firms in other countries have minimal environmental regulations with which to comply. This leads to the belief by some that environmental regulation is a curse on business in North America. Business strategy and environmental management is constantly changing and often reinventing itself, and this adds to costs as well. Regulation and forced compliance in North America will not likely fade, so the challenge for business and ecomanagement leaders is to create and take advantage of new opportunities for competitive advantage created by evolving environmental expectations.

The evolution of ecomanagement, greatly simplified, is as follows: (1) awareness of ecological problems by society and government leads to regulation and pollution control standards set by government; (2) costly regulation encourages the firm to examine the cost effectiveness of current processes and practices and the benefits of ecomanagement; and (3) the firm develops ecomanagement strategies resulting in greater sustainability of firm practice, thus creating competitive advantage.

Global and local environmental issues include concentrations of greenhouse gases in the atmosphere, the depletion of the ozone layer, air pollution, and water and ground contamination. Communities and governments place much of the responsibility for these nonsustainable consequences and polluting behaviors at the doorstep of industry. Lack of self-control and voluntary ecoenvironmental practice by industry leads directly to government regulation controlling corporate behaviors and setting standards. Being in compliance is becoming increasingly expensive as firms have already passed the more easily achieved initial standards of twenty-five years ago, and so firm attention has shifted to the prevention of pollution in an attempt to avoid regulators altogether. Being in compliance during the 1980s was seen by most corporations as the price to be paid in exchange for receiving permits and thus permission to operate, but minimum compliance today is seen as performance insufficient to maintain competitive advantage.

There is also increased consumer demand for environmental quality. We have moved from an industry-driven market to a consumer-driven market that demands certain quality or performance (including environmental performance) from industry. This results in the recasting of the environment as a competitive issue (Peters 1990). The influence of the environment on processes, products, and costs has grown, and so has the pressure on environmental managers to find environmental strategies to improve company performance. These environmental strategies could focus on management strategies, regulatory strategies, and/or product/service strategies (Piasecki, Fletcher, and Mendelson 1999). Questions raised by ecomanagers include: How can pollution be prevented in all stages of the manufacturing process? How can harmful materials be eliminated through substitution or process changes? How can waste quantities be reduced (waste = inefficient use of resources = cost)? How can energy and water be conserved?

Business must also cope with many unwanted stakeholders such as Greenpeace or other well-funded and well-organized environmental activists. The activist agenda is often antidevelopment or growth, and thus seen as antibusiness.

The regulatory climate protecting the environment is constantly becoming tougher. The government is increasingly turning to criminal sanctions against individuals regarding corporate practice, and so managers and ecoleaders today must be careful not to conceal or disregard a pollution problem or they may find themselves personally liable and in court. The business risks associated with compliance failures have escalated to the point where some of the "best practices" of a few firms in prior years are becoming universal practices required of all firms (Piasecki, Fletcher, and Mendelson 1999).

Life cycle costing is part of the process of ecomanagement awareness. The object of life cycle costing is to assign some monetary figure to every effect of a product, and the list of costs is expanding, including such things as landfill costs, potential legal penalties, or recycling costs. When all these costs are factored in, a "real" cost is projected, so pollution control can be considered as an opportunity to create a more effective and cost-saving organization (Denton 1994). Ecomanagement is usually framed in terms of risk reduction, reengineering, or cost cutting, however, and rarely linked to strategy or technology development (Hart 1997). The need for regulatory compliance combined with general management awareness of environmental issues often causes the proactive firm to realize an improved competitive position (Shelton 1994).

The era of dramatic leaps in cost savings and efficiencies in environmental behavior changes are likely behind us. We live in an age when continuous improvement means smaller, incremental, and more expensive changes requiring systematic and integrated effort within the firm.

Ecomanagement leaders face a challenging set of demands that are different from those faced by corporate leaders in other more established departments such as finance, sales, or marketing. The first goal of ecomanagers is to achieve compliance cost effectively, yet compliance is merely a starting point. Second, they must go beyond compliance to recognize business opportunities while accepting prudent risks. The third goal of ecomanagers is to meet public expectations by responding to key stakeholders (Piasecki, Fletcher, and Mendelson 1999), so they must work creatively with a wide range of external stakeholders, and not all of them are friendly. Ecomanagers require an extraordinary range of knowledge, political talent, dispute-resolution abilities, as well as basic business skills (1999).

Practitioners of corporate environmental management are keenly aware that their field is highly dynamic, and indeed the status quo is the enemy. Adequate environmental behavior yesterday is inadequate behavior tomorrow, as the ever-increasing accumulation of laws and regulations combined with new scientific findings and technologies demand continual adaptation. Complete overhaul of the way companies address their environmental responsibilities is sometimes required. Corporate policy in many firms has changed from being reactive (cleaning up after the fact) to proactive (preventing pollution from all stages of the process). Effective environmental managers need to be change agents and be capable of persuading line and staff organizations to alter their work routines, spending priorities, and plans

(Piasecki, Fletcher, and Mendelson 1999). Ecomanagement awareness can reshape all aspects of business functions, including acquisitions, facility operations, manufacturing, design, and distribution. Yet, most firms and corporate decision makers continue to respond to environmental opportunities in a limited manufacturing or waste management context, thereby limiting their strategic choices (1999). Many of the corporate changes required for effective adaptation of ecomanagement strike at fundamental business assumptions.

Ecomanagement is a complex, frustrating, and evolving perspective as a framework for firm management. Properly focused performance measures and improved process operations ultimately improve the overall quality and strength of a company, which is something that investors, analysts, regulators, and communities demand.

However, environmental management often involves decisions made in the face of uncertain environmental impact and thus uncertainty in how much to spend on changes above compliance minimums. The main reasons for these uncertainties include changing societal expectations and values, changing government expectations through regulation, changing technological knowledge and ability, and changing global pressures.

Global forces are generally a negative influence on ecomanagement because lower global costs mitigate against expensive environmental practices, but also because of the generally lower environmental standards in non-Western nations. Government pressures on ecomanagement are mixed, being both pro-growth yet supportive of ever-higher environmental standards, which are seen by many as being antigrowth. Societal support for ecomanagement is also mixed, generally in favor of a cleaner and safer environment, yet relatively unprepared to make sacrifice (including higher costs) to achieve these benefits. Business and industry are realistically stuck in the middle, forced to achieve compliance but financially constrained and unsupported by government or society from seeking environmental excellence. Many industries seem more interested in antiregulatory political lobbying than proenvironmental changes.

While several established management perspectives of the firm will fade over the next several decades, the ecomanagement perspective will stay with us, quite likely becoming prominent as societal expectations for nonpolluting practice become even stronger. Business and industry are the dominant social institutions on the planet and they play a key role in the shaping of the future for all of us. What is the implication of these points for readers and managers? Our understanding of the relationship between the environment and organizations is still in its infancy. The behavior of large-scale enterprises in this regard is still open to interpretation and direction.

What are the shortcomings of this field of inquiry? One set of concerns relates to the link between environmental management and performance:

> Research relating environmental management to performance has been fragmented, appearing in literatures on finance, corporate social responsibility, economics, accounting, and environmental management. Aggregate firm level financial performance has frequently been compared to environmental performance. Environmental performance has been measured with pollution control indexes, annual corporate reports and 10k's, Fortune reputational surveys, environmental awards, and independent third party ratings. The results reported by empirical studies . . . have often been conflicting or ambiguous, fostering ongoing debate in the literature. . . . [T]he mixed findings of corporate social performance studies are the result of their use of different methodologies such as surveys, event studies and content analysis and different measures of performance at the firm level. This research has also tended to rely on very small samples (often fewer than 20 firms), few control variables, and questionable performance measures. The ambiguous findings also suggest that various constructs may drive both environmental and business performance including management strategy and firm level resources. (Klassen and Whybark 1999, 600)

Many of the criticisms raised in Gladwin's review of research on the topic are also still relevant:

> Researchers have not offered precise definitions, often leading to confused and contradictory findings. Researchers have not produced, after three decades of attention, what anyone could rightfully consider as a great wealth of high quality empirical findings. Researchers have not based much of their work on rigorous hypothesis testing logic that rules out alternative explanations. Researchers have not conducted very much systematic comparison of their discoveries across industries, across firm size, and across societies. Researchers have not explicitly incorporated dynamics into their study designs, relying overwhelmingly on static cross-sectional methodology—few programmatic, long term, longitudinal research efforts on greening appear to exist. Researchers have not always distanced themselves from advocacy and ideology. (1993, 43)

Part II

Functional Organization Theories

Why are companies like General Electric, America Online, and Nortel Networks so successful? Responses to this question often depend on the viewpoint of who is doing the answering. Contributors to the field of organizational theory address issues of this nature. As theorists and researchers, these individuals are primarily concerned with explaining why organizations look and act as they do and why they are effective.

Organization theories exist within the functional paradigm—the lower right-hand quadrant of Burrell and Morgan's (1979) work noted in chapter 2. Functional theories are implicitly managerial in their orientation, while theorists in this tradition "seek to examine regularities and relationships that lead to generalizations" (Gioia and Pitre 1990, 590).

A number of issues differentiate organization theories from economic theories of the firm. First, the objects of analysis are organizations, not just business enterprises. Second, performance or organizational effectiveness is not limited to the corporate bottom line or externally imposed market measures. Desired outcomes may take many forms, including survival and legitimacy. Third, organizations are not necessarily considered singular decision takers. Fourth, firms or entities under examination are recognized as organizations encompassing multiple individuals. Finally, theorists of this tradition address the structures of internal organization and the relationships between constituent units and departments (Grant 1996). In this part, we continue to examine how a number of exemplar perspectives contribute to macro-organizational theorizing.

17

Bureaucracy Perspective

The term "bureaucracy" has a distinctly negative implication in contemporary Western culture. Generally, it brings to mind images of stifling, demotivating, inefficient, even inhumane organizations, structured in such a way that productivity is inhibited. From Franz Kafka's novel *The Trial* to Terry Gilliam's 1985 movie *Brazil*, both literary and pop culture characterizations of bureaucracy approach nightmarish proportions. For many people, bureaucracy represents the core of what prevents many of this era's major institutions from functioning efficiently. Interestingly, what few people realize is that the theory that gave us bureaucracy was originally attempting to describe the ideal type of organization, one that operated with the smoothness and efficiency of a machine.

There is some debate as to who first theorized about a bureaucratic system of organization. Some trace its origins to early twentieth-century writers who documented the trial and tribulations of the scientific management movement. Others suggest that the writings of thinkers such as Henri Fayol should be given some of the credit. Still others see the theory's roots in the spirit and thought surrounding the industrial revolution of the late eighteenth century.

More often than not, where one situates oneself in this debate is more a matter of one's critical perspective than of conclusive evidence. For those who take their investigative cues from sociology, the origins of bureaucratic thought might be found in the writings of the twentieth-century, German-born sociologist Max Weber. It was not until the late 1950s, however, when American sociologist Talcott Parsons translated Weber's works from German, that Weber became known to the wider English-speaking world.

Weber's theory of bureaucracy developed out of his concerns about industrialization. He theorized that as organizations grew and as the workplace became increasingly industrialized, organizations that structured themselves to complement this efficient, rational, systematic environment would operate most effectively. What he developed was a vision of the ideal organization that reflected the optimism that the twentieth century held for mechanization.

A bureaucratic firm, according to Weber, has certain rational features. Bureaucracies are organized in a clearly defined hierarchy of offices, with each level having clearly defined, explicit authority and responsibility. Each level is responsible not only for its own actions, but also for the actions of the department below it. This creates a chain of command. Employees are appointed, not elected, to positions on the basis of their technical competence. Each position is filled by a free contractual relationship. While they are completely free to do as they wish in their private lives, employees of a bureaucracy are subject to strict controls at work and must adhere to the rules and policies of the organization. The firm should also be the primary employer of each individual (Tawney 1958).

In return for their service to the firm, Weber felt that each employee should be compensated with a salary that is fixed to his or her position in the hierarchy. Most employees would also have the right to a pension. Employees should not be able to own shares in the firm. Ideally, employees are encouraged to make a career of their work at the firm. While they can resign if they wish, employees cannot as a general rule be fired, only demoted. Employees can be promoted to higher positions and salaries if their superiors deem them to be fit (Tawney 1958).

Weber also believed that all decisions made in a bureaucratic firm should be recorded on paper. This was so that documents could be referred to in the future in the event of a dispute. For this form of organization to function effectively, two stipulations need to be accepted by all members. First, the rules of the organization must be accepted without question. Second, there can be no disagreement as to the legitimacy of hierarchical authority (Tawney 1958).

The bureaucratic approach to organization was significant for a number of reasons. For one, it was the product of its time, evolving out of an era that placed an almost overwhelming amount of faith in the potential of machines, of technology, and of science to perfect human activity. Therefore, the rational organization of a bureaucracy was in touch with the spirit of its age. Also, Weber's theory was original in its comprehensiveness. It was one of the first theories to explain how an organization functions in such exact detail, which again appealed to the rational, scientific mind-set.

Weber's theory offered a new means of understanding authority as well, representing a break from the traditional justifications for decision making. Prior to Weber, people tended to rely on traditional and charismatic sources for authority. Traditional authority refers to a belief in traditions and in the legitimacy of those exercising authority through these traditions. Charismatic authority depends on the momentum and influence of an individual person and on the order set out by that person. Weber's ideas broke from both traditional and charismatic sources of authority, creating a decision-making process that based its justification on rational-legal authority. Rational-legal authority emphasizes the need for employees to believe in the rules of an organization and in the right of authority figures to issue commands based on these rules. On this basis, Weber argued that authority should be offered to those who displayed technical competence and adhered to the rules of the organization.

Bureaucracy theory fits within the social science tradition of structural-functionalism. Structural explanations seek to outline a feature of society as the predictable consequence of certain structural characteristics of society. Functional explanations seek to outline a feature of society in terms of the beneficial consequences it has for the larger social system (Burrell and Morgan 1979).

The primary criticism of bureaucracy theory is that it functions better as an idea than it does in the real world. In practice, this form of organization has proved to be extremely inefficient and inflexible, if not inappropriate in this era of employee empowerment and continuous change. One of the most important critiques is simply that contemporary organizations are different.

> Few would fail to acknowledge the emergence of new forms of organization. On the outside the boundaries that formerly circumscribed organizations are breaking down as individual entities merge and blur in chains, clusters, networks and strategic alliances. . . . On the inside the boundaries that formerly delineated the bureaucracy are also breaking down as flat, flexible . . . organizations . . . lose shape. (Clegg and Hardy 1996, 9)

This is also perhaps the most important implication for practitioners. Many who change initiatives seek to move an organization away from a bureaucratic structure yet how can a new organization be created without understanding the look and feel of the old one? Analysts and researchers might find it helpful to understand "what is" before they assess "what can be." A second implication is that despite the drawbacks listed earlier, the Weberian model of organization works well in many industries. Retail stores, fast food restaurants, recreation facilities, most militaries, some forms of government, and many manufacturing facilities, to list a few, function efficiently, albeit imperfectly, under this form of structure.

Weber himself suggested possible downsides to a bureaucratic organization, portraying it as a potential iron cage for those it employed. His resulting pessimism was significant enough for him to worry about the "freedom of the human spirit and the values of liberal democracy since those in control have a means of subordinating the interests and welfare of the masses" (Morgan 1986, 17). A number of early studies effectively portrayed the problems associated with bureaucracy. These unintended consequences included overall rigidity, managers who use control apparatus to build and control internal empires, conflict, and an inability to deal with exception or change (Daft 1983). Other criticisms include a lack of attention to the informal features of organizational structure (Bennis 1959; Pettigrew and Fenton 2001) and an assumption of this form of organization as a universal, ideal type.

In conclusion, despite these shortcomings, the bureaucratic form remains the dominant description of large-scale organization for much of the workforce. With that said, it is perhaps fitting to finish this discussion with a final critique of this style of thinking:

> People do not naturally group themselves in the same sort of units as those produced by rational organizational design. As formal organizations cut across human relationships and subjugate interests, other dynamics take over and begin to operate. Thus organization moves from being functional to dysfunctional. Parochialism, conflict and goal displacement occur from compartmentalization, labeling and separating people. Developing shared values and maintaining the commonality of purpose, the very reasons why organization members come together in the first place become organizational tasks in their own right. (Wilson 2001, 153)

18

Contingency Perspective

If one were to take a quick look over all the articles and books written about organizational theory by academics, one would quickly discover that the largest body of research falls under what could be broadly characterized as contingency theory. Throughout the 1960s and 1970s, researchers grew dissatisfied with the confining features of bureaucracy theory and sought new models for explaining and assessing large-scale organized behavior. In its original form, contingency theory "conceptualized Weber's bureaucracy as a variable within organizations rather than an undifferentiated ideal type" (Pettigrew and Fenton 2001, 14). They did this by bringing the issue of performance into play. Termed by some the "it depends" theory, one subcategory of theorizing, structural contingency theory, attempts to answer the important question: Which organizational structures achieve the highest performance?

At its core, structural contingency theory argues that the decision regarding how a structure should be designed depends on the particular situation that an organization faces. The environment, the technology, and the task the organization must perform are all important determining factors. Put another way, the contingencies or sources of uncertainty facing an organization shape the organizational design. The designer of an organizational structure must comply, or at least contend, with these constraints if the organization is to run effectively (Jones 1995).

Organizations ultimately seek to be both efficient and effective. Therefore, structures should be designed to respond to various contingencies or to things that could happen and must be planned for. The relationship between an organization's environment and its structure is deterministic. That is, aspects of an organization's context (environment, technology, task, size of firm, and so on) determine its structure. Structures that more closely mirror the requirements of an organization's context are more likely to be effective than those that do not. There is no single best way to structure an organization, though every individual situation has a best solution. If there is a simple rule of thumb that can be drawn from structural contingency theory, that rule might be that there can be only one best structural solution in a specific contextual situation. Within a given situation, there are no alternatives, only one best choice (Schreyogg 1980).

Among the factors to be weighed, the environment must always be considered a given, as it is always present and rests outside the control of the organization. Furthermore, since an organization has to achieve a certain level of economic performance in order to survive, the criteria against which the organization's performance is assessed are defined externally and therefore out of the control of the organization.

In applying this theory to an organization, it is necessary to consider specific categories of structural elements against specific categories of the organization's context. Structural elements include specialization of functions and roles, standardization of procedures, formalization of documentation, centralization of authority, span of control, and configuration of role structure. Generally, the structural elements are contingent, or dependent, on aspects of the organization's context (Pugh et al. 1969).

When applied to business settings, structural contingency theory is a powerful tool for explaining why NASA is set up as it is and why professional service firms are not organized along the lines of a manufacturing plant. It also explains why companies like General Motors or Microsoft are structured in a different manner than that of the Seattle Winter Olympic Games entity.

Many studies have been undertaken over the years in an effort to test the assertions of structural contingency theory. A complete discussion of the findings is beyond the scope of this chapter. Robbins (1990), though, notes some of the major insights. The findings related to the effect of technology on structure are inconclusive. In terms of the effect of environmental conditions, the evidence suggests that some organizational structures are more appropriate in some contexts while others are less appropriate. Finally, research into the relevance of an organization's size is somewhat more conclusive. Increased size was found to lead to decentralization, increased vertical differentiation, increased formalization, and a stronger administrative component.

Structural contingency theory fits within the social science tradition of structural-functionalism. These theories seek to explain a feature of society either as the predictable consequence of certain structural characteristics of society or in terms of the beneficial consequences it has for the larger social system (Burrell and Morgan 1979).

A number of criticisms have been directed toward the structural contingency perspective. A majority of these are summarized as follows:

> Structural contingency theory was too complicated to be easily comprehended or summarized, which is necessary if it is to be used by people who do not have the luxury of returning to the texts for guidance. The theory was too disconnected from decision variables actually controlled in organizations, employed concepts that were too abstract, and did not deal in robust parsimonious ideas. (Pfeffer 1997, 162)

In more detailed terms, studies in this realm usually leave the underlying process of decision making to be inferred and therefore fail to take into account that managers may choose the forms that they desire (Child 1972; Pettigrew and Fenton 2001, 17).

Evidence also suggests that a variety of organizational structures can survive in a given environment and that there is rarely one best model for securing success. Furthermore, most research in this area does not convincingly establish any cause and effect relationship between the various factors, making both proving or disproving this theory problematic (Schoonhoven 1981). More obviously in question is the theory's assertion that organizations have no direct influence on their contextual situation. Where used, profit maximization does not seem to supply a clear enough criteria to guide the decision-making process in the way that the theory suggests it should (Schreyogg 1980).

In light of these criticisms, what is the status of structural contingency today? The following statement offers an interesting point of view:

> With some notable exceptions (Donaldson 2001), structural contingency theory has virtually faded from the research and managerial literature scene. What happened to structural contingency theory reflects in part characteristics of the field of organization studies . . . : (1) an attraction to the new and unique, which makes following through on any cumulative program of research difficult and unlikely; (2) an interest in ideas that are readily translated into action; and (3) a fasci-

nation with economic logic which is almost invariable non-contingent.
(Pfeffer 1997, 158)

Although this chapter has focused on structural contingency theory,
it is worth noting that other variants do exist. A closely related variant
seeks to explain why some organization departments or subunits exert
more influence on corporate behavior than others. Termed the "strategic contingencies theory of intra-organizational power" (Hickson et
al. 1971), it offers insight into how power is wielded in some large
entities.

In conclusion, despite little in the way of recent research activity,
an important implication for readers is that structural contingency offers analysts an extensive and well-supported tool kit for describing
organizations operating in different contexts.

19

Strategic Choice Perspective

What many of us now take for granted—that the individuals who run our major institutions and corporations can affect their organizations' long-term profitability and survival—was once neither obvious to nor extensively explored by organizational theorists. Up until the early 1970s, one of the major proponents of this view was Chandler (1962), who explored the development of some of North America's most prominent multinationals in his now famous book *Strategy and Structure*. A prominent 1972 article by Child further popularized these ideas, complementing the work of classical management theorists such as Barnard (1938) and Selznick (1957).

Prior to 1972, most management theory addressed issues of large-scale organized behavior from a limited number of perspectives. Strategic choice theory and the research that grew out of it were in essence a reaction against the constraining insights of structural contingency theory. Most formal theoretical perspectives previous to strategic choice ignored or downplayed the active role of managers in the day-to-day running of corporations.

What separated Chandler (1962) from his predecessors was his interest in managerial innovation, or how new administrative forms and methods are created. Chandler conducted a preliminary study of the experiences of fifty of the world's largest industrial enterprises and discovered the rise of a new organizational form, the multidivisional or decentralized structure.

In order to learn more about this new form, Chandler then conducted an in-depth analysis of du Pont, General Motors, Jersey Standard, and Sears and compared his findings from these four organizations to the experiences of 100 similarly large corporations. He followed the development of this sample of firms using data spanning over thirty years, from 1909 to 1948. From this research, one overriding principle evidenced itself: Growth without structure leads to economic inefficiency. From this principle, Chandler developed the following thesis:

> *Structure follows strategy* and the most complex type of structure is the result of the combination of several basic strategies. *Expansion of volume* led to the creation of an administrative office to handle one function in one local area. Growth through *geographical dispersion* brought the need for a departmental structure and headquarters to administer several local field units. The decision to expand into new types of functions, *vertical integration,* called for the building of a central office and multi-departmental structure, while the developing of new lines of product, *diversification,* brought the formation of the multidivisional structure with a general office to administer the different divisions. (1962, 16–17)

From his research, Chandler (1962) also developed a number of other important propositions about managerial innovation. First, he asserted that administration is an identifiable activity. Second, an administrator must make two types of decisions. One type is a strategic decision, which deals with the long-term health of the company. Strategic decisions are entrepreneurial in nature and involve the allocation or reallocation of resources. The other type of decision is a tactical decision that deals with the day-to-day operational concerns of the company. It is this element of managerial autonomy that served to suggest choice in decision making and distinguished his work from the pure contingency theorists.

Chandler also suggested that executives carry out their activities from one of four offices. A general office oversees one or more industries and geographical areas. A divisional office oversees one specific industry. A departmental office oversees one specific function. And finally, a field office oversees one specific function in a local area.

Chandler's ideas set a new context for the study of organizational theory in the early 1960s. However, it was not until 1972 and the work of Child that the popular trend began shifting away from structural theories. Child argued that the analysis of an organization and its environment must recognize the ability of the organization's decision makers to exercise choice. These decision makers, he suggested, may well have some power to enact or favorably alter their organization's environment. Therefore, their decisions as to where the organization will be located, what clientele it will serve, or who it will employ may mitigate the effects of the organization's environment. In other words, strategic decisions may have a significant effect on how the organization performs in its environment (Child 1972).

According to Child, decision makers hold the power in an organization. Executives can be categorized into two groups on this front: those that are in the position to take organization-altering initiatives and those that are in the position of having to respond to such decisions. Child's ideas, in effect, force a choice on organizational observers, suggesting that top managers might be portrayed as either heroic crusaders or greedy tyrants. Most business academics have favored the former characterization, describing aggressive management in terms of heroism.

What was also new about Child's argument was that it weakened the prevailing notion that contextual factors exert a high degree of constraint on the choice of structural design. While many of his colleagues were engaged in a debate regarding the influence of such factors as the use of technology, the power of competitors, and the effect of industry relations on the structure of organizations, Child was suggesting that it was management, not outside forces, that really determined the structural style of organizations.

Child's thesis can be summarized as follows:

> The boundaries between an organization and its environment are similarly defined in a large degree by the kinds of relationships which its decision makers choose to enter upon with their equivalents in other organizations, or by constraints which more dominant counterparts impose upon them. In view of these essentially strategic and political factors, environmental conditions cannot be regarded as a direct source of variation in organizational structure. The critical link lies in the decision maker's evaluation of the organization's position in the environmental areas they regard as important, and the action they may consequently take about its internal structure. (1972, 382–383)

Not only could management determine its own structure, Child suggested that its decisions as to structure could also have a restrictive influence on performance levels. In other words, the way in which an organization structures itself can either help or hinder that organization's ability to be profitable. This notion places an incredible amount of importance on ensuring that the decisions taken by management are the right ones, as those decisions ultimately influence the success or failure of the organization, as well as the environment outside the organization.

A good example of this is Bill Gates and his efforts to build Microsoft into a world leader in the computer software industry. Not only has he influenced his own organization, but he has also had a significant impact in the development of many other organizations through the influence of Microsoft's software products.

The work done by Chandler (1962) and Child (1972) forms the basis for what is now referred to as strategic choice theory. In fact, within the last two decades, strategic choice has become the dominant viewpoint in management literature, replacing the structural determinism of previous perspectives with a notion more akin to organizational self-determination.

In the broader context of the social sciences, strategic choice theory falls under the general heading of interpretivist theories. Interpretivism suggests several basic ideas about how organizations work. First, organizations are open systems that process information from the environment. Second, an organization's interpretive process is somewhat different from an individual's interpretive process. Third, strategic or executive-level managers are the ones within an organization who decide how interpretation will occur. Finally, organizations differ systematically in the processes they employ to interpret their environments.

One major implication of strategic choice theory is that managers through their decisions can improve performance. In many ways, management becomes the primary link between the organization and the environment. Strategic choice theory describes the way in which management creates, learns about, and shapes an organization's environment. In this sense, numerous possible strategy-structure relationships exist. Ultimately, each organization chooses its target market and develops its own set of products or services. These domain decisions are supported by appropriate decisions concerning the organization's technology, structure, and processes (Child 1972).

Given that top management teams or dominant coalitions make the key decisions, they are also assumed, from this perspective, to be responsible when performance does not meet objectives. Thus, from an analyst's point of view strategic choice theory tells us that poor financial performance will often signal turnover in the executive ranks.

Another implication of this perspective is the existence of industry recipes (Spender 1990) or mental models among senior executives regarding how things are done in a specific industry. "How things are done" refers to normal competitor, customer, or supplier activity within an industry. Analysts who are able to learn these recipes may find themselves with an advantage over competing analysts who seek to predict corporate behavior.

A number of strong criticisms exist regarding strategic choice theory. First, it ignores the argument that aspects of an organization's institutional, competitive, or operating environment may determine features of its structure. Citing work by Palmer, Friedland, and Singh (1986), Hall argues that "[t]he industrial limits to choice are evident in the fact that the petroleum and agriculture industries were less diverse than other industries . . . the industrial context in which firms operated thus had a major impact on the form adopted" (1996, 105).

Second, empirical evidence suggests that managerial choice or adaptation may be but another contingency of structure (Donaldson 2001, 132). Interestingly, when tested in this vein evidence suggests that the "extent of choice over structure is at most, limited" (Donaldson 2001, 135). When adaptation of structure does occur, it occurs after a time lag (Dyas and Thanheiser 1976) and as a result of low performance (Donaldson 2001). Third, when tested empirically, it appears that the evidence for contingency explanations of organizational structure are stronger than for those of strategic choice (Donaldson 1996).

20

Resource Dependence Perspective

Health care is an issue dear to many of us. How will it be delivered five or ten years from now? Will a visit to a doctor's office, medical clinic, or hospital still be de rigueur? How will advances in communications and Internet technologies impact this area? Answers to questions such as these are as yet unclear. Even less clear are the identities of those organizations that will be the major players in health care delivery. How influential will doctors be in the future? Where will pharmaceutical companies and HMO's fit? What type of organizations will really control health care? Don't be surprised if the names Cisco Systems, IBM, and America Online are in the picture. Resource dependence theory is one perspective useful for those seeking to obtain a glimpse of the future.

Resource dependence theory suggests that the behavior and success of an organization can be accounted for by the environment within which it operates. Because they cannot supply all of their needs internally, organizations require resources from their operating environment. This interdependence most often leads to a complex set of relationships where one organization attempts to influence its resources, while in return its resources attempt to influence the organization. As such, organizations must attend to the demands of those environmental factors that provide resources that are necessary for their continued survival (Pfeffer 1982). The goal in attending to these influences is to reduce uncertainty. Therefore, to a certain extent organizations are dependent on their resources for stability (Pfeffer and Salancik 1978).

There are two basic premises to this argument. First, organizations are externally constrained. They will and should respond more to the demands of those organizations or groups that control critical resources or on which they are dependent. Of course, some competitors, regulators, allies, or industry participants will be more important to an organization than others. Those groups that control resources that are critical to an organization will be the most powerful and influential and will therefore see their concerns addressed first (Pfeffer 1982).

The second premise is that, for a variety of reasons, organizations attempt to manage their external dependencies, both in order to survive and in order to gain, if possible, more autonomy and freedom from the constraints placed on them by those external dependencies. In turn, organizations strive to make others dependent upon them in order to maintain power, stability, and the ability to adapt in the future (Pfeffer 1982).

The dependence of one organization on another may be determined by the following factors:

- The possession of some resource by itself
- The importance of that resource to the firm
- The inability of the firm to obtain that resource elsewhere
- The firm's ability to take desired action
- The firm's lack of control over resources critical to the environmental actor (Pfeffer and Salancik 1978)

Most firms do not simply respond to external constraints and controls by complying. Rather, there are a variety of strategies that might be employed in order to avoid compliance with the demands of those controlling necessary resources. These strategies may include the following actions:

- Restricting the flow of information about the firm
- Denying the legitimacy of the constraints imposed by the resource
- Merging, diversifying, or expanding to alter interdependencies
- Negotiating a new relationship with the environment through interlocking directorates
- Undertaking political action, such as lobbying (Pfeffer and Salancik 1978)

From this perspective, an organization is seen as functioning both as a coalition of varying interests as well as a market where influence and control are traded. Participants can and do have incompatible goals and interests, and an interplay of influences inevitably ensues. The issue of whose interests prevail is most often determined by which organizations have the most power and how they employ that power.

At the beginning of this chapter the issue of health care was raised. The ideas of resource dependence can be used to paint a picture of this sector in a number of ways. Consider the case of health care information Web portals such as Web MD, Caregiver, or McKesson. Online organizations such as these are striving to deliver medical services to the home, to caregivers, and to patients in traditional forms using website and communication technologies. But who really controls this type of information and service delivery? One answer arises by identifying the major investors in these online organizations. Large, cash-rich corporations should be noted. Another angle is to examine the origins of the members of the boards of directors of these firms. One may also want to consider the previous employers of the executives employed by these corporations. In these latter two cases, look for commonalities. Technologies are also important. Which vendors offer technologies that support the delivery of online health care through these portals? Investors, executives, directors, and technologies are all resources of one form or another. In this case, perhaps HMOs will not be as influential tomorrow as they are today. Alliances between Web cam manufacturers, such as Polycom, Logitech, or Kodak, and Internet or computer equipment manufacturers, such as Cisco Systems, IBM, or Intel, may prove to be the real power holders in the health care systems of the future.

Another example of resource dependency at work can be found in the personal computer industry:

> Manufacturers—such as Compaq, Packard Bell, and Apple Computer—are dependent on organizations such as Intel that supply memory chips and integrated circuits. They are also dependent on chains of computer stores and other retail stores that stock their products and on school systems and corporate customers that buy large quantitites of their products. When there are few suppliers of a resource, such as integrated circuits, or few organizaitons that distribute and sell a product, companies become very dependent on the organizaitons that do exist. Intel, for example, makes many of the most advanced microchips and thus has a lot of power vis-à-vis computer makers that need its fastest chips to compete successfully. The greater the dependence of one organization on another, the more power the latter has over the former, and the more it can threaten or exploit the dependent organization if it wishes to do so. (Jones 1995, 226)

Resource dependence theory is an intriguing analytical framework. One of a number of important implications for managers is that there are limits to organizational autonomy and limits to efforts to make other organizations dependent. The U.S. government's antitrust case against Microsoft is but one example of the limits placed on an organization's activities to make others dependent upon it.

Resource dependence theory does have its shortcomings. It may overplay the importance of power in explaining organizational behavior. That organizations may be goal- or objective-driven is an aspect that is not given much consideration (Hall 1996). Its focus on issues such as diversification, mergers, joint ventures, and vertical integration leads one critic, Donaldson (2001), to suggest resource dependence may not be an organization theory after all. It may really be a theory of corporate strategy. Donaldson (2001) also offers other arguments to counter the ideas of this approach. To begin, as a perspective that focuses its attention on interorganizational relations, its relevance for explaining the makeup and internal organizational structures is limited. It may also overemphasize the importance of politics. Although many organizations do interact with government, in most instances this is not a central role. Resource dependence perspective may also overemphasize the ability of an organization to influence or alter its operating environment. Furthermore, relatively few empirical studies have tested its assertions. In many cases where the ideas are tested, other explanations are available to support the findings. Finally, in conclusion its main proponent, Pfeffer (1982), suggests that its time may have passed as a viable explanatory tool given its relative simplicity.

21

Population Ecology Perspective

Which companies or organizations will be around 100 years from now? Will professional service firms, temporary entities, such as the Olympic Games organizing committees, or multidivisional structures, such as those found in major organizations, including the Royal Bank of Canada or IBM, still be prevalent in a few decades? Which industries are ripe for nurturing and supporting a series of initial public offerings? Why do so many restaurants tend to fail after short periods of operation while other entities such as banks seem to lead charmed lives? You may be interested to learn that ideas originating in the biological sciences can help answer questions such as these.

The language of ecology and its references to populations, niches, variation, selection, and retention provide clues as to what the future of organizations may look like. It also provides suggestions regarding why our current institutions look like they do.

Population ecology is a perspective that seeks to explain the factors that affect the life cycles of organizations in a given population of existing organizations (Hannan and Freeman 1977). Originating as a response to strategic choice theory, it also suggests why some organizations are around longer than others. One argument proposed by theorists in this tradition is that business environments within which organizations exist select those that will survive over time. Organizations do not adapt to their competitive environments. Corporate fates are determined by their surroundings. This emphasis on environmental determinism is among the most obvious of features of this perspective that sets it apart from other theories of organization (1977).

Within this school of thought, "performance," "success," and "effectiveness" refer ultimately to survival over time. "Survival" refers to a form of organization with the environment determining the distribution and form that a population of organizations may take (Jones 1995). "Population" refers to all organizations within a particular boundary that have a common form. Each population occupies a specific niche or a distinct combination of resources and other constraints that are sufficient to support an organization form.

From this perspective, organizations have distinct features. Each has a structure or blueprint for future action. This blueprint encompasses the organizations' stated goals, the forms of authority used within, a core technology, and a marketing strategy (Hannan and Freeman 1984).

Organizational forms follow a particular life cycle that includes three stages: variation, selection, and retention (Hannan and Freeman 1977). Variation across organizations occurs primarily at the time organizations are formed with much of this being the result of the creation of new structures and the replacement of old forms.

Organizational forms are then selected according to how well they fit their environment. In general, most organizations cannot freely change themselves. Inertial pressures keep them the same (Hannan and Freeman 1984). Indeed, selection processes tend to favor organizations whose structures are difficult to change. Difficult-to-change structures are those that reliably produce collective action and are accountable. Reliability and accountability are indicated by the extent that a form is reproduced.

What conditions create an environment conducive to selection? Four in particular are quite important (Hannan and Freeman 1984). First, there should exist a high rate of variation among organizational forms. Second, high organizational mortality rates should be evident. Third, competition within the industry should be intense. Finally, resources should not be relatively abundant.

Those forms that will survive are then retained. Mechanisms used to retain specific organizational forms include the development of standard operating procedures, the use of socialization processes developed for new employees, and the acceptance of common bureaucratic principals such as a clearly defined hierarchy of offices with each level having clearly defined, explicit authority and responsibility.

New, rapidly evolving industries and markets often offer good examples of the logic of population ecology. Jones (1995) offers the following illustration of the applicability of this perspective. First, he defines the terms "population" and "niche":

> A population of organizations is comprised of all the organizations that compete for the same set of resources in a specific environment. For

example, IBM, Compaq, Dell, Gateway, and the other personal computer companies constitute a population. They all seek to attract the
same environmental resources, in this case, the money which consumers
spend on personal computing. Some organizations within a population
often choose to focus on different environmental niches, or sets of resources. For example, Dell Computer chose to focus on the mail-order
niche of the personal computer environment whereas IBM and Compaq
originally focused on the business niche, while Apple focused on the
higher education niche. (422)

Using these ideas as a starting point, ideas from the same example
are then used to explain peaks and troughs of new start-up birth rates.
Of interest is its explanatory power for understanding situations where
companies are rapidly formed to provide services and capitalize on
resources that were previously nonexistent.

Two factors account for this rapid birth rate. First, as new organizations
are founded, there is an increase in knowledge and skills available to
generate similar new organizations. New organizations are often
founded by entrepreneurs who leave existing companies such as
Hewlett-Packard and IBM. A second factor that accounts for this high
organizational birth rate is that when a new kind of organization is
founded and it manages to survive, a role model is provided for other
would-be entrepreneurs. The success of a new organization breaks a
path, making it easier for others to attract investment and start similar
organizations, lending to such new organizations a certain measure of
legitimacy. . . . Once an environment is populated with a number of
successful organizations, the birth rate of new organizations tends to
taper off. Two factors working against new organizations at this point
are diminishing resources and the strength of the existing competition.
. . . Companies that start first and achieve success, like McDonald's or
Microsoft, have a competitive edge on later entrants because of *first-
mover advantages*. First-mover advantages include such things as customer loyalty, a recognizable brand name, and location advantages.
(Jones 1995, 423)

Summarized, population ecology suggests the following:

Environments define a strategic resource path that an organization must
follow to be selected for and survive over time. Niches provide the
resources that a firm needs to be selected for and survive over time.
Because limited environment resources constrain the number of popu-

lations a niche can support, some populations and organizations are selected against and disappear. (Ulrich and Barney 1985, 474)

Researchers have been exploring organizations from a population perspective for over a quarter-century. Their findings suggest a number of implications:

> What we have learned from the various ecological studies is that there is a liability in being young or new, a liability that recurs to some extent when there are reorganizations or important successions. There is also a liability to being small. We have learned that foundings are more likely and organizational mortality is diminished the fewer similar organizations there are and, conversely, that foundings are less likely and mortality is greater the more dense the population becomes. The studies of particular industries have also examined more specific effects such as political and economic conditions that are relevant for understanding organizational birth and death in the particular population. (Pfeffer 1997, 168)

This theory is open to numerous criticisms. First, among theorists of this tradition there is "a common rejection of individual organizational adaptation or any notion that management frequently guides such a process" (Donaldson 1995, 70). Second, borrowing ideas from the Darwinian theory of natural selection may be inappropriate for the study of organizations. Donaldson (1995) suggests that three mechanisms found in nature that allow natural selection to work— reproduction, genetic inheritance, and high birth and death rates—are not normally found in organizations. Third, "[a]s a theory of performance, population ecology focuses attention on factors that may be substantively important but over which there is virtually no organizational control except to the extent organizations can choose their competitive niche. . . . Consequently, population ecology . . . is . . . reasonably far from a theory that permits knowledge to be translated into action" (Pfeffer 1997, 168).

Another concern is that the time frame necessary for an effective study of organizational life spans is often inhibiting, as the lives of some entities may have to be measured in centuries or half-centuries. As a result, most studies are necessarily historical. Critics also argue that many population ecology studies focus their attention on exploring the relationship between density and performance as opposed to examining other factors that might cause organizational births or deaths (Pfeffer 1997). Many studies to date have also tended to focus on industries with large numbers of very small participants, such as the restaurant business or gas stations. This has led some observers to question the ability of a theory based on such studies to say anything relevant about established industries with very large organizations (Perrow 1986). However, a literature review by Baum (1996) does suggest that studies of large-entity industries are increasing and that the failure rate of these entities increases with the number of organizations of similar size in the population (Pfeffer 1997, 168). Many also question the definitions and measurements employed in population ecology studies. For instance, does a merged firm count as a death or birth? How are name changes or spin-offs accounted for? Finally, most research in this tradition is heavily empirical in nature. This has led to two other major concerns: absence of contextual realism and measurement imprecision. In short, the studies and their instruments don't always measure what their authors intended them to measure due to a dependence on the use of large-scale historical databases (107).

22

Institutional Perspective

Have you been to more than one conference or convention lately? Any type counts. Have you noticed that to some extent they all look somewhat similar? Regardless of location, topic, venue, or audience, the meals tend to taste the same, the rooms look the same, the schedules read alike, and the handouts are rarely original in appearance. There are very good reasons why most conferences are not too different in how they are organized. They are the topic of this chapter.

Why are organizations different? This question underlies many of the organizational theories addressed in this book. It also leads to an assumption that organizations are fundamentally distinctive from one another. Institutional theory inverts this assumption, asking instead: Why are organizations the same? It suggests that internal and external social pressures reduce the variation of structures and strategies found in today's world of commerce. These social pressures are on occasion quite complex, often difficult to identify, and can take many forms. One explanation is that "[f]irms operate within a social framework of norms, values and taken-for-granted assumptions about what constitutes appropriate organization level behavior. Economic choices are constrained not only by . . . technological, informational and income limits . . . but by socially constructed limits that are distinctly human in origin like norms, habits and customs" (Oliver 1997, 699).

The implication of these ideas is a picture or explanation of organized behavior that is nontraditional and thought provoking. In its simplest form, this perspective argues that

> [f]irms' tendencies toward conformity with predominant norms, tradition, and social influences in their internal and external environments lead to homogeneity among firms in their structure and activities, and that successful firms are those that gain support and legitimacy by conforming to social pressures. (Oliver 1997, 699)

Put another way, "organizations conform to social expectations because they are rewarded for doing so through increased legitimacy, resources and survival capabilities" (Scott 1987, 498).

> The institutional view sees organizations as having two essential dimensions—technical and institutional. The technical dimension is the day-to-day work technology and operating requirements. The institutional structure is that part of the organization most visible to the public. Moreover, the technical dimension is governed by norms of rationality and efficiency, but the institutional environment is governed by expectations from the external environment . . . which in turn . . . is composed of norms and values from stakeholders (customers, investors, associations, boards, government, collaborating organizations). As a result of pressures to do things in a proper and correct way, the formal structures of many organizations reflect the expectations and values of the environment rather than the demand of work activities. This means that organizations may incorporate positions or activities perceived as important by the larger society and thus increase its legitimacy but which are not . . . rational with respect to work flow and products or services. (Daft 2001, 183)

A good analogy for the way this works might be found in the world of fast food restaurant chains. Most of the newer restaurant chains somewhat mirror the two most popular ones: McDonald's and Burger King. Even these two industry leaders seem less the products of unique ideas and more the products of careful comparison and imitation. Indeed, aspects that appear to boost the popularity of one chain are quickly adopted in some faintly altered form by the other. Generally, the layouts are similar, the menus are similar, the labor forces are similar, and the promotional gimmicks are similar. Chains that are too different from these industry front-runners rarely survive. Why is this?

Well, earlier we noted a tendency toward conformity or imitation. In more detail, this occurs for a number of reasons (Dimaggio and Powell 1983).

One reason may have an economic basis. If one firm makes slight adjustments to its organizational structure that appear to increase its efficiency, other industry competitors are also likely to notice and incorporate these changes to ensure that they are not left behind. Conformity may also occur as a result of industry regulation. Often, laws are enacted that affect all industry players and force all managers to comply. Equally influential are the bylaws and policies of the various professional associations and bodies whose policies regulate the conduct of employees in so many industries.

Similarly, if the uncertainty facing one firm originates in its environment, it is likely that competing firms face the same form of uncertainty. In this situation, firms often alter their organizational structure along the lines of their successful competitors (Narayanan and Nath 1993).

Finally, organizations, like individuals, generally require a certain level of social acceptance in order to function. Few organizations wish to be perceived as "flouters" of industry norms. Nonconformity may upset investors and other stakeholders. If industry norms are consistent organizational goals, then it is in the best interest of the organization to conform.

Clearly, legitimacy matters to most organizations. Remaining legitimate in the eyes of the public or important stakeholders is not always a simple task, as members of the Canadian Armed Forces might attest in the wake of their experiences in Somalia. However, prior to any damage being done, most managers have a number of options at their disposal (Suchman 1995). The two most prevalent options are to protect their accomplishments to diligently work to spot problems ahead of time. Accomplishments can be protected by building a strong internal culture, such as that found in the nuclear industry; toning down highly visible efforts to build legitimacy; and policing internal operations so that problems do not occur.

Despite the best of efforts, some organizations find themselves in positions of declining legitimacy. In these cases, three strategies are commonly used in an attempt to repair the damage (Suchman 1995). The first is not to panic. Restructuring is a second strategy. Restructuring is the way an organization disassociates itself from the source of concern. Common restructuring tactics include firing executives, changing operating procedures, and occasionally shifting geographical locales. A final strategy for restoring legitimacy is to create a set of believable rationales. These may take the form of denying the problem, thus hoping that time will heal the wounds; excusing the organization by blaming others; justifying the problem through creative moral arguments; and explaining the problem in a positive light.

Another implication for readers is that some industries are more likely to display this tendency toward conformity than others. In the case of retail sales, competing chains often offer similar store layouts and products. In the service industry, procedures related to customer relations are often common to many firms. Many firms involved in manufacturing use similar raw materials and production techniques.

Conformity for many organizations also means change. When change does occur and new structures and ideas are incorporated, they tend to originate in strong sources such as personal and professional networks and in industry-dominant organizations such as America Online, IBM, or Intel.

A number of criticisms have plagued institutional theory. To begin, empirical evidence is simply lacking to support many of its major assertions (Donaldson 1995). Its detractors suggest that it does not sufficiently explain strategic or autonomous behavior by managers. Indeed, even in the most extreme cases, it is not implausible to suggest that most managers have some ability to manipulate, defy, compromise, avoid, or acquiesce influential environmental forces (Oliver 1991). There is also healthy debate regarding the generalizability of many of the insights of this theory to many for-profit entities. Can survival and prosperity truly rest on the assessment of formal structures as opposed to observed financial performance? A more direct concern is the applicability of the perspective (Tolbert and Zucker 1996). To which conditions does it apply? Although the range of such studies has broadened, traditionally they have focused on public-sector organizations (Hinings and Greenwood 1988) and more recently on professional service firms. Tolbert and Zucker pose a series of questions that highlight other shortcomings related to our understanding of the process of institutionalization:

> [I]t falls short in answering a number of other questions. How and when choices or alternative lines of action become socially defined; who acts to cause change and to diffuse that change to multiple organizations; what are the potential benefits of creating similar structures or converging to the same structures. (1996, 186)

Finally, many scholars find it difficult to accept the assumption that organizations passively accept the changes imposed on them by their environment (Narayanan and Nath 1993). Though recent commentators have attempted to recast this idea, much of institutional theory remains true to its initial hypothesis. We conclude our discussion of the institutional perspective with the following quote: "Probably the most important implication from our perspective is the need to develop more direct measures and better documentation of claims of the institutionalization of structures" (Tolbert and Zucker 1996, 184).

23

Chaos Perspective

How does knowledge of the natural sciences and progress in that domain apply to the world of contemporary organizations? If one is a believer in the tradition of Morgan (1986), then one's imagination is the only limit to potential applications. Others might suggest that a particularly innovative stream of thinking found within the sciences may have significant potential for increasing our understanding of these all-important phenomena. Originating in the study of fluid dynamics, chaos theory has been used to explain phenomena in fields as disparate as chemical solutions, social systems, biological evolution, mathematics, medicine, and international relations.

How do technological giants such as Hewlett Packard or Microsoft progress from garage-based or backyard operations to the position of global leaders? Life cycle models of large-scale change, theories of strategic management, and entrepreneurial studies programs all offer important insights and unique perspectives. Chaos theory offers an alternative means to understand these developments.

Chaos theory is a way of understanding how systems emerge in ways and with patterns that are not intended. It arose in response to traditional science's inability to explain the unexplainable. As a field, organization theorists have traditionally been open to adopting insights from different areas of the sciences and the humanities. In particular, the principles of chaos theory have helped organizational theorists tackle a number of different challenges. These include those of self-organizing systems in which innovative cultural patterns and increasingly complex structures repeatedly emerge, the operation of unique, extremely high-risk organizations, and the development of multifirm alliance relationships.

As with any other theory of the natural or social sciences, chaos theory has a language all of its own as well as a specific set of principles. A true connoisseur of the art of chaotic organization is well versed in the meanings of terms such as "fractals," "sensitivity dependence," "discrete bifurcation," "strange attractors," "sensitivity dependence," and "irreversible disequilibrium" or "irreversible actions." Organizational theorists have been creative in their application of such concepts to contemporary organizations. For example, in organizational terms, fractals refer to "similar patterns of structures and processes found at different levels of analysis." Strange attractors refer to "the forces that push one or more dimensions of a firm to look like another" (Thietart and Forgues 1995, 26). Other terms and definitions are as follows:

> *Chaos:* Because of the coupling of counteracting forces, organizations are potentially chaotic.
>
> *Discrete Bifurcation:* Organizations move from one dynamic state to another in an abrupt, noncontinuous manner. Dramatic change can occur unexpectedly. Periods of apparent stability are likely to be short lived.
>
> *Sensitivity Dependence on Initial Conditions:* When an organization is in a state of chaos, small changes can have big effects in the long term. Small disturbances multiply over time. Thus, long-term forecasting is impossible. However, short-term forecasting and planning are possible.
>
> *Strange Attractors:* When in a chaotic state, organizations are attracted to a recognizable configuration or pattern of structures and processes.
>
> *Fractals:* When in a chaotic state, similar patterns of structures and processes may be found at the organizational, group, and individual levels.
>
> *Irreversibility of Action:* No cause in one organization can have the same effect in another organization. No action taken twice in the same organization will have the same effect. History does not repeat itself, thus, studying the past will not lead to much learning in regard to the future.

In recent years, insightful corporate observers have noted the importance of understanding the notion of paradox for managing day-to-day organizational life. At its core, chaos theory describes the interaction of paradoxical forces and offers an intriguing means to describe the impact of two of these—change and stability—on large-scale enterprises.

Chaotic organizations are driven by the counteracting forces of change and stability. These forces contain the seeds of order and chaos. On the one hand the forces of change are stabilizing because of their tendency to push the system out of its orbit. Experimentation, incoherence, diverse and diverging activities from the organization thrust are all sources of instability. They create demands that are not necessarily consistent with planned objectives.

On the other hand, forces of order and stability are used to close a system which is considered too complex by most people. Search for order is an attempt to build islands of certainty where purposeful action can be undertaken. Furthermore, order is a means to create the illusion of management. This illusion is forged by individuals who are confronted with the impossible challenge of achieving a mission without having the capacity to succeed. Order can also create resistance to change and leave an organization in a state of limbo. (Thietart and Forgues 1995, 27)

What should be apparent from these terms and the twin forces of paradox is that chaos theory offers potential insights into how organizations change. The exact applicability of these ideas to our contemporary institutions is a subject of contentious debate among theorists. However, the following insight offers an example of how it might be used effectively:

At some point in time industries or organizations reach a point of complete and utter chaos characterized by decline and disarray. This is termed a point of *irreversible disequilibrium.*

Organizations then reach a bifurcation point or a *point of singularity,* juncture that allows the inherent tendencies toward equilibrium to be overcome.

A *bifurcation point* then ushers in a period of disequilibrium that reflects a break from the past and requires participants in a system to discommit themselves from existing processes and values. Out of this arises a self reinforcing or *self organizing system.* (Browning, Beyer, and Shetler 1995, 139–140)

In order to make sense of apparent chaos, managers and other stakeholders develop innovative corporate cultures and increasingly complex structures. This process repeats itself over time as new challenges arise. Unfortunately, the end results of these changes are never quite known ahead of time. Some old ways of doing things are destroyed, others improved, and still others are made permanent. Unpredictability, novelty, and a chance for something new to emerge accompany expansion (Browning, Beyer, and Shetler 1995).

How would one make use of a theory such as this for describing organizational phenomena? Where might it find a home? One suggestion is to picture an extremely complex organization. How about the operations of a 5,000-person Nimitz-class aircraft carrier? How does it function effectively in times of high anxiety? How about describing the formation processes and cooperative behaviors of an eight-company defense/high-technology industry consortium of former competitors? These examples suggest strongly that what appears as sheer and utter chaos on the surface may in truth be an example of regular and highly patterned activity.

A number of powerful implications arise from chaos theory for managers and analysts. To begin, its ideas can improve the practice of strategic planning. Levy (1994, 170–172) suggests the incorporation of five ideas by strategists. These include an awareness that long-term planning is difficult, industries do not reach a stable equilibrium, dramatic change can occur unexpectedly, short-term forecasts and predictions of patterns can be made, and guidelines are needed to cope with complexity and uncertainty.

Chaos theory can also be used to understand the behavior of complex political coalitions within organizations, the behavior of individual firms seeking to gain competitive advantage over a group of competitors (Phelan 1995), international supply chains (Levy 1994), the engineering of products such as kerosene fans (Aihara and Katayama 1995), the short-term prediction of contagious diseases, weather, and the economy (Ditto and Munakata 1995, 98), and the operation of a research and development consortium (Browning, Beyer, and Shetler 1995).

This last case offers a good example of how chaos theory helped researchers (Browning, Beyer, and Shetler 1995, 113) to explain how members of a semiconductor research and development consortium, SEMATECH, cooperated and persisted despite also being intense competitors. SEMATECH was formed during the 1980s by the U.S. government and fourteen U.S. semiconductors to pool resources and respond to the threat of Japanese dominance of the semiconductor market. During the early 1980s, the U.S. market share of semiconductor sales was falling quickly with the result that the U.S. Department of Defense feared that foreigners would soon control computing resources essential to the economic and military security of the country. Many American executives also came to the conclusion that no one company would be able to restore American supremacy in this area, so a pooling of efforts became an acceptable response.

SEMATECH proved a fascinating case application of chaos theory. Browning, Beyer, and Shetler (1995) arrive at a number of conclusions. Two of the most important are as follows:

> The successful founding and continued viability of SEMATECH demonstrates that cooperation between competitors can be achieved under certain conditions. The presence and activities of SEMATECH have not eliminated competition in this industry. Rather SEMATECH has provided a neutral ground on which "blood enemies" can cooperate with certain agreed-upon boundaries. The consortium has become the symbol and catalyst for many cooperative efforts. Complexity theory helps to explain how small, discrete events can have large consequences. Individual contributions became self-amplifying in this case because that gave birth to a moral community and created structures that in turn created other structures. Initial disorder made innovation mandatory. Complexity theory highlights the importance of an initial crisis or state of chaos that marks a break with the past and stimulates openness to radical new ideas. Members of the semiconductor industry knew that they could not continue to prosper unless they drastically changed their practices. Such recognition, relatively rare in organizations and industries seems to be a necessary radical precursor of change. (145)

What other organizations might researchers wish to apply the ideas of chaos theory in order to understand behavior?

> Imagine an organization with a globally respected brand name that is used by 23,000 institutions in 200 countries and territories; whose market-leading products are used by 355 million people to make more than 7 billion transaction worth $650 billion annually—the single largest block of consumer purchasing power in the world economy; that would have a value of around $150 billion in stock-market terms that can't be bought, sold or raided, since the 23,000 institutions that create its products are also its owners, members, customers, subjects and superiors, holding membership in the form of perpetual membership rights. . . . The name of the riddle? A little ubiquitous thing called Visa. (Caulkin 1995, 35)

At first glance, chaos theory appears to be an attractive explanatory tool for organizational researchers. Yet, some researchers suggest that the theory has serious shortcomings (Levy 1994), especially when applied to situations that are not of the natural sciences. To begin, it may not be a good fit. In many instances, it is simply difficult to demonstrate a link between chaotic behavior and organizational effectiveness.

> Despite its attractions, the application of chaos theory to the social sciences is still in its infancy, and there are those who think that expectations are too high. . . . Although real life phenomena may resemble the patterns generated by simple nonlinear systems, that does not mean that we can easily model and forecast these phenomena; it is almost impossible to take a set of data and determine the system of relationships that generates it. . . . In fact there is considerable debate in the economics and finance literature about how one tests a data series to determine if it is chaotic or simply subject to random influences. Moreover, it is important to realize that many systems are not chaotic, and that systems can transition between chaotic and non-chaotic states. (169)

At its core, chaos theory is a mathematical approach to understanding complex phenomena. As suggested earlier, this brings to mind an important question: Can the behavior of an entity that employs thousands of individuals, sells to millions of customers, maintains hundreds of suppliers, operates in tens of industries, and responds to dozens of stakeholders be meaningfully modeled by mathematical formula? This mathematical basis presents another concern. Many researchers may not possess the necessarily mathematical skills to model complex organized behavior. Finally, chaos theory is just that, a theory. It is continuously being tested and modified. But like all theories, the best that we can ultimately do is to attempt to falsify its underlying hypotheses.

Part III

Interpretive and Social Constructionist Perspectives

A number of common themes exist to tie together the often disparate series of frameworks and perspectives that cumulatively form the body of insight known as organization theory. Among the most of important of these themes is the idea that efforts to improve the corporate bottom line do not always drive the behavior of large organizations. Despite the popular conception among lay observers and commentators that profit dictates business policy, many actions taken by managers of corporations are taken for reasons other than raising revenues and cutting expenses. A guiding principle underlying any such suggestion is that people in organizations are autonomous and capable of acting on the choices they make.

One theoretical basis of these ideas is the paradigm or school of thought known as interpretivism—the lower left-hand quadrant of Burrell and Morgan's (1979) work noted in chapter 2. Theories in this quadrant provide an important response to functionalist theories. In contrast to the oversocialized, passive, determined role taker presented in functionalist theories, interpretive theories provide for an undersocialized, active, role maker. "This perspective is based on the view that people socially and symbolically construct and sustain their own organizational realities" (Gioia and Pitre 1990, 588). Of importance to theorists of this tradition are the descriptions, insights, and explanations of events that reveal the system of interpretations and organizing processes that are associated with modern organizations.

In this part, we will consider five of the most relevant interpretive and social constructionist approaches for organization theorizing: symbolic interactionism, dramaturgy, the use of metaphors, sensemaking, and organizational rules perspective. We complement these five perspectives with a sixth, the culture perspective. As with the others in this book, these theories contribute to macro-organizational theorizing.

24

Symbolic Interactionism Perspective

Deborah Hurst and Conor Vibert

News flash: January 11, 2004—Vibcorp announces quarterly profits and revenues that exceeded those of the previous year by 10 percent and 15 percent, respectively.

This sounds familiar doesn't it? But is it good news? What appears on the surface to be stellar results for Vibcorp may be perceived by the market to be something quite different: suboptimal performance. What is the real story? If one follows the market, it should be obvious within minutes. Vibcorp's share price will probably rise or fall depending on the behavior of a legion of analysts and investors.

Does personal interpretation matter? If one considers that day in and day out armies of analysts are employed for the sole purpose of interpreting corporate actions, deciphering signals, and translating symbols, be they those of competitors or potential investments, then an answer of yes is probably reasonable. Given that these same individuals and their employers then pronounce judgment in terms of their recommendations or their buy and sell behavior, this same yes is resounding.

Why do large organizations behave as they do? In the world of publicly traded corporations, one answer is to manage and then meet the expectations of important external stakeholders. If one also considers the connection of most CEO compensation packages to share-price performance, then it is perhaps understandable that managing the expectations and interpretations of Wall Street analysts is also one of a CEO's most important responsibilities.

Interpreting performance and managing expectations is big business, whether the interpretations belong to twenty-eight-year-old Wall Street analysts or engineers reporting to senior management. The rise of corporate public and investor relations departments, the existence of a highly educated workforce, the creative and lucrative nature of many employee retention programs, and the existence of a cottage industry of change management consultants all suggest the acceptance by employers of the disparate viewpoints and beliefs that exist within and beyond their empires. Not only do interpretations need to be recognized and understood, especially when held by important and influential outsiders, they also need to be managed and created internally. One consequence

> is that leaders come to be symbols. . . . The leader as a symbol provides a target for action when difficulties occur, serving as a scapegoat when things go wrong. . . . Successful leaders, as perceived by members of the social system, are those who can separate themselves from organizational failures and associate themselves with organizational success. . . . For instance, if a manager knows that business in his or her division is about to improve because of the economic cycle, the leader may, nevertheless, write recommendations and undertake actions and changes that are highly visible and that will tend to identify his or her behavior closely with the division. A manager who perceives impending failure will attempt to associate the division and its policies and decisions with others, particularly persons in higher organizational positions, and to disassociate himself or herself from the division's performance, occasionally even transferring or moving to another organization. (Pfeffer 1977, 110)

Of course, these ideas are not new and their origins are widespread. Two important theoretical bases for these ideas are symbolic interactionism and the social construction of reality.

Symbolic interactionism is broadly defined as the human capacity to create and use symbols to communicate. Meaning is derived from social acts, gestures, and the creation of significant symbols. World creation flows from human ability to symbolically represent not only each other, but also objects, ideas, and virtually all aspects of experience. With the capacity to create symbols and use them in human affairs, patterns of social organization among humans are created, maintained, and changed. Humans rely on their symbol-using powers to adapt and survive in a complex world (Turner 1986).

Social life depends on the ability to imagine oneself in another social role. Taking on the role of the other depends on the capacity for reflexivity or having internal conversations, which means that the self, reflexivity, and the generalized other are the crucial concepts in this perspective. Key exemplars are George Herbert Mead and Herbert Blumer.

Therefore, symbolic interaction suggests that individual actions and beliefs are understood through a process of interpretation by which the inquirer attempts to discover the meaning or significance underlying those actions or beliefs. As there is radical diversity across cultures in the ways in which social life is conceptualized or understood, such interpretations are both unstable and ever changing. As social practices (bargaining, promising, working, parenting, and so on) are constituted by the meanings that their participants attribute to them, their meanings are always shifting and as shifts are confronted, meanings are reinterpreted. In short, there are no hard and fast definitions in the discipline of social science. Symbolic interactionists and other writers of the interpretive tradition are antipositivists. They seek to understand organized behavior by seeking out uniqueness and particularity. Unlike positivists, they do not stress the primacy of facts or the hypothetical deductive mode of explanation. Instead, they emphasize an inductive approach that works from the data up (Glazer and Strauss 1967; Strauss 1987).

Numerous organizational writers have drawn from these ideas to theorize about the behavior in organizations. Daft and Weick (1984) propose that our modern institutions be understood as systems of interpretation based on four assumptions: organizations are open systems that process information from the environment, their interpretive process is somewhat different than the individual's interpretive process, strategic- or executive-level managers decide how interpretation will occur, and different organizations use different processes to interpret their environments.

In order to understand the competitive environment facing them, Daft and Weick (1984) suggest that organizational actors may enact or learn by doing, discover by doing research with surveys, act on undirected viewing based on hunches, rumors, or chance opportunities, or act on conditioned viewing based on formal measures and data.

Organizations typically follow three steps in interpreting their competitive environment. First, they scan it in order to obtain important information. They then interpret the data or impose meaning on it. Finally, they take action in accordance with their interpretation of their findings—that is to say, they learn.

Other interpretive theorists also offer insight that can be used to understand how organizations make sense of their competitive and operating environments. A good example is work by Berger and Luckman (1967) that is termed the "social construction of reality." Their analysis deals with issues such as the makeup of knowledge, the order found within that knowledge, the existence of multiple realities or multiple viewpoints of events, and how knowledge intersubjectively guides everyday life. An implication for practitioners of social constructivism is the need to be aware that the executives and workers employed in corporations, institutions, and other entities do not always think alike. Statements made on behalf of an organization may not be widely accepted within it. Indeed, as is discussed in chapter 29, many organizations are comprised of competing subcultures, each with its own distinctive outlook on its purpose and function.

Social constructivists believe that we create social structures through knowledge-generating exercises. Unfortunately, we also become slaves to the structures that we have created. Our ideas become the basis of organizational inertia! This idea is highlighted in Berger's other work on the sacred canopy, where he discusses the human creation of religion as a ruling, ordered structure (Berger, 1990).

Another interpretive approach builds on the ideas of Berger and Luckman (1967). Smircich and Stubbart (1985) suggest that work environments are socially constructed. Organizational managers actually reshape their environments by observing, interpreting, and acting on their interpretations. For example, if Bill Gates and Microsoft decide that the future lies in the development of a certain software product, their decision to research, produce, and market that product can actually impact and change the business environment. By developing Microsoft Windows, Gates effectively constructed a new business reality that had not existed previously.

Among the most important implications for readers is the idea that managers or executives may create organizational realities through their clever use of symbols or interpretation of critical incidents, organizational history, and environmental challenges or opportunities. Thus, for researchers seeking to retrospectively understand corporate actions, corporate websites may not be the best sources for information. For instance, despite wide-spread and well-publicized allegations of improper business practices during the dot.com boom, researchers would be hard pressed to find specific details about the improprieties on Worldcom's website. Despite seeing its share price fall to penny-stock status from well over $100 per share in 2001 and subsequently laying off tens of thousands of employees, much of the discussion of recent Nortel Networks history found on its website currently deals with new technology innovations and their market launch dates. All too often, despite employing tens of thousands of individuals, all contributing in different ways to the corporation's success, many corporations portray the CEO as the face of their organization. Describing the actions and behavior of these executives in almost romantic terms is more a norm than an exception in many cases.

Symbolic interactionism is not without its shortcomings. It offers little insight into the issue of acceptable organizational performance or effectiveness. Indeed, from this perspective it appears that managers' interpretations are what matter. It also is silent in regard to the issue of organizational boundaries. It ignores the suggestion that there are clear, concrete manifestations of organized behavior as well as nonsymbolic consequences, such as layoffs, pay cuts, and unions. Finally, there is not a large body of empirical research to support assertions found in this literature.

25

Dramaturgical Perspective

The stage is set. The regulator is set to shut down the utility operator—your client! The client is set to sue and possibly push into bankruptcy the power plant simulator builder—your firm! The project director's career is in jeopardy—that's you. The project is salvageable but only if the resources of the company are not distracted with a legal action. The outcome hinges on the meeting scheduled for next week.

The script is flowing. The simulator site will be cleaned and polished. Although nonfunctional, the indicator lights and panels will be lit up. A main control panel and related functioning software will be temporarily borrowed from the site of a less demanding client.

The actors know their lines. Your company's chairman will be on hand to ease the worry and concern of his old friend, the client firm's CEO. The software and hardware integration teams will work through the weekend to perfect the ruse of a working simulator. Although weeks from completion, a simulator that appears to work well holds the key to pleasing an audience that includes potential future clients, stock analysts, journalists, energy sector players, and, of course, the industry regulator.

Theorizing about organizations occurs in many forms. One interesting example uses a format that is fairly easy to recognize. It is termed the "dramaturgical approach" and it builds on the ideas of symbolic interactionism and the social construction of reality. Here, social role construction is taken very seriously. In many ways, we spend most of our lives acting out various symbolic social roles and constructing and reconstructing our image, both at work and at home. The dramaturgical approach takes us one step farther by describing organizations as stages and employees as actors who are playing roles.

The idea of describing social phenomena in terms of drama dates way back in our literary tradition, but was formally developed in modern thought by Goffman (1959). Goffman provides many insights regarding life as a drama from his studies on total institutions and gender advertisements. His major interests include role analysis, social interaction, chance encounters, gatherings, and small group dynamics. In particular, Goffman attempts to chart and describe the dynamics of the fleeting, chance, and momentary social encounters that make up such a large part of our everyday lives. In order to express the extent to which such interactions are ordered, or scripted, Goffman employs the metaphor "drama."

It is useful to understand organizations in terms of their fit within the symbolic interactionism perspective. According to this perspective, organizational life revolves around our ability to imagine ourselves in other organizational roles. This imaginary "taking on" of other roles depends on our capacity for an internal conversation with ourselves. In essence, we have to be able to role-play various parts in our heads.

Dramaturgy describes social orders (in this case business organizations) as always being precarious or risky ventures because they are frequently disrupted by embarrassment, by withdrawal, and by breakdowns of communication (Abercrombie, Hill, and Turner 1984). Picture a play where the actors forget their lines, withdraw and ignore each other on stage, and miss their cues. This, in essence, is how organizational drama often functions, or misfunctions.

The basic premise of dramaturgy is that when interacting, individuals tend to put on shows for each other, stage-managing the impressions that others receive. Social roles are like acting roles. Employees and managers project images of themselves, usually in ways that serve their own best interests, because such images help to define situations and create appropriate expectations. Within this context, organizational activities often take on a particular symbolic significance for the society at large. Organizational events taking place within corporations (mergers, takeovers, criminal allegations, and so on) become dramas that are followed by the society via the mass media.

In accordance with the previous perspectives within the interpretive paradigm, dramaturgy views organizations as systems of shared meanings between employees, managers, customers, suppliers, and society at large. This implies that the real task facing managers is that of building and maintaining shared meanings about how and why their organization does business. In this sense, managers construct reality. As well as being actors, they are directors.

A number of organizational writers have been very successful at developing their insights on this front. Pfeffer (1982) suggests that corporations such as IBM produce two types of output. One type of product is tangible and measurable, such as computer hardware. The second type is symbolic, intangible, and not so easily measured. It consists of attitudes, values, and perceptions held both within the organization and by outsiders (1982).

Not surprisingly, managers tend to have much more influence over symbolic outputs than tangible ones. An implication is that their attempts to focus or alter their organizations—direct their dramas—occur primarily through means of organizational restructuring (altering symbols), executive successions (making use of ceremonies), organizational development (creating new and shared languages), and restructuring of the physical workplace by moving desks or changing the wallpaper (altering physical cues) (Pfeffer 1982). While these actions all involve practical change components, their key aims are symbolic.

These processes help executives to influence their corporate employees by creating and popularizing myths and metaphors. However, a problem with this approach is that the benefits of myth making and other forms of symbolic interaction are not necessarily found on a corporation's bottom line. Creating and re-creating a more effective organization does not necessarily make it more profitable. In fact, this approach is not really concerned with the organization and its business at all. It merely describes the acting of individuals and how their activities can be analyzed. But it does help organizations to avoid problems such as conflict, resistance, high turnover, and absenteeism.

Why might practitioners have an interest in dramaturgy? One important reason is its practical application in impression management. An understanding of an event can be improved if one thinks of it as a drama involving actors unfolding over time. For example, consider the use of impression management in collective bargaining negotiations in a university setting. On one side of a table sit faculty members, many of them tenured. On the other side of the table sit administrators who know that the only major tool of influence on the faculty side is the threat of strike. Yet, both sides realize that an unhappy body of faculty members can seriously damage the culture of the institution by collectively reducing teaching effort and minimizing contact time with students. So how does one side wring concessions out of the other side? Create drama in the negotiating room and with the union members, and carefully manage impressions on the campus, in the community, and in the media.

Indeed, Goffman (1959) uses collective bargaining on many occasions to illustrate life as a theater.

> There are the public or on-stage activities such as face-to-face bargaining, press releases, public forums and the highly symbolic activity of renting and setting up of strike headquarters. There are also backstage activities such as developing the scripts to be employed during the bargaining process, preparation of bargaining positions, press releases and caucuses during negotiations to develop, revise or improvise scripts. All of these activities are designed to manage or manipulate the impressions or messages received by the many stakeholders as the two directly engaged actors (management and union bargaining teams) attempt to curry favour (and thereby gain bargaining power) with the other actors as the acts of the drama unfold. (Kondra and Hurst 2003, 7)

Another reason for a practitioner to pay attention is to think of events where impression management is very effectively handled and events where ineffectiveness reigns. The 2003 outbreaks of SARS in Toronto and the Mad Cow disease in Alberta are two cases in point. In the latter case, within a day of the announcement to the media that one cow in an isolated herd in Alberta had contracted the disease, the United States closed its border to Canadian beef products. The responses of the governments of Alberta and Canada were swift. U.S. meat inspectors were invited to help assess the extent of the problem. Government and public health officials quickly reassured the public that Canadian beef was safe to eat. Also within a day of the announcement, the Canadian prime minister and his agriculture minister were photographed at separate events eating freshly cooked Canadian beef.

The impression management surrounding the outbreak of SARS in the Toronto region was not quite as effective. Critics pounded the Canadian government in the media suggesting that it was too slow to act and did not take seriously a disease that would eventually kill more than twenty Canadians. One consequence was the temporary placement of Toronto on a World Health Organization travel advisory list. To compound the problems, the mayor of Toronto accepted an invitation to appear on CNN and was subsequently berated in the media for his ill-informed comments on the matter.

Practitioners may also want to consider the role of impression management in job interviews. How might the wrong individual be chosen for a job? Consider the impact that an interview coach might have. Advice on what to say, how to look, and who to have as a reference on one's résumé all can be scripted in advance. Insight as to the identities of the interviewers and their likes and dislikes can all be communicated and acted on. The result is often an impression that fades quickly once the candidate starts work. How might a candidate be convinced to accept an offer? The context and the environment of the interview can be planned ahead of time. Interviewees can be met at the airport, put up in first-class hotels, taken to the finest restaurants, and offered opportunities to exercise. Tours can be arranged to visit real estate properties and schools in the anticipation for a potential move. The candidate's background can be researched. Accomplishments can be praised in the interview and a corner office assigned. Access can be granted during the interview to influential senior executives, an opportunity not normally offered to other candidates.

Understanding organizations in terms of drama is open to numerous criticisms. The strongest of these involves conflicts between the theory's imaginative take on organizational life and the hard realities of real-life organizations. Occasionally, viewing corporate life as a drama is useful, but it is an incomplete picture. Taking it too seriously might be disastrous. Also, just as with real drama, a perspective that understands organizational life as a drama is somewhat at the mercy of the broad range of audience response. Audiences inevitably produce a range of responses that are unmanageable, inconsistent, and impossible to interpret. Furthermore, it is difficult, if not unfair, to generalize the failure of one actor, or employee, to an entire cast, or organization.

26

Metaphorical Perspective

In recent years, a number of innovative organizational theorists (Morgan 1980; Pondy 1983; Trice and Beyer 1985) have moved beyond the boundaries of traditional management thinking in search of more contemporary ways to explain the concerns facing our major institutions. One approach has been to incorporate metaphors into the ways that we look at organizations:

> Although originally examined as a literary troupe, metaphors are more than ornaments that decorate language. They operate at multiple levels of analysis to provide insights into how we understand organizational life. A metaphor is a way of seeing a thing as if it were something else (Lackoff and Johnson 1980). . . . For some theorists, metaphors link abstract constructs to concrete things while for others metaphors tie the familiar to the unknown. Perhaps even more significantly, metaphors legitimate actions, set goals and guide behaviour. Metaphors also . . . facilitate the creation and interpretation of social reality. In effect, metaphors shape how we see and make sense of the world by orienting our perceptions, conceptualizations and understanding of one thing in light of another. (Putnam, Phillips, and Chapman 1996, 396)

One theorist in particular, Morgan (1980, 1986, 1993), a York University scholar, has taken the lead in incorporating this important perspective into the toolbox of techniques used by business and organizational analysts.

Many people may think of metaphors as being of concern only to those who study poetry and literature. However, the language we use every day is utterly dependent on the use of metaphors. In fact, numerous metaphors have become entrenched in the language we use to explain organizations. Most of our conventional ideas about organizations and management are both shaped and limited by a small number of images that we have come to take for granted. Machines, organisms, brains, and cultures are just a few of the metaphors commonly used to explain organizations. The following examples of organizational metaphors are based on those found in Morgan's critically acclaimed book *Images of Organization* (1986).

The most common metaphor employed to explain organizations is that of the machine. This metaphor assumes that if a machine could be constructed to function in an efficient, reliable, and predictable fashion, then certainly an organization could also be similarly constructed.

Another popular way to view organizations is as organisms. That is, we think of organizations as living systems existing in an environment, vying for the resources on which they depend for the satisfaction of their various needs. This image parallels the distinctions and relations made in biology between such concepts as molecules, cells, species, and ecology with the relationships between individuals, groups, organizations, and populations found within a business environment.

Organizations may also be thought of as behaving like brains. An organization, like a brain, is a system that is able to both learn and self-organize. Because organizations consist of both specialized and generalized functions, they are able to compensate if any one specialized aspect malfunctions or is eliminated, thereby keeping the organization functioning as a whole.

Organizations are often compared to cultures. Like a culture, organizations create their own shared meanings, shared understandings, shared goals, and, in a sense, they construct a unique organizational reality.

Organizations may also be explained as political systems. Like governments, organizations employ a system of "rule" as a way of creating and maintaining order among their members. Basically, organizational politics arises when there are conflicting opinions as to what actions should be taken. This diversity creates a tension that must be resolved through political means.

Another metaphor is a psychic prison. From this perspective, organizations are ultimately created and sustained by conscious and unconscious processes. The implication is that people can actually become imprisoned or confined by the images, thoughts, and ideas that they consciously or unconsciously hold.

These represent only a few of the metaphors that have been used as ways of understanding how organizations function. Others have included jazz bands, clouds, soap bubbles, strategic termites, and spider plants (Morgan 1990). Interestingly, the use of metaphors has not been limited to theories of organization. Other areas where they have been employed include information technology, decision making, human resource development, leadership, production management (Palmer and Dunford 1996), and mergers and acquisitions (Hirsch and Andrews 1983).

An interesting example of the use of the "storytelling" metaphor illustrates how an analyst might find him- or herself closer to the truth when seeking to understand taken-for-granted organizational histories.

> In organizations, storytelling is the preferred sense-making currency of human relationships among internal and external stakeholders. People engage in a dynamic process of incremental refinement of their stories of new events as well as on-going reinterpretations of culturally sacred story lines. When a decision is at hand, the old stories are recounted and compared to unfolding story lines to keep the organization from repeating historically bad choices and to invite the repetition of past successes. In a turbulent environment, the organization halls and offices pulsate with a story life of the here and now that is richer and more vibrant than the firm's environments. (Boje 1991, 106)

As an example, Boje explores the origins of the creation of Mickey Mouse:

> Early official versions of how four animators left Disney characterize them as disgruntled employees . . . preferring instead the security offered by a cutthroat distributor, Charles Mintz. As the story goes, . . . Mintz hired away most of Walt's animators, except Iwerks, and threatened to produce Oswalt the Rabbit at a lower cost in a new firm, saying, "Either you come with me at my price, or I'll take your organizations away from you." . . . In these early days at Disney, Ub Iwerks did 700 drawings a day and, as the genius journeyman, stood between Walt and the junior animators and apprentices. In early official accounts, Walt and no one else created Mickey Mouse after Mintz stole Oswald the Rabbit. In later versions, "Exactly how that character was created has been the subject of so much myth—often of Walt's own devising—that it is difficult to be certain of the facts" (Holliss and Sibley 1988, 15). The early versions of the official story state that on the way back from New York on a train, Walt drew the mouse that would change the cartoon industry (Miller 1957; Thomas 1967). . . . In 1948, Walt recalled how Mickey Mouse "popped out of his mind onto a drawing pad at a time when disaster seem just around the corner" (Holliss and Sibley 1988, 15). Walt mythologizes Mickey Mouse in the official tale: "a

struggling young artist, he [Walt] had befriended a family of mice that took up residence in a waste-paper basket. . . . But Dave Iwerks, Ub's son, recalls a quite different version of this story: "It's pretty clear now that Mickey was Ub's character" (Eliot 1993, 36). Ub had taken a sketch of Oswald the Rabbit and rounded the eyes and the ears to steal Oswald back from Charles Mintz (Crafton 1982, 210–215). (1995, 1010)

Overall, the use of metaphors offers the analyst a different angle for thinking about organizing and organizational structures. An important implication of this approach concerns how metaphors are used by organizations. In many instances, they guide behaviors and legitimate actions (Lackoff and Johnson 1980). Thus, if analysts can identify prevalent metaphors operating within an organization, they can often explain behavior.

Where might analysts or researchers find examples of revealing metaphors? Consider the speeches made by executives found on the websites of many organizations. In many instances, the texts of these metaphor-laden speeches will reveal much of a company's strategy, its industry outlook, its performance, or its activities. In the mind of a researcher, understanding how metaphors are used by a particular organization can help clarify its behavior. One may also want to consider the language of press releases. Changes in metaphor usage can signal changes in structure, direction, or performance. They can also signal which careers are on the rise and which, by their absence, are not. A further implication for researchers is to consider the use of metaphors in conversation by company employees. Are metaphors in use complimentary or derogatory to the organization? In this way, the use of metaphors can offer insight into the working culture of the organization. Tracked or observed over time, change in metaphor usage can also provide clues as to whether an organizational transformation is succeeding or failing, at least in a culture sense (Ford and Ford 1995).

Metaphors can help practitioners in other ways. They are an effective tool for communicating difficult to understand concepts such as those sometimes found in science. A metaphor may help expose the incomplete nature of a particular idea or argument simply by the obvious state of its own incompleteness. It can also induce critical thinking by forcing a researcher or practitioner to look at the underlying assumptions of a seemingly popular or controversial idea (Alvesson 2002).

This approach does, however, have its share of shortcomings. A first problem is fairly straightforward. How might metaphors be operationalized? Morgan (1993) offers frameworks for a number of examples. Unfortunately, not all metaphors are easy to apply in practice. A second major concern relates to the incomplete nature of almost all metaphors. While the metaphor of the "machine" may capture many aspects of organizational life on an assembly line or in a fast food restaurant, it also misses a big part of the picture.

> Being aware of what each metaphor captures—and what it neglects—adds insight to organizational studies and reflexiveness to research. The conduit and lens metaphors, with their concern for transmission, instrumentality, and message fidelity, highlight the container images of organizations and neglect meaning, context, and social interaction. The linkage metaphor captures elements that the conduit and lens metaphors miss, namely the give and take of transactions, organizations as relationships, and the erosion of physical of physical boundaries. . . . The symbol metaphor adds representation to the process of organizing but it often reproduces the meanings that service organizational elites. (Putnam, Phillips, and Chapman 1996, 396)

Metaphors are also appealing to use. Unfortunately, risks associated with this popularity include their adoption for seductive as opposed to analytically helpful reasons; the potential development of a supermarket attitude by researchers is their adoption and tendency to oversimplify complex actions and interactions (Alvesson 2000). A final problem concerns the issue of performance. Does their use help explain organized behavior more effectively? The answer is unclear.

27

Sensemaking Perspective

Jean Helms Mills

Consider the following organizational outcomes. In 1977, 583 people died when two jumbo jets collided on the ground. Although no one factor can be attributed to the crash, a series of nonroutine events played a part. A diversion, from Las Palmas airport to the smaller island airport of Tenerife, resulted in a series of conflicting instructions from the control tower, requests for changes in these instructions, and ambiguous communications between the tower and the pilots of both 747s, during what should have been a routine takeoff.

In 1949, a forest fire in Man Gulch, Montana, claimed the lives of a number of firefighters, who against the instructions of their leader refused to let go of their heavy equipment and were unable to outrun the smoke and flames.

During the past decade, large and diverse organizations, such as Nova Scotia Power, Imperial Oil, and General Electric, have introduced major change programs that have cost millions of dollars. Yet, despite significant gain, these organizations continue to switch from one change technique to another as the latest management fads and fashions come and go. In the case of Nova Scotia Power, between 1987 and 2002 the company implemented a planned culture change, reengineered itself, and undertook different strategic approaches, including a balanced scorecard approach, to name but a few.

Air Canada and British Airways have fostered a culture over the years that has specific views of women as sexualized objects, which in turn has contributed to the categorization of women's and men's work and has led to discriminatory and gendered employment practices (Helms Mills and Mills 2000a).

So, how can we make sense of these organizational events? What organizational theory do we use to explain how these events have occurred? Weick (1995), a prominent American social psychologist, has fine-tuned what he calls a sensemaking framework, which he first applied to both the Tenerife air disaster and the Man Gulch fire (Weick 1990, 1996) in order to explain how a series of distinct yet small failures can lead to such catastrophic outcomes. Since the mid-1990s, his sensemaking approach, which he describes as "a developing set of ideas with explanatory possibilities" (1995, xi), has gained popularity as an organizational analytical tool because its focus on understanding organizational processes makes it flexible enough to be applied to a diverse range of organizational outcomes. This approach sees "organizing as a process of sensemaking" (Colville, Waterman et al. 1999). For example, Helms Mills and Mills (2000a) use sensemaking to explore the development of discriminatory practices in Air Canada's and British Airway's cultures, and Helms Mills (2000) uses sensemaking to explain why Nova Scotia Power continues to engage in a series of organizational change programs, despite evidence of high failure rates.

At first glance, the concept of sensemaking seems deceptively simple. It appears to be an individual exercise that is about drawing on our experiences to make things that we see and experience sensibly. For example, a student might decide to take more courses in accounting if he or she has had a good experience in another accounting course. Likewise, someone who has never taken an accounting course might be apprehensive about such a course because he or she has no prior experience with the subject matter.

Yet, sensemaking is more complex because, as Weick (1995) explains, it is not a solitary process. Indeed, the crux of sensemaking is about different meaning that is assigned to the same experience, which, in turn, has implications for organizational outcomes. For example, at Nova Scotia Power, some employees thought the changes that were introduced by the company were great. Others were strongly opposed to them. Yet, all employees experienced the same training procedures.

There are seven properties that have become the cornerstone of sensemaking and each property has greater or lesser influence on the individual process of making sense, which explains certain behaviors in organizational situations. By examining each of these properties in some detail, we will be able to gain insight into the subjectivity of the process and see the value of the sensemaking approach in understanding how organizational outcomes occur that often seem to contradict common sense or defy rational beliefs.

The first, grounded in identity construction, suggests that our sense-making is influenced by our identity. Furthermore, it argues that our identity is influenced and shaped by the environment we face. Thus, identity is a result of work experience and of roles that we assume in family and societal relationships. In the case of the Man Gulch fire, one of the reasons the firefighters may have been reluctant to drop their heavy tools while trying to outrun the fire was that the tools defined who they were as firefighters and to drop them would have been contradicting their identity.

Second, the social property refers to the fact that our sensemaking is an activity that takes place within the context of (organizational) rules, routines, symbols, language, and scripts, but it is also contingent on the behavior of others, so that our expression of a situation will be partly how we see the situation and partly how we want our sense-making to be received by others. Weick explains the Tenerife air disaster using the social property to show how the breakdown of the pilots' normal routines forced them to regress to habitual responses. In other words, they reverted to individual sensemaking in the face of disruption to their expected routines and this led to the tragic outcome.

Third, sensemaking is focussed on and by extracted cues. This means individuals draw on familiar events, or structures, to help them develop the larger picture and flesh out the sensemaking event. In the case of Nova Scotia Power, four values were introduced as central cues to introduce their culture change. These cues became reference points for employees' understanding of the change process. And at Air Canada, images that portrayed women in terms of their physical attributes and men in terms of their intelligence reinforced the notion that women's work was less meaningful.

Fourth, sensemaking is ongoing. According to Weick (1995), people are constantly making sense, and while sensemaking does not have a starting point, it does have a series of interruptions that precipitate the extraction of cues. This property addresses the breakdowns that can occur in organizations. A case in point being Nova Scotia Power's move from one change program to another. This property suggests that the company's continual re-creation of change was the result of changing scripts (change fads and fashions) acting as reference points for making sense of new events.

For Weick, retrospection, the fifth property, is the single most "distinguished characteristic of sensemaking" (1995, 24). He argues that people act and then make sense of their actions. Indeed, sensemaking is retrospective because we are always reflecting on what has occurred but, at the same time, influenced by what is occurring in the present. This dichotomy helps explain senior managers' inability to recognize how new projects, such as Nova Scotia Power's switch from one change program to another, opened up new meanings and how old meanings had the potential to influence how people made sense of these new projects. Specifically, managers had difficulty in understanding that previously created expectations of a "humanistic" company were influencing how employees were responding to the reengineering program.

Weick (1995) maintains that people act as if they have complete and accurate information. But sensemaking is driven by plausibility, the sixth property, rather than accuracy because in most cases people make decisions based on incomplete and sometimes inaccurate and often conflicting information. This is done because plausibility is about what feels right and fits with what we know. This usually depends on the context in which the sensemaking is taking place. Thus, the culture change at Nova Scotia Power was made plausible by the belief that the culture of the 1980s was unsuited to the times, and Air Canada's enforced "retirement" for married female employees reflected societal values at that time.

Finally, and critically, Weick (1995, 30) argues that sensemaking is inactive of sensible environments. Simply put, this means that we create an activity that reflects our making sense of the experience within our environment. These environments then constrain how we behave. For example, Air Canada's senior management enacted an environment (i.e., by defining what was women's work and what was men's work) that reflected how it wanted employees to behave.

Sensemaking has been described as "a new fundamental unit for organizational analysis" (Nord and Fox 1996) and is a valuable analytic tool for exploring existing data. By applying sensemaking to organizational theory, Weick offers a way of thinking about organizations that deviates from mainstream approaches (Calás and Smircich 1992). The main strengths of sensemaking lie in its ability to tie together strands of various social theories into a comprehensive framework, to conceive of organizations as processes rather than outcomes (Colville 1994; Ferguson 1994), and to uncover uncertainty and ambiguity in organizations (Gherardi 1995). Yet, it is still underutilized as a framework for making sense of organizational outcomes.

Why might analysts and managers have an interest in understanding the dynamics of organizational sensemaking? Consider the following description of one special type of organization:

> Imagine that it's a busy day, and you shrink San Francisco Airport to only one short runway and one ramp and one gate. Make planes take off and land at half the present time interval, rock the runway from side to side, and require everyone who leaves in the morning return that same day. Make sure the equipment is so close to the edge of the envelope that it's fragile. Then turn off the radar to avoid detection, impose strict controls on radios, fuel the aircraft in place with their engines running, put an enemy in the air, and scatter live bombs and rockets around. Now wet the whole thing down with sea water and oil, and man it with 20 year olds, half of whom have never seen an airplane close-up. Oh and by the way, try not to kill anyone. (Rochlin, Laporte, and Roberts 1987, 78)

The description, of course, is that of an aircraft carrier. It exemplifies one form of organization in which the "consequences and costs associated with major failures in some technical operations are greater than the value of the lessons learned from them" (Laporte and Consolini 1991, 19; Weick and Roberts 2001, 277). In other words, when accidents occur far too often, people die. Fortunately, in most instances accidents are rare because, along with organizations such as petrochemical plants, hospital emergency rooms, nuclear reactors, and natural gas pipelines, aircraft carriers are, out of necessity, highly reliable.

> High reliability organizations such as aircraft carriers differ in many ways from organizations usually portrayed as . . . high-efficiency organizations. Typical efficiency organizations practice incremental decision making, their errors do not have a lethal edge, they use low hazard technologies, they are governed by single rather than multi-layer authority systems, they are more often in the private than the public sector, they are not pre-occupied with perfection, their operations are carried on at one level of intensity, they experience few nasty surprises, and they can rely on computation or judgement as decision strategies. (Weick and Roberts 2001, 277)

What is the major implication of this perspective? The practice of organizational sensemaking enables analysts to understand why some organizations remain safe when appearances would suggest otherwise. In the example of the aircraft carrier, Weick and Roberts (2001) suggest in summary that much of the close to error free nature of its existence may be the result of an ongoing struggle for alertness by its personnel and, metaphorically speaking, a more complex mind than that of a typical high-efficiency organization.

While there are some specific criticisms of the individual properties of sensemaking relating to subjectivity, there have been limited criticisms of the overall model of sensemaking. What there is seems to center on its inability to address issues of power, control, and gender by ignoring the role of rationality in the sensemaking process (Calás and Smircich 1992; Reed 1992). More recently, Helms Mills (2000) suggests that sensemaking lacks the ability to explain why and how some "inventions" come to be developed in the first place, or how and why these "inventions" are mediated through a series of ongoing interactions that are guided by rules of behavior. Other weaknesses of the model include placing too much attention on the "imposition of ideas on situations that have consequences for those beyond the primary sensemakers" and a "failure to explain how the factors that shape culture are the result of sensemaking and inform sensemaking" (Helms Mills and Mills 2000b, 8). Finally, the model offers little insight into the all important issue of organizational boundaries.

28

Organizational Rules Perspective

Albert J. Mills

The first time I ever watched ice hockey was in the mid-1980s when I emigrated from Britain to Canada. I quickly learned that the game consisted of three "periods," each lasting twenty minutes. Thus, I expected it to be over in just over an hour. After all, where I had come from was a place where they played soccer, which was divided into two forty-five minute "halves" that lasted just over ninety minutes. How surprised I was when I found the hockey game still underway three hours later. That was just the first of my problems in following the game. I cheered when a player hit the puck the length of the rink, from behind his own goal to behind the goal of his opponents. My cheering stopped when the play was called for "icing." There were many other rules that I had to learn before I could understand and then appreciate what was going on. This is true of any other game with which you are unfamiliar. It is hard to understand what is going on until you know the rules. The same is also true of organizations.

One of my very first jobs was as a "trainee estimator" with a large, United Kingdom–based, multinational company. One day I wore to work an open-neck pink shirt that my grandmother had sent me for my birthday. I was promptly called before a senior manager and told that it was an office rule that male staff should wear ties. The next day I came to work in the same shirt but now with a matching red tie. Again I was called into the senior manager's office and this time I was fired. It turned out that I had missed the subtle clue that office employees are expected to wear a tie with a white shirt. The manager had not thought to tell me what should have been obvious: that I was the only male employee not wearing a white shirt, let alone a tie. I had failed to understand an elementary rule of office life.

Rules are a very important element of organizational life and by understanding not only specific rules, but also how rules in general develop and are maintained, we are better placed to manage and survive the world of work.

But what do we mean by "rules"? To begin with, we can say that "rules, in the broadest sense, are outline steps for the conduct of action, and depending upon combinations of circumstances and actors, those steps will be experienced as controlling, guiding and/or defining" (Mills and Murgatroyd 1991, 30). This means that every organization has a variety of written statements that let employees know what is expected of them (e.g., employment contracts), the tasks that they are expected to carry out (e.g., job descriptions), and the types of action that they are prohibited from doing (e.g., rules and regulations). In many ways, these rules control workplace behavior. For example, a rule that says that certain work can only be carried out by qualified electricians controls the behavior of nonelectricians by prohibiting them from certain tasks. It also controls the behavior of electricians by restricting them to do work that is defined as "electrical." But control is only one side of the story. In this example, the rule may help define who does what task and, in some cases, how that task is to be carried out. Therefore, the same rules can be experienced as a form of control, guidance, and definition. In short, there are "both enabling and constraining aspects of rule governed conduct" (Reed 1992, 183).

If the formal written rules of an organization were all there was, we would have no need of an organizational rules approach. You would just have to read the rules of an organization and you would know much of what you need to know. But there are different rules and people stand in different relationships to any given set of rules. Thus, there are two elements of the rules approach: "the rules themselves and the actors who engage in the process of establishing, enacting, enforcing, misunderstanding, and/or resisting rules" (Helms Mills and Mills 2000, 59).

The different forms of rules—or established sets of expectations—include formal and informal rules, written and unwritten rules, and legalistic, moralistic, and normative rules.

Formal rules arise out of the development of an organization and are "the expectations and requirements that are routinely associated with the pursuit of organizational purposes, activities, or goals that are perceived as legitimate or 'normal' " (Helms Mills and Mills 2000, 59). When people establish organizations (e.g., a company, a political party, and so on), they do so with some purpose in mind (e.g., profit, political power, and so on). To that end, they lay down some basic rules that define the organization and its goals. As the organization begins to grow, more rules develop so that employees or new members know what is expected of them. Essentially, these formal rules lay down expectations about the "manner in which groups and individuals combine to get things done" (Eldridge and Crombie 1974, 89). Quite soon, there are rules about which level of the organization each person is at (e.g., employee, supervisor, or manager), which division or department a person is in (e.g., marketing or accounting), who reports to whom and when (i.e., communication rules), and who does what job, where, and over what time frame (e.g., job descriptions, employment contracts, and so on). Many of these rules are written down and many are unwritten expectations. For example, as a young machine operator in a rope factory, written rules made it clear that I had to punch a time clock when I arrived and left the workplace and that I would lose fifteen minutes of pay for every one minute that I arrived late or left early. But, even though there was nothing in writing, I also knew that I was not allowed to leave my workplace to go to the toilet without permission and that I was not allowed to spend more than five minutes in the toilet. These expectations were made very clear to me by my supervisor, who would yell when I requested a toilet break and would yell if, in his opinion, I took too long away from my machine.

Informal rules refer to those expectations that develop out of workplace interactions. As people do their work, they tend to establish some form of relationship with their coworkers. Workplace relationships can take many forms, including romantic attachments, friendships, informal groups, and factions. In each case, expectations centrally revolve around behavior toward other members in the relationship. In the case of informal groups, some of the expected behaviors may have a direct link to formal rules, when group members are pressured to not work too hard or too little.

These informal rules often run counter to formal rules of command and productivity requirements. In such cases, people respond to peer pressure rather that supervisory direction and productivity levels are lowered rather than maximized. In those cases when members of an organization develop conflict relationships, they often develop rules that discourage people from different groups from working or socializing together. Again, such rules can run counter to formal expectations. Romantic relationships and friendship groups often develop expectations that have little to do with the formal rules of the organization. Often, such informal rules neither support nor hinder the formal rules, although in certain circumstances they can do either. A group whose friendship is based on a mutual hate for its company, for example, can contribute to a negative atmosphere, whereas friendship based on workplace satisfaction may well contribute to an improved workplace.

Legalistic rules refer to those expectations that are determined by legal requirements imposed from outside of the organization. These are formal and invariably written rules. "No smoking" regulations are an obvious example that can be seen in numerous signs throughout a building.

Moralistic rules refer to values that people hold about what is right or wrong. Sometimes, they are expressed as formal, written rules, as in the example of sexual harassment policies. But they are also felt as informal pressures that inhibit people from acting in certain ways. There is no law that says employees cannot cross a picket line, but many people refuse to do so because they think it is morally wrong. Sometimes, formal and informal pressures come together in equal measure as in the case of cheating. Not only are there formal rules in universities against cheating, but often students will exert moral pressure on fellow students trying to cheat.

Normative rules refer to expectations that develop out of people's relationships. It is expected that people will behave in a way that has come to be accepted as "normal" or "the norm." This is characteristic of informal and unwritten rules. For example, many years ago the average student dressed smartly for class; those who dressed very casually were seen as not fitting the norm. Similarly, today's students dress casually for class, often wearing jeans and baseball caps. They would think it odd if someone came to class dressed in a smart suit or dress.

It should be clear by now that people stand in different relationships to organizational rules. Some people make the rules (e.g., founders, entrepreneurs, or senior managers), others enforce the rules (e.g., managers or supervisors), and still others are expected to follow the rules (e.g., employees). Some people are good at following rules (e.g., conformists), others have problems understanding the rules (e.g., the socially inept), and yet others resist the rules (e.g., rebels). Nowhere is this better explained than in Clegg and Dunkerley's metaphor of the chess game:

Power in an organization [is] . . . rather like a game of chess. . . . [It] is a function of the relationship of pieces (units) to rules, in that rules invest a certain power in a piece, independently of its position on the board. Imagine a game more analogous to social reality. In this game the rules are frequently changing and not all clear. Whoever was able to exploit this uncertainty, and rule in his interest, would in this sense have power. . . . To the extent that all pieces were able to negotiate their positions, more or less, then in a game with a fixed number of pieces, that piece which ended up ruling on the greatest number of pieces, serving its interests in preference to theirs, would be the most powerful. But obviously a piece like the Queen would start in a more privileged position than a pawn, simply because the extant rules, which are now open to interpretation, enable her to begin the sequence with more potential moves to make. (1980, 444)

The airline industry offers a compelling example of why readers and analysts might want to pay attention to the rules-based perspective. As noted in the following paragraphs, when left untouched, adherence to the wrong formal and informal rules can lead to the development of deviant work cultures:

It is formal rules that provide guidelines for desired behaviour in organizations and create the opportunity for these rules to be resisted and enacted, according to meaning that is bestowed on them by the organizational members. For example, an important formal rule at Air Canada/TCA that contributed significantly to the gendering of its culture was the requirement that married female employees must resign when they married. So important was this rule to organizational members that with the exception of the war years, the rule was upheld until the late 1950's. Indeed, it was expected that women's primary role was marriage.

This viewpoint shaped and reinforced a certain identity for women that impacted on subsequent employment opportunities for them. For example, in an organization where promotion was based on seniority, TCA's rule narrowly defined work options available to women, which in turn created pay inequities. Whereas most of the female workforce of TCA was comprised of women under thirty years of age, this left little chance for advancement, if a woman was still to fulfill her first role!

Informal rules differ from formal rules because they are not created to meet the goals of the organization. Informal rules are similar to group norms, because they develop out of social interactions and they are greatly influenced by the development of associations at work beyond those that are officially defined. While they do not necessarily affect the enactment of formal rules (i.e., informal rules of dress and commitment may not be critical to the goals of the organization), informal rules develop from and reflect the dominant ideology and values of the members of those social groups. In the case of TCA, whose workforce was predominately male, the policy on work/marriage legally defined work parameters, but informal rules arising from the interpretation of this rule through social interactions, did lead to many of the discriminatory practices that affected how women were perceived, how they were treated, and what types of work they should engage in. As such, a particular type of identity began to be constructed for female employees, which is evident in both verbal and pictorial evidence in Between Ourselves which overwhelmingly supports traditionally held views about women and women's employment. In general, informal rules that materialized during the airline's early years suggested that; i) women's work was not as valued as men's work; ii) women were viewed as sexualised objects, whose physical attributes should be used to promote the airline; and iii) women's goal in working for the airline was to find a husband. (Helms Mills, Mills, 2000, 57)

In recent years, there has been criticism of the rules-based approach for its lack of explanation on how individuals and groups translate and express rules as an active process. This has led to the incorporation of sensemaking theory in the development of a revised approach.

This new model can be found in Helms Mills and Mills (2000). There are also other concerns with this model. It is still a relatively young theory. Thus, relatively few studies have been undertaken to test or support its main ideas. Those that do may overemphasize its potential as an approach for "destabilizing existing frameworks of power" (70). Although originally conceived as a social constructionist model of organized behavior, much of its recent application is critical in nature. Thus, it shares a number of the concerns directed toward the works of critical theorists. It may unnecessarily portray managers in a negative light and as a stable elite who make decisions and think alike.

In summary, in order to understand behavior and structure in an organization we need to understand the complex rules that help to characterize it and something about the actors involved in the development of those rules. This approach can contribute to our understanding of organizational culture by exploring the ways that different rules come together to give an organization a unique character. The major implication of this perspective is that if we understand the rules of an organization, we understand why actions are taken. If we can change the rules, we can change the actions. In fact, organizational culture can be viewed as "being primarily composed of a particular config-uration of 'rules,' enactment and resistance" (Mills 1992, 111). The value of this approach lies in its ability to deal with such important issues as organizational change and employment equity. Part of the problem faced by those dealing with organizational change is that they often fail to take into account existing expectations and the values put on them by those involved. A rules approach encourages examination of the underlying rules and ways to end, modify, or strengthen those rules in light of desired organizational change. In a similar way, much needed employment equity programs face numerous problems when they deal with the symptoms but not the deep-rooted rules that create discrimination. For example, British airlines refused to hire female flight attendants until the mid-1940s. Up to that point, it was clearly a man's job. Although a number of women became "stewardesses" over the next two decades, underlying rules ensured that they were largely viewed as sex objects rather than professionals (Mills 1997). In short, when certain jobs open up to women they may not lessen discriminatory expectations where the underlying rules are left intact.

29

Culture Perspective

It was such a relief. In this company I am well paid and respected for my work. My tasks are challenging and my coworkers are supportive. As I don't work directly with clients, I don't have to worry about formal dress attire. As opposed to a cubicle, I work out of my home but share an office when at the company's premises. Profits are going up and the company is slowly adding more employees, so, all in all, the overall mood is good. About half of my colleagues are female, most are between thirty and fifty years of age, and almost all of them are professionals. Unlike my previous employer where the almighty clock seemed to rule workplace, I am now judged on the quality of my work and my ability to meet deadlines. The perks are pretty good as well. It is amazing how two companies can be so different in how employees are treated and business is conducted.

Does this sound familiar? It is, of course, one individual's comparison of one work environment with another. It is also a description of a corporate culture. In it, it is fairly obvious why one might want to work in such an environment. But is this really the case? Would another person's thoughts be any different? Is culture something to be manipulated or is it simply something that an organization has? Is it something that is shared or is it simply a state of mind that exists only in the eyes of the beholder? For instance, Mills and Murgatroyd (1991) view culture as the way organizational rules are enacted. In the world of management, few concepts are as pervasive yet as poorly understood as that of organizational culture. Is it an important topic? Consider the following. In a foreword to a recent book on the topic, Pettigrew's (2000) summary of its contents subtly suggests why practitioners and researchers might want to learn more about this important subject matter. According to Pettigrew, the benefits of learning about corporate culture include knowing

> how to understand and explain patterns and divergences in attitudes, perceptions, and values; how to make sense of language and symbols;

how to balance continuity and change; and how to intervene in organizations to deliver cultural change, improve climates for service and innovation, influence career development and manage mergers and acquisitions. (xi)

Culture, be it organizational or societal, is part of our lives. It is not something from which we can simply escape. However, are there other reasons why practitioners should take note? Well, yes. To begin, managers talk about it, so we should understand it (Schein 2000). In another sense, "senior organizational managers are always, in one way or another, 'managing culture'—underscoring what is important and what is less so and framing how the corporate world should be understood" (Alvesson 2002, 1). As a result, it may be beneficial for managers and practitioners to develop a "capacity to think in terms of organizational culture" as it "facilitates acting wisely" (2). But what is meant by acting wisely? Think about how an organizational change may now be handled. Knowledgeable executives would most likely perceive it in terms of a comprehensive transformation. Acting wisely may also be thought of in terms of what leaders do. Furthermore, it may include visioning, a practice that has been added to the portfolio of services that leaders might provide.

Consider again the case of a transformation. Acting wisely would take into account the need to address the underlying values of the employees (Ashkanasy, Wilderom, and Peterson 2000). Culture may also explain how employment discrimination practices arise (Helms Mills 2002). Finally, efforts to understand and improve a corporate culture may be viewed by workers as an attempt by managers to improve employee morale (Barney 1996).

Culture matters. Few will disagree with this statement. Some will even suggest that "culture has become a powerful way to hold a company together against a tidal wave of pressures for disintegration, such as decentralization, de-layering, and downsizing" (Goffee and Jones 1996, 133). But, what is culture? The answer is not simple. In many instances, our understanding of this difficult concept often corresponds to the same features that researchers look at when they study culture. These are termed "cultural manifestations" and refer to the rituals, organizational stories, jargon, humor, physical arrangements, and formal and informal practices, values, and assumptions as inferred by interviewees (Martin 2001, 343).

Despite these specific notions, culture has no fixed or broadly agreed on meaning even in its field of origin: anthropology. As a result, it is a tricky concept that can be used to cover everything and nothing (Alvesson 2002). Indeed, in one review of writing on this topic (Martin 2001), thirteen different definitions are found in the management literature. These range from one-sentence definitions such as "culture is the set of important understandings (often unstated) that members of a community share in common" (Sathe 1985, 6) to paragraph-length versions (Schein 1985; Meyerson 1991; Feldman 1991).

Seeking to make sense of the bewildering array of researcher and writing efforts on this topic, Martin (2002) groups studies and under-standings of the term "organizational culture" under three categories whose origins can be found within functional, critical, and postmodern schools of thought. The terms used as labels for these categories are "integration," "differentiation," and "fragmentation," respectively.

> The integration perspective assumes consistency across manifestations, organization-wide consensus, and clarity. According to this view of culture, if something is ambiguous it is not part of culture. The differ-entiation perspective offers interpretations of manifestations that are inconsistent with each other, finds consensus only within subcultural boundaries, and allows for ambiguity—but only in the spaces between subcultures which are therefore islands of clarity. Subcultures can re-inforce, conflict with, or exist independently of each other. The frag-mentation perspective focuses on interpretations of manifestations that are not clearly consistent or clearly inconsistent with each other. Al-though particular issues may generate interest, these issues do not create clusters of people who feel the same way about more than one issue, so little organization-wide or subculture specific consensus is found. Ambiguity, rather than clarity is the heart of a culture. (344)

Clearly, culture is important for the operation of most organizations. However, does it impact the bottom line? An extensive literature ar-gues yes (Wilmott 1993).

Unfortunately, once this question is examined more closely the re-sponse is not as clear. To begin, Alvesson (2002, 54) suggests that there really are four schools of thought in this regard. From the stand-point of one group of scholars, cultures capable of responding to the environment are the key to good performance. A second school of thought argues that profit levels can be directly tied to the commitment of an organization's employees and managers to the same set of values, beliefs, and norms.

An example of this latter school of thought can be found in Handy's 1989 best-seller *The Age of Unreason* (1989). Handy argues that three generic types of organization will dominate the future. He terms them respectively "Shamrock," "Federation," and "Triple I." Handy's Shamrock organization is composed of three distinct groups of workers. These include core workers or the full-time professionals and specialists, the contractual fringe or individuals contracted to carry out certain tasks and paid a fee based on results, and the flexible labor force or a pool of part-time workers. In a Shamrock organization, judicious use of employment practices, structure, technology, and machines allows profits to grow while the size of the company remains small.

The second form of organization, a Federation, refers to a network of individual organizations allied together under the same banner with a shared identity (Handy 1989; Burns 2000). Finally, a Triple I organization is built around core workers "who use their intelligence to analyze the available information to generate ideas for new products" (Burns 2000, 114).

Still, a third school of thought reverses the arguments of Handy and others by suggesting that a strong homogenous corporate culture is the result of high performance.

Finally, one last perspective suggests that under certain competitive situations, a particular type of culture may be more appropriate than others. An example of this last school of thought can be found in the work of Goffee and Jones (1996). According to these researchers, corporate cultures can be characterized by, and positioned in, a two-by-two matrix with high and low levels of sociability or friendliness on one axis, and high and low levels of solidarity on the other. Solidarity in this instance refers to the "ability to pursue shared objectives quickly and effectively regardless of personal ties" (138). When analyzed and plotted in one of the four quadrants of the matrix, the studied corporate cultures are labeled as either mercenary in nature, fragmented, communal, or networked. As for their main argument, they suggest that there is no right or best culture for an organization, only the appropriate culture for a particular business environment (Beam 1999).

Handy's (1989) and Goffee and Jones's (1996) studies are but two of many on the topic of organizational culture. Unfortunately, this body of literature and research is characterized by a number of conceptual and methodological weaknesses. In many instances, individual case studies are used as the basis for generalizing findings. When multiple companies are examined, often the number of participating organizations under examination is limited. In the case of surveys, respondents are frequently unrepresentative of the entire organization. Indeed, in some cases only executives respond, while in other instances no executives are included. But most worrisome is that it is often unclear if the variables measuring performance and culture are operationally valid (Wilderom, Glunk, and Maslowski 2000, 196).

So what does the evidence really suggest? The idea of a corporate culture cannot be linked simply and tightly to corporate results (Denison 1984; Siehl and Martin 1990; Wilderom, Glunk, and Maslowski 2000; Alvesson 2002). Although there is some empirical evidence to suggest a link, it is not convincing (Alvesson 2002). Indeed, in some studies the results suggest that the direction of the relationship between culture and performance is not as hypothesized, while in other cases performance appears to drive the culture of a company rather than vice versa (Wilderom, Glunk, and Maslowski 2000, 196).

Aside from the organizational culture-performance concern, other weaknesses hamper knowledge creation in this area. Some of the concepts underlying corporate culture may have been inappropriately borrowed from anthropology and sociology without the historical criticisms attached to the original notions (Meek 1988; Alvesson 2002). The result is that practitioners tend to "oversimplify the meaning of organizational culture as they borrow, adapt or are fed the latest theory of organizational culture" (Frost and Martin 1996, 614).

The legitimacy of the researchers examining culture has been questioned. Meek terms them " 'pop cultural magicians' or 'tricksters' who make their living by convincing corporate executives that they can equal the productivity of Japanese industry through the mechanical manipulation of organizational symbols, myths, and customs" (1988, 365). In a related sense, "many studies of culture seem unduly linked to the interest of management and which promulgate the idea that 'culture' is the collective consciousness of the organization, owned by management and available to management for manipulation" (365).

Furthermore, despite the existence of a vast literature and a literal cottage industry of consultants, "few cultural management approaches appear to help improve the lives of people who work in organizations and no one theory of culture management can claim superiority over another" (Martin and Frost 1996, 613).

Finally, corporate culture is an abstraction.

To conclude this discussion about corporate culture, it might be safe to say that most practitioners and researchers agree that a sense of common, taken-for-granted ideas, beliefs, and meanings are important for ongoing organized activity (Smircich 1983). Yet, it is also fitting to quote the following description of the state of research:

> For there is chaos rather than order, conflict rather than consensus and little sense of a cumulative building of what would generally be regarded as advances in knowledge. These problems are compounded because so many cultural researchers for good reasons prefer qualitative methodology developing context specific descriptions of cultures rather than collecting quantitative data that lend themselves more obviously to . . . the development of empirically based theoretical generalizations. (Martin and Frost 1996, 600)

Part IV

Radical Humanist and Structuralist Perspectives

Conor Vibert and Deborah Hurst

Two important paradigms, radical structuralism and humanism, are rarely associated with managerial theorizing due to their confrontational and oppositional nature. Yet, a close inspection of the ideas found within these schools of thought suggests that organizational scholars do indeed make use of these perspectives to understand many phenomena.

Unlike the more conservative thrusts of the functionalist and interpretive approaches, theories in the radical structuralist and radical humanist traditions (Burrell and Morgan 1979) serve to challenge and critique existing taken-for-granted beliefs, assumptions, and institutions (Gioia and Pitre 1990). Radical theories add an important perspective to our thinking about organizations, particularly for the complacent among us. From a radical humanist approach, we examine organizations from the perspective of postmodernism, critical theory, and configuration theory. Two important areas of writing that fall within the structural side of this paradigm, and are discussed in the following chapters, are the Marxist and poststructuralist feminism perspectives. But first, what do the terms "radical humanism" and "radical structuralism" imply?

Radical humanism is a well-established style of theorizing quite common to the discipline of sociology. When applied to modern organizations, theorists in this tradition seek to "free organization members from sources of domination, alienation, exploitation and repression by critiquing existing social structure with the intent of change" (Gioia and Pitre 1990, 588). Theories found under this heading seek radical change by examining the legitimacy of the social consensus on meaning, uncovering communicative distortions, and educating individuals about the ways in which these distortions occur.

Theorizing in the tradition of radical structuralism is somewhat different. Before defining this school of thought, it might be useful to understand the meaning of the term "structuralism." Structuralism is a term applied by analysts of theory to describe the undertakings of those theorists who seek to discover a logic underlying social meaning. Structuralists assume that the world is a product of ideas and that there is a logical order that underlies general meaning. They also believe that individual social action and meaning emerges from underlying structures. However, there appears to be some variation in the way "structure" is analyzed. Does structure emerge from society or is it part of the way the human brain is constructed? At first glance, it seems that determinism is implied by the distinction between individuals and society. However, the term "emergent" may be used to better describe the relationship. This means that meaning emerges from structure rather than being caused by it.

Structural theorists have been broadly influenced by the French sociological tradition of Émile Durkheim, the German idealism tradition of Immanuel Kant, and the structural linguistics tradition of Ferdinand de Saussure. Two methodological models are most often associated with this style of theorizing: linguistic and semiotic. The linguistic model suggests that language is the vehicle for communication, that language is composed of signs, and that the meaning of sign is binary opposition. On the other hand, the semiotic model, or the science of signs, provides for the analysis of modern myths. For its adherents, structuralist methods offer the advantage of a clear logic of undertaking depth classification, a useful conception of structure, and underlying structural levels that offer clear explanatory power. The disadvantages of this approach include reductionism, static analysis, as well as an inability to explain transformations over time and to absorb metaphysical assumptions.

Radical structuralists share an ideology for change, seeking to remove from society, industries, and organizations the sources of domination forced on lower members of the social hierarchy by dominant elites. The normal operation and makeup of modern corporations and organizations are viewed as dysfunctional, capable of transformation only through conflict and revolution. Not surprisingly, theories found under this heading seek to understand, explain, criticize, and act on the dysfunctional features of our modern institutions (Gioia and Pitre 1990).

In this part, as with the others in this book, we deal with how the theories contribute to macro-organizational theorizing.

30

Configuration Perspective

Are accounting firms all alike? Are the services offered by management consulting firms such as Bain and Co., McKinsey and Co., and the Boston Consulting Group all that different? If you are agreeable with statements such as "an audit is an audit is an audit," then you probably perceive a similarity in the look and feel of professional service firms such as these. Yet, partners and managers of many of the most well-known consulting and auditing organizations would suggest very strongly that numerous inherent features do actually serve to differentiate one firm from another. Indeed, the recent failure of a number of high-profile merger efforts may indicate that these executives have a point. The real answer is, of course, somewhere in between. Theories falling under the guise of the configurational perspective recognize the complex makeup of large entities, be they of a public, private, or not-for-profit nature. They also recognize that organizations take their meaning from the whole (their operating environments) and cannot truly be understood in isolation (Meyer, Tsui, and Hinings 1993).

This style of theorizing acknowledges that there is more than one way for an organization to succeed in a given operating environment (Meyer, Tsui, and Hinings 1993). However, it also suggests that there is a limited range of organizational forms:

> The argument for the prevalence of common configurations is based on the population ecology (Hannan and Freeman 1977) premise that firms will converge upon viable configurations thereby limiting the available repertoire of strategic and structural configurations. Secondly, organizations are driven towards common configurations in order to achieve internal harmony among strategy structure and context. Finally, organizations will remain with successful configurations for fairly long periods because of the disruption and expense of change. (Pettigrew and Fenton 2001, 18)

As with many other perspectives, this approach has multiple research agendas. Among the most influential of studies have been those that argue for unique configurations of strategy and environment (Miles and Snow 1978), strategy and structure (Miller 1986), structure (Mintzberg 1979), and strategy, structure, and environment (Miller and Friesen 1978).

It also has its own distinct vocabulary. For instance, the treatment of the term "structure" differs according to the overarching paradigm:

> From a functionalist perspective, organizational structure is usually viewed as a stable objective characteristic; from an interpretive perspective, structuring is often viewed as a socially constructed, ongoing process of accomplishment; from a radical humanist perspective deep structure is frequently seen as a subjective construction of those in power that should be exposed and changed; and finally, from a radical structuralist perspective, social class structures are considered as objective realities that demand examination and radical change. (Burrell and Morgan 1980, 26)

From this frame of reference, configuration as a concept is inherently tied to the notion of structure. Indeed, structure is usually understood to imply a configuration of activities that are characteristically enduring and persistent. One opinion suggests the dominant feature of organizational structure is its patterned regularity (Ranson, Hinings, and Greenwood 1980). Structure also refers to the parts of an entity. Configuration theorists try to explain how order emerges from the interaction of those parts of an organization as a whole.

Its gets more complicated. Bureaucracy and structural contingency perspectives are but two areas of intellectual thought that might reasonably lay claim to forming a basis for a configuration approach that fits within the functionalist quadrant of theories. Strong arguments could also be made to support other bodies of thought. One important alternative is to suggest structuration theory as a basis for this style of theorizing. Using this lens, we situate the following exemplar in the radical humanist quadrant of theories. We do so because of the attention placed on a number of distinct patterns of regularity, in this case, values, interests, and power. In this vein, organizational structures consist of institutionalized structural arrangements and supporting cultural idea systems.

To begin, try thinking about some of the major institutions of our era in a nontraditional manner. How about defining the structures of corporations such as Microsoft or IBM, not-for-profit organizations such the Cancer Society or the Red Cross, and government organizations such as the Food and Drug Administration in terms of "mutual dependency, rather than opposition, of human agency and social structure" (Abercrombie, Hill, and Turner 1984, 245)? Think of "structure" as the "properties of social systems that provide the means by which people act and they are also the outcomes of those actions" (245). From this perspective, "organizations are a complex medium of control that are continually both produced and reshaped in interaction with what they structure" (Giddens 1979, 16).

The insights of one group of researchers (Ranson, Hinings, and Greenwood 1980; Hinings and Greenwood 1988a) represent one example of a stream of work fitting under the configuration heading. Their model is the result of a study of the change efforts of twenty-three British municipal government organizations. Spanning ten years from the mid-1970s until the mid-1980s, they developed a unique interpretation of a structure's role in organizations. Three ideas summarize their main findings:

- Members create interpretive schemes that articulate values and interests.
- Alternative interpretive schemes vie for dominance.
- Contextual constraints influence and are influenced by interpretive schemes.

Their initial idea was that members of organizations tend to create "provinces of meaning" that incorporate interpretive schemes, or structures. These interpretive schemes are intermittently articulated as the values and interests that shape the direction and strategy of the organization. Within any given organization, there will be alternative interpretive schemes, values, and interests at work, each vying for dominance. The resolution of these differences is determined by the various interdependencies of power and domination that exist within this entity (Ranson, Hinings, and Greenwood 1980). In other words, the most powerful managers decide which values and interests get articulated.

Interpretive schemes and structures do not exist in a vacuum. The ideas that underline them are influenced by and incorporate the constraints existing within the organization's operating environment. Members of organizations are constantly involved in a process of both proactively altering operating environments and reactively responding to contextual changes. The effects of these interactions are always dependent, though, on both the opportunities that arise and the levels of influence of the affected individuals.

In considering this model, it becomes necessary to view our society's important organizations in a holistic manner, as archetypes. At their core, most organizations represent a set of structures and systems that are held together with a specific set of values and beliefs; in a way, they are a corporate culture.

Archetypes can be thought of in terms of organizational design. They describe patterns in different aspects of structures, systems, and meanings. They may also be maintained or destabilized by a number of dynamics, including the organization's operating context, deep-seated employee values, the conflicting interests of various groups within an organization, the power these groups have to implement ideas, and the capacity these groups have to transform ideas into concrete action (Hinings and Greenwood 1988a).

When broken down further, the terms "structure" and "system" can be best understood to mean the sets of roles and responsibilities of the employees, the decision-making mechanisms that allow policies to be made and resources to be allocated, and the organization's recruitment, appraisal, and compensation procedures and policies.

Values and beliefs, on the other hand, refer to ideas about the organization shared by most employees. Most employees can be expected to share the same values in regard to three different areas (Hinings and Greenwood 1988b). The entity's overall purpose is generally well accepted within an organization, as are its basic organizing principles. Furthermore, the criteria by which outsiders judge an organization's performance (share price, ability to meet performance expectations, and ability to deliver services without controversy) are usually well accepted by an organization's employees.

What is one implication that may be derived from research in this perspective? There are common patterns of organization. From these patterns, lessons can be learned about success and failure that may be generalized to other similar organizations. To illustrate this point, the following example offers insights from a different body of configuration research (Miller 1990) to suggest that organizations may follow coherent trajectories over time.

Charles "Tex" Thornton was a young Texas entrepreneur when he expanded a tiny microwave company into Litton Industries, one of the most successful high-technology conglomerates of the 1960s. By making selective, related acquisitions, Litton achieved an explosive rate of growth. And its excellent track record helped the company to amass the resources needed to accelerate expansion still further. Sales mushroomed from $3 million to $1.8 billion in just twelve years. But Litton began to stray too far from familiar areas, buying larger and more troubled firms in industries that it barely understood. Control systems were overtaxed, the burden of debt became unwieldy, and a wide range of problems sprang up in the proliferating divisions. The downward spiral at Litton was no less dramatic than its ascent.

Builders are growth-driven entrepreneurial companies, with a zeal for expansion, merger, and acquisition. They are dominated by aggressive managers with ambitious goals, immense energy, and an uncanny knack for spotting lucrative niches of the market. These leaders have the promotional skills to raise capital, the imagination and initiative to exploit magnificent growth opportunities, and the courage to take substantial risks. They are also master controllers who craft acute, sensitive information and incentive systems to rein in their burgeoning operations.

But many Builders develop into Imperialists, addicted to careless expansion and greedy acquisition. In the headlong rush for growth, they assume hair-raising risks, decimate their recourses, and incur scads of debt. They bite off more than they can swallow, acquiring sick companies in businesses they don't understand. Structures and control systems become hopelessly overburdened. And a dominant culture of financial, legal, and accounting specialists further rivets managerial attention on expansion and diversification, while stealing time away from the production, marketing, and R&D matters that so desperately need to be addressed. (13)

Configuration theory is not beyond criticism. Among its most vocal critics is Donaldson (2001, 152). He suggests a number of shortcomings that characterize this body of research. To begin, Donaldson argues that few of the existing organizational configurations have been identified. Indeed, there exist far more configurations than suggested by the major proponents of this perspective. He also argues that most configurations change frequently and incrementally. Indeed, strategy-structure fits or configurations are best thought of as existing along continua on which they may move. In general, they do not change through occasional quantum jumps. Furthermore, Donaldson questions the empirical support for many of the assertions of the area of research. He offers evidence that suggests many of the forms identified within this perspective are contradicted by empirical research linking these configurations to specific contingencies. Pettigrew and Fenton are even more damning when they suggest that "what has been lacking . . . is any dedicated empirical work to support arguments" (2000, 19).

Aside from these and Donaldson's (2001) suggestions, other criticisms are noteworthy. This perspective assumes a systems approach to the study of organizations, one that may not always be appropriate. Finally, as with other theoretical perspectives, the eye of the beholder may often dictate the identity and importance of structures to be examined. In short, researchers pose the questions and often find what they are looking for.

31

Postmodern Perspective

Is there a theory of organization that mirrors Western society? North American society? American society? Many would consume more than one pot of coffee simply pondering the query. The obvious dilemma for many is being able to describe the makeup of any particular society. Demographics and the interpretations that accompany studies in that area offer some insight as to why developing such an understanding is never quite as simple as it might seem.

Expressions such as the "War Generation," "Baby Boomers," and "Generation X" serve as headings to mark the disparate values and beliefs held by just one of many societies, that of North America. With descriptors ranging from extroverted traditionalists and cosmopolitan modernists on the one hand to aimless dependents and autonomous poststructuralists (Adams 1997) on the other hand, all that is needed to understand the great divide between the world of those in their sixties and seventies and those in their late teens and early twenties is a vivid imagination. An interesting example of such a divide might be the large number of unsuccessful efforts of many a high-profile advertising firm or creative artist to build advertisements that effectively capture the imagination of the early twenties set.

Perhaps two overarching perspectives might be proposed as a means to understand the makeup of any contemporary society. One perspective would suggest that it is possible to paint a portrait of humanity—to construct a grand narrative (Montagna 1992). This is the modernist perspective. A second perspective suggests that such a feat is not possible. Efforts to write grand narratives are meaningless and doomed to failure. This is the perspective of the postmodernists. Most of the theories found within this book fit within the domain of modern thought. The challenge of this chapter is to paint a portrait of a postmodern theory of organization.

Before tackling that question, a more urgent query needs addressing. What does the term "modernism" mean? What are its underlying assumptions? "Modernism is the moment when man invented himself; when he no longer saw himself as a reflection of God and nature" (Cooper and Burrell 1988, 93). The modern era is characterized by four imperatives: (1) a revival of Enlightenment beliefs in the power of reason and observation, (2) a search for fundamentals and essentials, (3) a faith in progress and universal design, and (4) absorption in the machine metaphor (Gergen 1991).

These four imperatives imply a belief in reason and its manifestations in the form of science, empiricism, and positivism as the means of achieving progress. If humans can understand the world and nature—that which is "out there"—they can control it. At the core of the modernist project is an unchangeable rationalism and a faith that the results of inquiry can be communicated to other rational beings.

The modern era is also characterized by criteria of normality, consensus, determinacy, unity, and the official (Cooper and Burrell 1988). To allow confident predictive statements about organizations, the modernist assumes a superior objective standpoint. This is achieved by two means.

First, using a positivist, empiricist approach to science, explanation and prediction about the social world are sought by the search for regularities and causal relationships between its constitutive elements. Underlying this approach are a number of axioms (Parker 1992). To begin, all knowledge is deemed to be found in sensory experience, while meaning is grounded in observation. Next, the ideal pursued is knowledge in the form of a mathematically formulated universal science deductible from the smallest number of axioms. Statistical and empirical techniques are used to derive our theories. Following this, conceptual entities do not exist in themselves. They only represent the particulars from which they have been abstracted. Facts are observations. Values are not facts, and hence, cannot be given in sensory experience. Finally, since all knowledge is based on sensory experience, value judgments cannot be accorded the status of knowledge claims. As a result, attempts are made to quantify values through observations of physical artifacts and the use of questionnaires.

Second, if humans can understand the world, then they can explain it. Knowledge is cumulative. Grand narratives of the world may exist (Montagna 1992). Unity is possible. There is a reduction of analysis to one identity, the rational economic actor.

Modernism refers to both a way of life as well as a state of being.

Postmodernism may be described in the same manner. Its origins are numerous. Chaos theorists from the domain of the physical sciences, social analysts working in the tradition of workplace and the economy, critics of contemporary art forms such as a painting, literature, and architecture, and intellectuals of a distinctly European tradition whose discussions led to the rise of fields of inquiry, such as feminism, deconstruction, critical theory, structuralism, and poststructuralism, all may be given credit for the rise of postmodern thought (Bergquist 1993).

Little agreement exists within the literature as to a definition of the term "postmodern." If a unifying concept does exist, it is one that counters the four modernist imperatives stated earlier. Postmodern thinking attacks the grand narratives of modernism, including a single set of irresistible and empirical tendencies that use the rationalization of the world and bureaucratization as the primary means of its achievement. Postmodern thinking argues that it is no longer possible to take for granted the idea that the modern world is capable of producing endless human progress. This mode of thinking suggests that systems do not have meanings or purposes; these are human projects in which we uncritically assume that the world exists only for us and by which we locate ourselves at the controlling center of things (Feyeraband 1975).

Postmodernists believe that humans are essentially observers who construct interpretations of the world around them. No interpretations are universal. Multiple realities reign. What is real is what we socially define as real and, as such, reality is constantly changing (Montagna 1992). Reality is the possession of the individual.

Postmodernity, within a socially constructed world, is the total acceptance of discontinuity, heterogeneity, difference, multiple realities, and contradiction (Derrida 1973; Cooper 1988). As the French philosopher Jean-François Lyotard (1984) argues, if there is one theme that links the various interests in postmodernism, it is that of pluralism. This pluralism is captured by the informal nature of relations where local and immediate interests resist categorization and rationalization.

Given the postmodern ideas that unified visions of the world cannot exist and that multiple realities reign, an implication is that reality is specific to the individual. According to one theorist, a postmodern individual is

> a member of many communities and networks, a participant in many discourses, an audience to messages from everybody and everywhere— messages that that present conflicting ideals and images of the world, even different beliefs about belief. (Gergen 1991, 268)

What might a postmodern world look like? Anderson offers a portrait of such a world whose origins may be found in the pressures of globalization, the freer mobility of vast numbers of people, and the sheer enormity of recent technological change:

> All regions of the world become pluralistic, with people of different races, religions, worldviews and traditions living in close contact with one another and exposed to global events. There are not only many beliefs, but many beliefs about belief. People inhabit cultures in different ways, improvise, and create new forms. "Culture wars" between traditionalists and innovators continue to be a familiar part of social and political life everywhere. (1995, 8)

The postmodern perspective suggests that corporations or large-scale institutions supportive of the development of multiple realities will prosper. The acceptance of multiple realities may be important for another reason. Contestations of consensus within organizations may actually be beneficial. This is an important implication of postmodern theorizing. When faced with multireligious, multiethnic, complex, and continually changing competitive environments, corporations that strive to plug into the vast pool of knowledge found within their global employee base will be those that gain a competitive edge.

How might a postmodern corporation or entity be organized? Clegg offers the following insight:

> Within the core enterprises and countries of postmodern organizational forms, control will become less authoritarian in the workplace as new forms of market discipline substitute for the external surveillance of supervision, and changes are fostered by extensive deregulation. Internal markets within large organizations will increasingly be created as cost centers and profit centers, and surveillance will be lessened as more flexible manufacturing systems are adopted within which workers become their own supervisors.
>
> Where modernist organization was rigid, postmodern organization is flexible. Where modernist organization was focused on the strategic business unit and specific end products, postmodern organization is

centered on the management of the workforce core competencies. Where modernist consumption was premised on mass forms of consumption, postmodernist consumption is premised on niches. Where modernist organization was premised on technological determinism, postmodernist organization is premised on technological choices made possible through de-dedicated micro-electronic equipment. Where modernist organization and jobs were highly differentiated, demarcated and de-skilled, postmodernist organization and jobs will be highly de-differentiated, de-demarcated and multi-skilled. Employment relations assume more complex and fragmentary relational form, such as subcontracting and networking. (1992, 35)

Clegg (1990) offers another interesting insight. Despite the intriguing theorizing of many within the field, postmodern organizations still need to be responsible for meeting a number of concerns. They must have some means for articulating their goals or strategies. Somehow, they must arrange or align the functions that their personnel perform. They must identify the mechanisms that are used for coordination and control within their confines. Some thought needs to be given as to who is accountable for what and the roles played by individuals. Planning and communication of ideas must take place and rewards need to be linked in some capacity to performance. Finally, when hundreds or thousands of employees are involved, the term "effective leadership" should mean something to somebody. Clegg (1990) suggests that a good means to specify the makeup of a postmodern organization might be to describe it along these dimensions. In his view, mainstream Japanese corporations, with their emphasis on building and maintaining internal harmony, are one model of how this might be done.

Are there any problems with such a perspective? Yes, a number do exist. To begin, there are few empirical studies that offer evidence to support the ideas proposed by postmodern researchers. Although "part of the criticism arises from a narrow view of the notion of 'empirical' . . . researchers can still be faulted for doing many conceptual essays without extended field experience and reports" (Alvesson and Deetz 1996, 212). Second, although complex in its definition (if a common one can be found), the use of the term "postmodern" is quite fashionable among organizational theorists. Indeed, despite the absence of a large body of empirical research, the ideas of this perspective are slowly attracting legitimacy among mainstream organizational thinkers. Many consider it to be an alternative body of work useful for understanding organized behavior at a conceptual level. This awareness of the major themes suggests that postmodern theorizing may not be so different after all. Indeed, one may simply consider Bergquist's (1993) descriptions of postmodern organizations. Almost a decade since the descriptions were published, these organizations now appear fairly common, leading one to ask: What is so different about these organizations?

> The social structure of organizations of the future will have some unique characteristics. The key world will be "temporary." There will be adaptive, rapidly changing temporary systems. These will be task forces organized around problems to be solved by groups of relative strangers with diverse professional skills. The groups will be arranged on an organic rather than mechanical model; it will evolve in response to a problem rather than to programmed role expectations. The executive thus becomes coordinator or "linking pin" between various task forces. He must be a man [or woman] who can speak the polyglot jargon of research, with skills to relay information and to mediate between groups. People will be evaluated not according to rank but according to skill and professional training. Organization charts will consist of project groups rather than stratified functional groups. . . .
>
> Kaiser is a very fragmented institution in that there is no common goal throughout its distinctly different areas. It is as if it is two different organizations, holding together in a symbiotic relationship for profit, while pretending to be a nonprofit organization. The two different halves of the whole are the doctors and hospitals and the health plan which sells the memberships and generates the revenue which supports the hospitals. The two sides are constantly battling with each other for control of the organizations and for the financial backing of expenditures from the common budget. This power struggle is at the crux of all important decisions. (188, 221)

Third, this perspective appears quite susceptible to the liberal use of programmatic slogans. This may be the result of a confusion among readers as to whether postmodern writers are to trying to identify postmodernity or are being postmodern (Parker 1992; Alvesson 1995). Although "resistance" is a favorite topic of many writers, most of the discussion is theoretical with little being grounded in the day-to-day lives of specific individuals (Alvesson and Deetz 1996).

Fourth, if it is true that, "for post modernists, the world is not a stage but a text to be read . . . [and] multiple and conflicting readings may be held simultaneously" (Marsden and Townley 1996, 670), where does that leave us? Parker is even more blunt in his criticism: "If the real world does not exist in anything other than discourse, then is the act of writing one interpretation of a discourse a worthwhile pursuit?" (1992, 11). In many instances, the meaningful application of postmodern themes to organized behavior is difficult. Although some researchers have built strong cases for its application (Townley 1993), these successes are few and far between.

Finally, Alvesson delivers perhaps the most damning of critiques of postmodern organizational theorizing:

> Pomo is an unhelpful, if not hopeless term as an organizing principle for academic debates, which (too easily) stands for everything and nothing . . . can be summarized in terms of intertextual and intratextual meaningless. (1995, 16)

32

Critical Theory Perspective

Picture this: You have just graduated and started work with an exciting, growing company in the manufacturing sector. As part of your training, you have been assigned to work for three months on the shop floor of one of the most successful plants in your firm's portfolio of operating facilities. Two hours into your first shift, a number of troubling aspects of the work environment become apparent to you. First, all employees operate under a timecard. Entrance into and exit from the building is timed and noted. Breaks are limited to ten minutes in the morning and in the afternoon with a lunch allocation of fifty minutes. Pay is docked for late arrivals, early departures, and lengthy breaks. Washroom visits are limited to the same two-break and lunchtime slots. The company does not provide a cafeteria although a number of dispensing machines are available for snacks, soft drinks, and coffee. Workers are allotted fifteen pencils or pens per month and must pay for any usage above this amount. Four video cameras mounted high above in the ceiling record all movements on the shop floor. The building itself is over 100 years old and looks it. The machinery and materials used in the production process are occasionally greasy. Your employer does not provide work clothes for the employees. Unlike your management group, there is no pension plan, dental plan, or health benefits of any form for these individuals. Workers are typically employed on contracts that range from six months to one year, with most being renewed on a regular basis. The remainder of the day proceeds as the beginning. Each hour is filled with more insight about this work environment that you did not really grasp when you began considering it as an employer of choice. At the end of your first day of work, you are quite content with one aspect of this experience. Your understanding is quite clear as to how the shop floor of one arm of this successful corporate entity really works. Implicit in the question, How *do* organizations work, is a second and equally important question: How *should* organizations work? Living as we do in an age of globalization, rapid technological change, and the social upheaval of downsizing, it is necessary to approach such questions both self-consciously and critically.

Critical theory asks us not only to be critical of organizations, but also to be critical *of* theory. Rising out of the Frankfurt School of sociology in the early 1920s, critical theory was in many ways the result of a growing disenchantment with Marxism being more directly interested in establishing a truly critical approach. As Abercrombie, Hill, and Turner suggest:

> Critical theorists also had a deeper perception of the value and importance of the term critique. By its very nature, criticism has to be self-critical. Consequently, the Frankfurt School developed an open attitude which held out the hope for emancipation. They also recognized that since Marxism had changed fundamentally in form, it was impossible to remain entirely within the framework of nineteenth century capitalism. The principal target therefore became the claims of instrumental rationality (in particular natural science) to be the only valid form of genuine knowledge. (1988, 57)

Critical theory offers several common theses that unite writers and researchers operating under its umbrella (Grimes 1982). First, it aims to enlighten individuals or to help them understand their own true interests. This takes the form of a commitment to emancipate humanity from all forms of exploitation, domination, and oppression. By doing so, it strives to free these same individuals from a straitjacket that is partly self-imposed. Second, it rejects positivism—the separation of facts from values. As a metatheory, it is analytical in the search for the sources of domination, but abandons the idea that only a revolution will result in meaningful change to work environments. Third, it is a body of knowledge in itself. Finally, it examines both the theories of society and the natural sciences and the individuals who create those theories and operate within associated paradigms.

Critical theory reminds us that no one way of thinking is beyond question. Specifically, theorists of this tradition are interested in identifying and altering the rationales or ideas that dictate our understanding of organizations. They also suggest that our organizations are in serious decline. Their agenda is to make them more humane.

Critical organizational theorizing recognizes a bias in the direction of corporate interests in much of the mainstream literature and the way in which organizations are defined. The critical perspective takes this problem as its starting point. Critical theorists look for what is missing in organizational theorizing and endeavor to include issues defined as unimportant.

With the critical perspective as a basis, Alvesson (1985) offers an alternative theory of organization that describes the workings of our major institutions. Despite critical theory's break from Marxist thought in the 1920s, the language used by theorists such as Alvesson frequently echoes Marxism in that it is more likely to take the viewpoint of the common worker over that of management, shareholders, or owners.

Accordingly, Alvesson notes that

> [b]usiness companies and quasi-industrial organizations can be regarded as instruments for reproducing technological rationality. At the same time, they can be viewed as being determined by, and dependent on, the dominance of the rationality in society. In other words, organizations create, maintain, and propagate this rationality and its concrete forms of expression in economic, social and cultural contexts. (1985, 129)

In real terms, what Alvesson (1985) suggests is that large organizations survive by manipulating economic, social, and cultural factors to work to their best advantage. Furthermore, organizations promote themselves and their interests by promoting technological rationality— a certain way of thinking that includes these organizations' own values and goals. Technological rationality eventually becomes accepted by the society as reasonable and beyond question.

In simple terms, what organizational problems does a technical or instrumental rationality cause? Reviewing the literature, Alvesson and Deetz (1996, 203) suggest a number of concerns including constrained work conditions, unbalanced social relations between experts and nonexperts, gender bias, extensive control of employee minds, use of mass media and lobbying to control beyond organizational boundaries, and destruction of the natural environment.

For example, one form of technological rationality that is prominent in our society is that of progress. For the greater part of the past century, progress has been a cultural value that has been beyond question. Progress, for all intents and purposes, has been equated with societal good. What critical theory suggests is that the dominance of a rationality like progress must be approached critically. Progress has achieved and maintained its high status in our society because it is in the best interest of our society's largest and most powerful business organizations. If society questioned the technological rationality of progress too frequently, there would be no market for the latest automobiles, no funding for research and development, and no interest in the latest software upgrades. The extent to which this rationality has effectively infiltrated our thinking is impressive. Consumers dutifully purchasing the latest software upgrade are less likely to feel manipulated than they are to feel up to date.

Working from this premise, Alvesson (1985) offers four observations about large organizations. First, they exist in a constant state of tension between technological rationality and the negation of that rationality. Negation in this instance refers to efforts to escape the mind-set of practical reason in order to maximize individual freedom and minimize repression in the organizational workplace.

Second, this tension between the dominant mind-set and the forces negating it may be reduced by sharing profits with employees, decreasing the de-skilling of the workforce, reducing labor-management strife, and striving for fewer contradictions between technological rationality and its negating forces.

The third point covers the dominance of technological rationality over the operational processes of large organizations. The dominant mind-set of technological rationality usually corresponds quite neatly with the interests of society's elite groups (i.e., business and political leaders). Because these problems exist predominantly among senior managers, any management principles designed to address them should to be aimed at that same group (Alvesson 1985).

Finally, Alvesson (1985) suggests that a society built around the dominance of technological rationality—that is, around an accepted mind-set dominated by organizational interests—requires a highly developed ideology capable of covering the contradictions and criticisms of that perspective. In other words, large political and corporate organizations routinely pull the wool over our eyes in order to keep the system running to their best advantage. Thoughts and actions aimed at disturbing the status quo and reducing the dominance of technological rationality (complaints, protests, and so on) will be obstructed and avoided.

Critical theory suggests a number of implications for managers and readers. Among the most important is an awareness of the positive role to be played by "doubt" (Saul 1994). It also suggests that we become more questioning of organizations and their rational style of decision making. Historical examples such as the role of the London-based British General Staff in sending hundreds of thousands of soldiers to their deaths in the World War I trenches of France or the decision by the U.S. government to fight the Vietnam War from the White House offer extreme illustrations of the problems associated with an instrumental rationality and a lack of questioning until it is too late.

In today's society, critics such as Saul (1994) suggest that we pay attention to the role of multinationals and their influence on our lives. Corporatism is his target and he defines it as follows:

> A corporation is any interest group: specialist, professional, public or private, profit-oriented or not. The one characteristic shared by all corporations is that the primary relationship of individual members is to the organization and not to society at large. In a corporatist society, the corporation replaces the individual and therefore supersedes the role of democracy. In their own relationship with the outside world, corporations deal whenever possible with other corporations, not with individuals. . . . Corporatism is the persistent rival school of representative government. In place of the democratic idea of individual citizens who vote, confer legitimacy and participate to the best of their ability, individuals in the corporatist state are reduced to the role of secondary participants. They belong to their professional or expert groups—their corporations—and the state is run by ongoing negotiations between those various interests. This is the natural way of organizing things in a civilization based on expertise and devoted to the exercise of power through bureaucratic structures. . . .
>
> These groups function as almost independent states. The large banks and industrial corporations are so complex that their presidents are often reduced to glorified princes who read what is written for them travel in a cocoon, fulfilling predetermined activities. (74, 79)

One needs to simply ponder the implications of the Enron scandal to understand that Saul (1994) and other critical theorists may have a point.

Critical theorists have made important contributions to our understanding of organizations. Yet, they also leave themselves open to a fair amount of criticism from defenders of the status quo.

First, critical theorists may underestimate the good that has been derived from the overarching technical rationality that they claim is pervasive to organizations. Advances in communication technologies now allow individuals to educate themselves in the home through the use of the Internet. Many of these same technologies allow geographically dispersed individuals to communicate instantly and organize themselves online to address commercial or societal issues. This same disciplined rationality has served to dramatically increase awareness of the costs associated with drinking and driving while decreasing the number of road accidents. The same can be said for the use of cell phones in automobiles. A technical rationality has quickly inspired researchers to discover that the use of a cell phone while driving is extremely dangerous. The result is tightened usage restrictions in many countries. As well, an entire discipline, ergonomics, has arisen to improve the comfort of individuals who use technology on a regular basis.

Second, empirical studies to test the ideas underlying this perspective are not numerous: "What is lacking in particular are serious efforts to ground ideas of local resistance in specific empirical context" (Alvesson and Deetz 1996, 212). In other words, where is the evidence?

Third, an assumption underlying critical theory is of a stable managerial elite that make decisions and think alike:

> Yet this idea of the unity of the ruling class is challenged by the plethora of hostile takeovers as well as by the greater activism on the part of boards of directors in the 1990's to dismiss poorly performing CEO's—friends don't raid each other or fire each other. (Pfeffer 1997, 196)

Fourth, there is a distinctly antimanagement tone to the language of critical theory. While critical theorists are justified in their attempts to overcome the marginalization of all organizational participants, they do themselves few favors by expressing their ideas in a tone that berates and alienates the very people they need to address to produce change: the business elites. Of course, this is what makes theory so interesting. Defenders suggest that a critical perspective is not likely to kowtow to elites when the central notion is to expose sources of domination and managerial bias.

33

Marxist Perspective

"Firms exist to meet the needs of shareholders." If you are one of the many thousands of analysts employed in the financial services industry, you may have little reason to disagree with this statement. If, however, you are among the millions of unionized individuals employed throughout the private sector, chances are your view of the role of corporations may be somewhat different. Despite record-breaking advances in stock markets prior to the new millennium, labor strife continues in many areas of the economy. While share price performance often accurately reflects the financial performance of a firm relative to its competitors, it rarely offers a compelling portrait of life within the physical or virtual walls of the organization. Unfortunately, aside from glowing media portrayals in 2000 of working technology sector millionaires, a significant number of North American workers have seen their workloads grow without a corresponding increase in time off or financial remuneration. While the look and feel of many office and work environments have changed, many of the issues that led to the rise of unions decades ago remain. Although rarely admitted by union leaders, Marxist theory underlies many of the ideas that drive their efforts to improve the work environments of their members.

Marxist theory originates with the writings of the nineteenth-century political thinker Karl Marx (1859) and falls under the general social science category of "materialism." This school of thought argues that by looking at the use of technology and at the social arrangements that govern production, we can explain important features within a given society. According to materialism, the idea that human beings satisfy their material needs through productive social labor creates a fundamental set of constraints and imperatives. These constraints and imperatives in turn influence a variety of social phenomena, such as political institutions, social conflict, and systems of norms and values (Elster 1985).

Materialism begins with the observation that all societies must have institutions through which the basic needs of the population are satisfied. From there, it suggests that various societal features can be best understood in terms of their appropriateness to the workings of a society's production systems. That is to say, materialism explains features of politics, culture, and organization by analyzing human needs and the ability of a society's production systems to meet those needs.

In relating these ideas to organizational theory, the basic assumption underlying Marxist theory is that capitalists are primarily interested in maximizing their accumulation of wealth and power in society. While debate continues as to what an appropriate interpretation of Marx's writings might look like, many scholars would agree that a Marxist view of organization might be summarized as follows:

> Employers seek an inexpensive, relatively powerless labor force that can be controlled to work in concert with their interests. . . . Means of production (technologies) are selected that have the effect of de-skilling the labor force, thus ensuring social control over the labor force. . . . Employment relationships are structured so that the power and control are largely hidden, yet largely achieved. . . . Attempts to de-skill and control the labor force have within them forces that produce resistance on the part of the labor force. These forces include lack of motivation and effort, absenteeism, turnover, and collective action taken through labor unions. . . . A cycle of conflict and change is endangered by the struggle between capital and labor. (Pfeffer 1982, 163)

As noted earlier, Marxism fits within the radical structuralist paradigm of organizational theories. A structuralist reading of Marx is not simply about economics, but also of underlying structures of society. It begins with the assumption that society is a totality, not just a base and superstructure. Researchers in this tradition seek to understand how it all fits together the units of analysis in a totality (Gioia and Pitre 1990). Reality in this case is a process not a relationship between variables in which parts are thought to work for the maintenance of the system that is built around contradictions. The ultimate contradiction is between labor and capital, or forces and the relations of production in organizations. This contradiction is built into the logic of the approach and cannot ever be resolved.

At least two major implications come to mind when contemplating the insights of Marx. A first implication is, quite simply, the existence of unions. When seeking to understand the behavior of an organization that is unionized, managers and analysts need to take into account that workers will resist. A second implication is that workers may be correct. Oppression may indeed be present in the work environment. Edwards (1979) uses the following example by Aronowitz (1973) to illustrate the existence of oppression:

> At Lordstown, efficiency became the watchword. At 60 cars an hour, the pace of work had not been exactly leisurely, but after [new managers] came in the number of cars produced almost doubled. Making one car a minute had been no picnic, especially on a constantly moving line. Assembly work fits the worker to the pace of the machine. Each work station is not more than 6 to 8 feet long. For example, within a minute on the line, a worker in the trim department had to walk about 20 feet to a conveyor belt transporting parts to the line, pick up a front seat weighing 30 pounds, carry it back to his work station, place the seat on the chassis, and put in four bolts to fasten it down by first hand-starting the bolts and then using an air gun to tighten them according to standard. It was steady work when the line moved at 60 cars an hour. When it increased to more than 100 cars an hour, the number of operations on this job were not reduced and the pace became almost maddening. In 36 seconds the worker had to perform at least eight different operations, including walking, lifting, hauling, lifting the carpet, bending to fasten the bolts by hand, fastening them by air gun, replacing the carpet, and putting a sticker on the hood. Sometimes the bolts fail to fit into the holes; the gun refuses to function at the required torque; the seats are defective or the threads are bare on the bolt. But the line does not stop. (1973, 22)

Edwards then suggests how workers might resist oppressive work environments such as this:

> These illustrations involve assembly-line productions, but the basic relations exist in all workplaces; indeed, the shop floor, the office, the drafting room, the warehouse, the hospital ward, the construction site, and the hotel kitchen all become places of continuing conflict. Workers resist the discipline and the pace that employers try to impose. At most times the workers' efforts are solitary and hidden; individual workers find relief from oppressive work schedules by doing what their bosses perceive as slacking off or intentionally sabotaging work. At other times resistance is more conspiratorial; informal work groups agree on how fast they will work and combine to discipline rate-busters; or technicians work to rules, sticking to the letter of the production manual and

thereby slowing work to a fraction of normal efficiency. More openly, workers or even union locals (often against the commands of their leaders) walk off the job to protest firings, arbitrary discipline, unsafe working conditions, or other grievances. More public still, established unions or groups seeking to achieve bargaining rights strike in order to shut down production entirely. (1979, 14)

Theorizing in the tradition of Marxism and structuralist Marxism has some following in the field of organizational analysis due its ability to explain the traditionally confrontational and troubled relationship between labor and management. However, among management academics, it is not normally highly acclaimed or accepted as a mainstream perspective. There are a number of important reasons for this. To begin, Marx wrote of a society that existed well over 100 years ago. Much has changed. For instance, the capitalists to whom he referred now have, in many instances, pension and mutual funds that manage money for workers. Regardless, for over a century, theorists and scholars have been interpreting and reinterpreting his work. Marx, of course, has not been around to answer back. The language of Marxism is often labored and rhetorical. "Liberation through revolution" may have been an attractive creed in the early twentieth century, but it no longer is the case in much of the West. Although many employees may desire improved working conditions, pay, or benefits, most are either quite happy to leave these concerns at the office or will simply find another job when possible.

Hall offers two other criticisms of the Marxist approach:

First, the evidence in regard to the extent of the deskilling of labor is actually quite mixed (Attewell 1987). Indeed, there is evidence of skill enhancement for some kinds of work. The second problem is that, just as a "perfect solution" to a design issue is unlikely, so too is the likelihood that managerial attempts at control will work perfectly. In addition, labor will strongly resist efforts at control (Edwards 1979). (1996, 105)

Finally, Marxist thinking has an image problem. Many of the worst atrocities of the twentieth century were committed in the name of Marx or by regimes committed to or against his ideas (Buss 1993, 11). One need simply to think of the Cold War, the Vietnam War, Joseph Stalin, Pol Pot, and Augusto Pinochet to understand the impact of Marx and his ideas.

34

Poststructuralist Feminism Perspective

Deborah Hurst

Mary returned to work as a new mother. Given her change in circumstance, she decided to investigate the possibility of flexible work hours with her manager. She was told that, although her manager was sympathetic, in her position there was no provision for flexible work hours in policy. Besides, her colleague Gary had also just become a parent and did not need such assistance. Her inability to cope with her new work-family demands was a "personal" and not an "organizational" issue. To change, this issue would need to be brought forward in negotiations. As Mary reviewed the policies, she became clearly aware of the lack of flexibility and underlying assumptions that employees were to dedicate themselves to work and not be encumbered by outside personal responsibilities like childcare. Policies still used the term "man" and "he" as the stand-in term for all employees as well. Mary became discouraged and started to update her résumé.

Many conventional organizational theory perspectives do not fundamentally question the assumptions of patriarchy as they bear on the relationship between work-family concerns and the structuring of women's work (Mills and Tancred 1992). Instead, these organizational theory perspectives accept conventional definitions and valuation of women's work experience and existing job categories. Organizational practices mirror ideas perpetuated in the literature about the position of women in the workplace and give little time to questioning the underlying assumptions. Even where managers are sympathetic in practice, provisions to allow discretion in dealing with difficult situations are at times not available. The reality of experience of subordinated groups is considered within the existing worldview, but not in a way that allows for silenced voices to be heard. There appears to be a reluctance to challenge the fundamental assumptions of male dominance. Distinctions made in organizations continue to rationalize a division of labor that is hierarchical, gendered, and justifies the claim that those on top are those who know best (Jagger 1988). Those defined as peripheral or marginal to the organization by the dominant discourse remain silent and collaborate in this approach (Mills and Murgatroyd 1991).

The discourse of liberal feminism, although interested in change to the reality and inequitable experience of women in the workplace, does not appear to self-consciously question the source of women's exclusion in the first place. Forms of oppression and exclusion are obscured for not allowing for structural and political avenues to change and to address the exclusions in a meaningful way. As illustrated by the points raised, we need to find a way to consider how gendered subjectivities and male dominance embedded in organizations relate. For meaningful change to occur, we suggest that what is needed is a deconstructive, poststructuralist feminist approach (Calás and Smircich 1990; Mills and Tancred 1992).

Poststructuralist feminism is a form of critical organizational analysis. This approach examines how organizations shape experience, the social consequences of managerial practice, and how language perpetuates disparities of power and opportunity. Poststructuralist feminism questions how social power is exercised and how social relations of gender, class, and race might be transformed (Weedon 1987). This approach offers a corrective to many forms of organizational analysis that obscure or ignore the experiences of "other" people—those of different gender, race, and ethnicity (Calás and Smircich 1992). Feminist perspectives result from the conflicts and contradictions between dominant institutionalized definitions of women's nature and social roles existing within the sexual division of labor, structure of the family, access to work, politics, and medicine.

The poststructuralist feminist method involves textual analysis, the deconstruction and examination of text for different meanings and of taken-for-granted assumptions within a context. We can question things that seem generic and considered to be appropriate for all people in the organization or to stand for all people in an organization. Deconstructing the text allows us to learn something about the character and application of particular approaches in the organization in terms of the relative impacts across different groups of people. This approach allows us to move beyond concerns for equity and sex differences to the production of knowledge. The approach questions the values, voices, and experience that appear privileged in organizational research. It also gets us much closer to uncover the voices of those silenced, excluded, trivialized, or omitted in organizational analysis. The approach also questions the stability of cultural categories, such as gender, race, and class, and in doing so casts doubt on the idea of validating knowledge by experience. Rejected is the "essentially" male or female reality or structure and considered instead is how ideas are culturally constituted as categories, products, and/or producers of social and material relations.

The normative goal of poststructuralist feminism appears as a form of politics used to change power relations between men and women in society. While this includes politics in the family, education and welfare, culture, leisure, and politics, it also quite clearly includes the workplace. The approach allows for an examination of women's concerns, the very question of what it is to be a woman in an organization, and how femininity and sexuality are defined and used at times to redefine women. Patriarchal relations are assumed to be the starting point in this approach, referring to the power relations that subordinate women's interest to that of men. Patriarchal power is derived from social meaning given to biological differences and is supported by discourse regarding the nature and social role of women in relation to men. This is found by the use of "he" and "man" as generic to include all humans in the claim presented. Such patriarchal relations are assumed to be structural and outside of the good or bad intention of individuals. This suggests, however, that we need a theory of subjectivity to allow for explanations of why individuals oppress one another, for conscious and unconscious thought, and for emotion to account for the relationship between the individual and the social. Subject positions of men and women are learned along with how institutions operate and who and what are valued within.

Substantively, poststructuralist feminism helps us to better understand the relationships between subjectivity and meaning, meaning and social value, the "normal" subject positions open to women, and the degree of power or powerlessness within these roles (Weedon 1987). The three key concepts central to this perspective are language, meaning, and subjectivity.

Language is examined for how possible forms of social organization and likely political and social consequences are defined and contested. Language is thought of as discourse in this perspective. Discursive fields structure and locate social structures and processes in institutions. A dominant discourse reflects values, class, gender, and racial interests within. Language is the site in which individuals are defined and where subjectivities are constructed. In fact, within language "poststructuralism theorizes subjectivity as a site of disunity and conflict, central to the process of political change and to preserving the status quo" (Weedon 1987, 21).

Meaning is inscribed symbolically often by devaluing one side of a linguistic pair, for example, female and family, while enthroning the other of the symbolic pair, for example, male and work. The relationship between discourse and institutional forms are then explored in terms of how meanings are created historically and institutionally and reproduced linguistically. Meaning is constituted within language. Gender and work-family issues are good examples of meaning that is socially produced and variable in different discourses.

The concept of subjectivity is central to the poststructuralist feminist perspective. Subjectivity, which refers to an individual's conscious and unconscious thought and emotion, is precarious and contradictory, and in the process meaning is constantly constituted and reconstituted in discourse. This allows for subjectivity to change—almost invites it to do so—which makes the term extremely precarious as well as a product of society and culture that is produced historically and institutionally. In feminist poststructuralism, the individual always becomes the site of conflicting forms of subjectivity that through language gains meaning.

By understanding the competing views and experiences of the individual, the signifier, and the signified within the organization that are rooted in different assumptions and depicted in the written word, we gain a deeper understanding. Poststructuralist feminism offers an alternative perspective that can help resist the acceptance of any one particular focus, set of concerns, or analysis as the "one right way" of doing things organizationally. Weedon (1987) provides an excellent summary of this approach:

> Feminist poststructuralism is a mode of knowledge production that uses poststructuralist theories of language, subjectivity, social processes and institutions to understand existing power relations and to identify areas and strategies for change. Through the concept of discourse, the structuring principle of society, in social institutions, modes of thought and individual subjectivity, feminist poststructuralism is able, in detailed, historically specific analysis, to explain the working of power on behalf of specific interests and to analyze the opportunities for resistance to

it. It is a theory that decenters the rational, self-present subject of humanism, seeing subjectivity and consciousness, as socially produced in language, as a site of struggle and potential change. Language is not transparent as in human discourse, it is not expressive and does not label a "real" world. Meanings do not exist prior to their articulation in language and language is not an abstract system, but is always socially and historically located in discourses. Discourses represent political interests and in consequence are constantly vying for status and power. The site of this battle for power is the subjectivity of the individual and it is a battle to which the individual is an active but not sovereign protagonist. (41)

Poststructural feminism is not beyond criticism. Four points are noteworthy. First, it does not really allow us to fully account for different forms of meaning at times or changes in meaning over time.

Second, poststructuralist feminism is but one of a number of different schools of thought falling under the broader heading of "feminist approaches." Others include liberal, radical, psychoanalytical, Marxist, socialist, and Third World/(post)colonial feminist viewpoints. "Each school of thought gives alternative accounts for gender inequality, frames the problem differently and proposes different courses of actions as solutions" (Calás and Smircich 1996, 219).

Third, many poststructural feminists now consider the interests of women to be only one of a number of agendas that need to be pursued in order to change organizations for the better. Its advocacy of pluralistic politics may actually make it harder to "eliminate systems of exclusion and oppression historically and culturally located in patriarchal and capitalist arrangements" (Calás and Smircich 1996, 245).

To illustrate this point, consider one description of an ideal feminist organization. Calás and Smircich (1996) offer Woodul's description as one example:

> The nature of business will be changed by feminist operation of it. There should be structures for worker input, working toward meaningful worker control. Salaries should be set within a narrow range with consideration of each women's particular needs as well as her role in the company. Structures should be clear to all and determined on concrete bases. Decision-making methods should be set out, with the understanding that decision-making must presume responsibility. There must be a consciousness of accountability to the women's community. There must be a commitment to channel more money back into the

community or movement. Finally, there must be a commitment to radical change—to the goals of economic and political power of women. (1978, 197)

Unfortunately, as Calás and Smircich (1996) note, descriptions such as this pose a problem for feminists. If equality is the goal, how can the interests of women take precedence "in the face of differences of class, race, sexuality, education, skills, dependents and financial resources" (229)?

Finally, the normative dimension, although a worthy undertaking, may in fact limit success due to the antagonistic exclusionary stance that is often perceived by readers. In other words, the style of writing may be perceived as "elitist, inaccessible and full of jargon, making it difficult to utilize by most analysts despite the democratizing impetus that is among the aims of the analysis" (Calás and Smircich 1996, 245).

To conclude, poststructuralist feminism, like all perspectives, is not without its flaws. However, it does offer information on where experience comes from, why it may be contradictory, and why and how it can change. And what is the implication of this perspective? Equality!

35

Conclusion

Are all organizations alike? Peter Drucker does not think so:

> What we mean by organizations is indeed changing. . . . The first def-
> inition of an organization comes from the way the Prussian king Fred-
> erick the Great in the mid-eighteenth century defined his invention of
> the modern army. "An army" he said, "has three parts: infantry walks;
> cavalry rides; artillery is being pulled." An organization, in other words,
> is defined by how different work is being done. . . . But now a totally
> different approach is emerging, not replacing the older approaches but
> being superimposed on them: it says that the purpose of organizations
> is to get results outside, that is, to achieve performance in the market.
> But as important as these shifts may be in the theory of the organiza-
> tion, and the resulting shifts in structure, even more important is the
> fact that we are rapidly moving away from the belief that there has to
> be one theory of the organization and one ideal structure. (1997, 2002)

The ideas found in this text demonstrate the validity of Drucker's
remarks. Organization theory seeks to explain why large-scale organizations look and act as they do and why they are effective. This book
provides readers with a tool kit of theoretical lenses for pursuing these
explanations. These lenses represent the theories that underlie practice.

This text also provides readers with a broad overview of the field,
in the form of summaries of thirty-two different theories of organization and economic organization beginning with a primer for the
uninitiated. These summaries are organized under four separate headings that incorporate thinking from Burrell and Morgan (1979) and
Gioia and Pitre (1990). These headings include functional economic
theories of the firm, functional organization theories, interpretive and
social constructionist perspectives, and radical humanist and structuralist perspectives.

Our hope is that we have informed readers of the main issues confronting organizations, the main theoretical ideas within the different

paradigms, why it is important to theorize about organizations, how these theories are constructed, and how learning is improved by scanning multiple perspectives. Insights from this discipline may also help readers and practitioners understand, among other things, how operating entities might be led, organize themselves, protect their workers and society in general, correct deficiencies or deviant behavior, and compete.

References

Chapter 1. Introduction

Dodge, B. 1999. "The Webquest Page." Educational Technology Department of San Diego State University, http://edweb.sdsu.edu/webquest/ (accessed April 20, 2001).

Fleisher, C.S. 2003. "Are Competitive Intelligence Practitioners Professionals?" In *Strategic and Competitive Analysis: Methods and Techniques for Analyzing Business Competition,* ed. C. Fleisher and B. Bensoussan, 29–44. Upper Saddle River, NJ: Prentice Hall.

Fleisher C.S., and B. Bensoussan. 2003. *Strategic and Competitive Analysis: Methods and Techniques for Analyzing Business Competition.* Upper Saddle River, NJ: Prentice Hall.

Gergen, K.J. 1985. "The Social Constructionist Movement in Modern Psychology." *American Psychologist* 40, no. 3: 266–275.

Gioia, E., and D.A. Pitre. 1990. "Multiparadigm Perspectives on Theory Building." *Academy of Management Review* 15, no. 4: 588–590.

Grant, R.M. 1996. "Toward a Knowledge-Based Theory of the Firm." *Strategic Management Journal* (Winter Special Issue) 17:109.

Hall, R.H. 1996. *Organizations: Structures, Processes, and Outcomes.* Englewood Cliffs, NJ: Prentice Hall.

Kuhn, T. 1962. *The Structure of Scientific Revolutions.* Chicago: University of Chicago Press.

Langley, A. 1995. "Between Paralysis by Analysis and Extinction by Instinct." *Sloan Management Review* 36, no. 3: 63–76.

Machlup, F. 1980. *Knowledge: Its Creation, Distribution and Economic Significance.* Vol. 1. Princeton, NJ: Princeton University Press.

Meyerson, D., and J. Martin. 1987. "Cultural Change: An Integration of Three Different Views." *Journal of Management Studies* 24:623–648.

Pfeffer, J. 1982. *Organizations and Organization Theory.* Boston: Pitman.

Prescott, J.E. 1999. "Debunking the 'Academic Abstinence' Myth of Competitive Intelligence." *Competitive Intelligence Review* 2, no. 4: 22–27.

Smith, M.J. 1998. *Social Science in Question.* London: Sage.

Vibert, C. Forthcoming. *Competitive Intelligence: A Framework for Web-based Analysis & Decision-Making.* Mason, OH: South-Western Thomson.

Windle, G. 2003. "How Can Competitive Intelligence Practitioners Avoid

Relying on the Internet?" In *Strategic and Competitive Analysis: Methods and Techniques for Analyzing Business Competition,* ed. C. Fleisher and B. Bensoussan, 85–97. Upper Saddle River, NJ: Prentice Hall.

Chapter 2. A Primer on Organization Theory

Burrell, G., and G. Morgan. 1979. *Sociological Paradigms and Organisational Analysis: Elements of the Sociology of Corporate Life.* London: Heinemann Educational.

Gioia, D.A., and E. Pitre. 1990. "Multiparadigm Perspectives on Theory Building." *Academy of Management Review* 154:584–562.

Hayagreeva Rao, M.V., and W.A. Pasmore. 1989. "Knowledge and Interests in Organization Studies. A Conflict of Interpretations." *Organization Studies* 102:225–239.

Kuhn, T. 1962. *The Structure of Scientific Revolutions.* Chicago: University of Chicago Press.

Part I. Functional Economic Theories of the Firm

Axelrod, R. 1980. *The Evolution of Cooperation.* New York: Penguin.

Bain, J.S. 1968. *Industrial Organization.* New York: Wiley.

Boatright, J.R. 1996. "Business Ethics and the Theory of the Firm." *American Business Law Journal* 34, no. 2: 2–12.

Burrell, G., and G. Morgan. 1979. *Sociological Paradigms and Organisational Analysis: Elements of the Sociology of Corporate Life.* London: Heinemann Educational.

Coase, R.N. 1937. "The Nature of the Firm." *Economica* 4:386–405.

Connor, K. 1991. "A Historical Comparison of Resource-Based Theory and Five Schools of Thought within Industrial Organization Economics: Do We Have a New Theory of the Firm?" *Journal of Management* 17:121–154.

Cyert, R.M., and J.G. March. 1963. *A Behavioral Theory of the Firm.* Englewood Cliffs, NJ: Prentice Hall.

Gioia, D.A., and E. Pitre. 1990. "Multiparadigm Perspectives on Theory Building." *Academy of Management Review* 15, no. 4: 590.

Grant, R.M. 1996. "Toward a Knowledge-Based Theory of the Firm." *Strategic Management Journal* (Winter Special Issue) 17:109.

Hart, O., and J. Moore. 1990. "Property Rights and the Nature of the Firm." *Journal of Political Economy* 98, no. 6: 1121.

Jensen, M.C., and W.H. Meckling. 1976. "Theory of the Firm: Managerial Behavior, Agency Costs and Ownership Structure." *Journal of Financial Economics* 3:305–360.

Machlup, F. 1980. *Knowledge: Its Creation, Distribution and Economic Significance.* Princeton, NJ: Princeton University Press.

Nelson R.R., and S.G. Winter. 1982. An *Evolutionary Theory of Economic Change.* Cambridge, MA: Harvard University Press.

Shoemaker, P.J.H. 1990. "Strategy, Complexity and Economic Rent." *Management Science* 36:1178–1192.

Spender, J.-C., and R.M. Grant 1996. "Knowledge and the Firm: Overview." *Strategic Management Journal* (Winter) 17:5–9.

Stigler, G. 1968. *The Organization of Industry.* Chicago, IL: University of Chicago Press.

Stigler, G.J. 1961. "The Economics of Information." *Journal of Political Economy* 69:213–225.

Williamson, O.E. 1976. *Markets and Hierarchies: Analysis and Anti-trust Implications.* New York: The Free Press.

Chapter 3. Neoclassical Economics Perspective

Conner, K. 1991. "A Historical Comparison of Resource-Based Theory and Five Schools of Thought within Industrial Organization Economics: Do We Have a New Theory of the Firm?" *Journal of Management* 17:121–154.

Demsetz, H. 1997. "The Firm in Economic Theory: A Quiet Revolution." *The American Economic Review:*1–4.

Milgrom, P., and J. Roberts. 1992. *Economics, Organizations, and Management.* Englewood Cliffs, NJ: Prentice Hall.

Rutherford, D. 1992. *Dictionary of Economics.* London: Routledge.

Williamson, O.E., and S.G. Winter. 1993. *The Nature of the Firm: Origins, Evolution and Development.* New York: Oxford University Press.

Chapter 4. Chicago School Perspective

Barney, J. 1986. "Types of Competition and the Theory of Strategy: Toward an Integrative Framework." *Academy of Management Review* 11, no. 4: 791–800.

Conner, K. 1991. "A Historical Comparison of Resource-Based Theory and Five Schools of Thought within Industrial Organizational Economics: Do We Have a New Theory of the Firm?" *Journal of Management* 17: 121–154.

Den Tandt, M. 2002. "Capitalist Ethos Too Strong in the '90s But Now It Has Become Hamstrung." *Globe and Mail,* 17 June, B9.

Saul, J.R. 1994. *The Doubter's Companion: A Dictionary of Aggressive Common Sense.* Toronto, ON: Viking-Penguin.

Stigler, G.J. 1957. "Perfect Competition, Historically Contemplated." *Journal of Political Economy* 65:1–17.
———. 1961. "The Economics of Information." *Journal of Political Economy* 69:213–225.
Strebel, P. 1992. *Breakpoints: How Managers Exploit Radical Business Change.* Cambridge, MA: Harvard Business School Press.

Chapter 5. Bain-Mason Perspective

Bain, J.S. 1956. *Barriers to Competition.* Cambridge, MA: Harvard University Press.
———. 1968. *Industrial Organization.* New York: Wiley.
Barney, J. 1986. "Types of Competition and the Theory of Strategy: Toward an Integrative Framework." *Academy of Management Review* 11, no. 4: 791–800.
Mason, E.S. 1939. "Price and Production Policies of Large-Scale Enterprises." *American Economic Review* 29:61–74.
———. 1957. *Economic Concentration and the Monopoly Problem,* Cambridge, MA: Harvard University Press.
Porter, M. 1980. *Competitive Strategy.* New York: The Free Press.
———. 1981. "The Contributions of Industrial Organization to Strategic Management." *Academy of Management Review* 6, no. 4: 609–620.
Scherer, F.M. 1980. *Industrial Market Structure and Economic Performance.* Chicago: Rand McNally.
Teece, D.J. 1984. "Economic Analysis and Strategic Management." In *Strategy for Decision Making in Complex Organizations,* ed. J.M. Pennings, 78–101. San Francisco: Jossey-Bass.
Tsoukas, H., and C. Knudsen. 2002. "The Conduct of Strategy Research." In *Handbook of Strategy and Management,* ed. A. Pettigrew, H. Thomas, and R. Whittington, 411–435. London: Sage.

Chapter 6. Transaction Cost Perspective

Donaldson, L. 1990. "The Ethereal Hand: Organizational Economics and Management Theory." *Academy of Management Review* 153:369–381.
———. 1995. *American Anti-management Theories of Organization: A Critique of Paradigm Proliferation.* Cambridge: Cambridge University Press.
Geroski, P., Machin, S.J., and C.F. Walters. 1997. "Corporate Growth and Profitability." *The Journal of Industrial Economics,* 45, no. 2: 171–189.

Ghoshal, S., and P. Moran. 1996. "Bad for Practice: A Critique of Transaction Cost Theory." *Academy of Management Review* 21, no. 1: 13–47.

Moran, P., and S. Ghoshal. 1996. "Theories of Economic Organization: The Case for Realism and Balance." *Academy of Management Review* 21, no. 1: 58–72.

Mosakowski, E. 1991. "Organizational Boundaries and Economic Performance: An Empirical Study of Entrepreneurial Computer Firms." *Strategic Management Journal* 12, no. 2: 115–133.

Ouchi, W.G. 1980. "Markets, Hierarchies and Clans." *Administrative Science Quarterly:* 129–141.

Tsoukas, H., and C. Knudsen. 2002. "The Conduct of Strategy Research." In *Handbook of Strategy and Management,* ed. A. Pettigrew, H. Thomas, and R. Whittington, 411–435. London: Sage.

Williamson, O.E. 1976. *Markets and Hierarchies: Analysis and Anti-trust Implications.* New York: Free Press.

———. 1985. *The Economic Institutions of Capitalism.* New York: Free Press.

Chapter 7. Network Perspective

Barney, J., and W. Hesterly. 1996. "Organizational Economics: Understanding the Relationship between Organizations and Economic Analysis." In *Handbook of Organization Studies,* ed. S. Clegg, C. Hardy, and W.R. Nord, 115–147. London: Sage.

Burt, R.S. 1992. *Structural Holes.* Cambridge, MA: Harvard University Press.

Carroll, G.R., and A.C. Teo. 1996. "On the Social Network of Managers." *Academy of Management Review* 39, no. 2: 421–440.

Clegg, S.R., C. Hardy, and W.R. Nord. 1996. *Handbook of Organization Studies.* London: Sage.

Granovetter, M. 1985. "Economic Action and Social Structure: The Problem of Embeddedness." *American Journal of Sociology* 91, no. 3: 481–510.

Gulati, R. 1995. "Does Familiarity Breed Trust? The Implications of Repeated Ties for Contractual Choice in Alliances." *Academy of Management Journal* 38:85–112.

———. 1998. "Alliances and Networks." *Strategic Management Journal* 19: 293–317.

Gulati, R., N. Nohria, and A. Zaheer. 2000. "Strategic Networks." *Strategic Management Journal* 21: 203–215.

Hitt, M.A., R.E. Freeman, and J.S. Harrison. 2001. *The Blackwell Handbook of Strategic Management.* Oxford: Blackwell.

Kilduff, M., and K.G. Corley. 2000. "Organizational Culture from a Network Perspective." In *Handbook of Organizational Culture and Climate,* ed.

N. Ashkanasy, C. Wilderom, and M. Peterson, 211–221. Thousand Oaks, CA: Sage.

Krackhardt D., and J.R. Hanson. 1993. "Informal Networks: The Company behind the Chart." *Harvard Business Review* (July–August): 104–111.

Moss Kanter, R., and R.G. Eccles. 1992. "Making Network Research Relevant to Practice." In *Networks and Organizations: Structure, Form and Action,* ed. N. Nohria and R.G. Eccles, 521–527. Boston: Harvard Business School Press.

Nohria, N. 1992. "Is a Network Perspective a Useful Way of Studying Organizations?" In *Networks and Organizations: Structure, Form and Action,* ed. N. Nohria and R.G. Eccles, 1–22. Boston: Harvard Business School Press.

Pettigrew, A., H. Thomas, and R. Whittington. 2002. *Handbook of Strategy and Management.* London: Sage.

Powell, W.W. 1990. "Neither Market nor Hierarchy: Network Forms of Organization." *Research in Organizational Behavior* 12:295–336.

Putnam, L.L, N. Phillips, and P. Chapman. 1996. "Metaphors of Communication and Organization." In *Handbook of Organization Studies,* ed. S. Clegg, C. Hardy, and W.R. Nord, 375–408. London: Sage

Stevenson, W.B. 1990. "Formal Structure and Networks of Interaction within Organizations." *Social Science Research* 19:113–131.

Stevenson, W.B., J.L. Pearce, and L. Porter. 1985. "The Concept of 'Coalition' in Organization Theory and Research." *The Academy of Management Review* 10, no. 2: 256–269.

Tolbert, P.S., G.R. Salancik, D. Krackhardt, and S.B. Andrews. 1995. "Review Essay—Wanted: A Good Network Theory of Organization." *Administrative Science Quarterly* 40, no. 2: 343–347.

Uzzi, B. 1996. "The Sources and Consequences of Embeddedness for the Economic Performance of Organizations: The Network Effect." *American Sociological Review* 61:674–698.

Williamson, O.E. 1991. "Comparative Economic Organization: The Analysis of Discrete Structural Alternatives." *Administrative Science Quarterly* 36:269–296.

Chapter 8. Agency Theory Perspective

Barney, J. 1996. *Gaining and Sustaining Competitive Advantage.* Reading, MA: Addison Wesley.

Barney, J., and W. Hesterly. 1996. "Organizational Economics: Understanding the Relationship between Organizations and Economic Analysis." In *Handbook of Organization Studies,* ed. S. Clegg, C. Hardy, and W.R. Nord, 115–147. London: Sage.

Demsetz, H. 1997. "The Firm in Economic Theory: A Quiet Revolution." *The American Economic Review:* 87, no. 2:1–4.

Eisenhardt, K. 1989. "Agency Theory: An Assessment and Review." *Academy of Management Review* 14:57–74.

Jensen, M.C., and W.H. Meckling, 1976. "Theory of the Firm: Managerial Behavior, Agency Costs and Ownership Structure." *Journal of Financial Economics* 3:305–360.

Lubatkin, M.H., P.J. Lane, and W.S. Schulze. 2001. "A Strategic Management Model of Agency Relationships in Firm Governance." In *The Blackwell Handbook of Strategic Management,* ed. M.A. Hitt, R.E. Freeman, and J.S. Harrison, 229–258. Oxford: Blackwell Business.

Pfeffer, J. 1997. *New Directions for Organization Theory: Problems and Prospects.* New York: Oxford University Press.

Rousseau, D.M., and J.M. Parks. 1993. "The Contracts of Individuals and Organizations." *Research in Organizational Behavior* 15:1–41.

Chapter 9. Stakeholder Perspective

Donaldson, T., and L. Preston. 1995. "The Stakeholder Theory of the Corporation: Concepts, Evidence and Implications." *Academy of Management Review* 20, no. 1: 65–91.

Freeman, R.E. 1984. *Strategic Management: A Stakeholder Approach.* Boston: Pitman.

Freeman, R.E., and J. McVea. 2001. "A Stakeholder Approach to Strategic Management." In *The Blackwell Handbook of Strategic Management,* ed. M.A. Hitt, R.E. Freeman, and J.S. Harrison, 189–207. Oxford: Blackwell.

Garud, R., and A.H. Van de Ven. 2001. "Strategic Change Processes." In *Handbook of Strategy and Management,* ed. A. Pettigrew, H. Thomas, and R. Whittington, 206–231. London: Sage.

Jones, T.M. 1995. "Instrumental Stakeholder Theory: A Synthesis of Ethics and Economics." *Academy of Management Review* 202:404–437.

Chapter 10. Resource-Based Theory Perspective

Barney, J. 1996. *Gaining and Sustaining Competitive Advantage.* Reading, MA: Addison Wesley.

Barney, J.B., and A.M. Arikan. 2001. "The Resource Based View: Origins and Implications." In *The Blackwell Handbook of Strategic Management,* ed. M.A. Hitt, R.E. Freeman, and J.S. Harrison, 124–188. Oxford: Blackwell.

Coase, R.H. 1937. "The Nature of the Firm." *Economica* 4:331–351.

Cool, K., L.A. Costa, and I. Dierickx. 2002. "Constructing Competitive Advantage." In *Handbook of Strategy and Management,* ed. A. Pettigrew, H. Thomas, and R. Whittington, 55–71. Thousand Oaks, CA: Sage.

Hart, S. 1995. "A Natural-Resource Based View of the Firm." *Academy of Management Review* 204:996–1014.

Mahoney, J.T. 1992. "Organizational Economics within the Conversation of Strategic Management." *Advances in Strategic Management* 8:103–155.

Penrose, E.T. 1959. *The Theory of Growth of the Firm.* New York: Wiley.

Porter, M.E. 1980. *Competitive Strategy.* New York: The Free Press.

———. 1985. *Competitive Advantage: Creating and Sustaining Superior Performance.* New York: Free Press.

Chapter 11. Behavioral Perspective

Ackoff, R.L. 1981. "The Art and Science of Mess Management." *Interfaces* (February): 20–26.

Aoki, M. 1984. *The Cooperative Game Theory of the Firm.* London: Oxford University Press.

Bromiley, P., K.D. Miller, and D. Rau. 2001. "Risk in Strategic Management Research." In *The Blackwell Handbook of Strategic Management,* ed. M.A. Hitt, R.E. Freeman, and J.S. Harrison, 259–288. Oxford: Blackwell.

Chakravarthy, B.S., and R.E. White. 2001. "Strategy Process: Forming, Implementing and Changing Strategies." In *Handbook of Strategy and Management,* ed. A. Pettigrew, H. Thomas, and R. Whittington, 182–205. London: Sage.

Cohen, M.D., J.G. March, and J.P. Olsen. 1972. "A Garbage Can Model of Organizational Choice." *Administrative Science Quarterly* 17:1–25.

Cyert, R.M., and J.G. March. 1963. *A Behavioral Theory of the Firm.* Englewood Cliffs, NJ: Prentice Hall.

Mahoney, J.T. 1992. "Organizational Economics within the Conversation of Strategic Management." *Advances in Strategic Management* 8:103–155.

Nelson, D.L., and J.C. Quick. 2000. *Organizational Behavior: Foundations, Realities and Challenges.* Cincinnati, OH: South Western College Publishing.

Pugh, D.S., and D.J. Hickson. 1989. *Writers on Organization.* 4th ed. Newbury Park, CA: Sage.

Simon, H.A. 1947. *Administrative Behaviour.* New York: Free Press.

Chapter 12. Game Theory Perspective

Aoki, M. 1984. *The Cooperative Game Theory of the Firm.* London: Oxford University Press.

Axelrod, R. 1980. *The Evolution of Cooperation.* New York: Penguin.

Bowman, E.H., H. Singh, and H. Thomas. 2002. "The Domain of Strategic Management: History and Evolution." In *Handbook of Strategy and Management,* ed. A. Pettigrew, H. Thomas, and R. Whittington, 31–54. London: Sage.

Gulati, R., T. Khanna, and N. Nohria. 1994. "Unilateral Commitments and the Importance of Process in Alliances." *Sloan Management Review* (Spring): 61–69.

Hofstadter, D.H.R. 1983. "Metamagical Themas." *Scientific American* (May): 16–26.

Rapoport, A. 1960. *Fights, Games and Debates.* Ann Arbor: University of Michigan Press.

Tsoukas, H., and C. Knudsen. 2002. "The Conduct of Strategy Research." In *Handbook of Strategy and Management,* ed. A. Pettigrew, H. Thomas, and R. Whittington, 411–435. London: Sage.

Chapter 13. Property Rights Perspective

Alchian, A., and H. Demsetz. 1972. "Production, Information Costs, and Economic Organization." *American Economic Review* 62:777–797.

Barzel, Y. 1989. *Economic Analysis of Property Rights.* Cambridge: Cambridge University Press.

Fisher, I. 1923. *Elementary Principles of Economics.* New York: Macmillan.

Grossman, S.J., and O.D. Hart. 1986. "The Costs and Benefits of Ownership: A Theory of Vertical and Lateral Integration." *Journal of Political Economy* 94:691–719.

Hart, O., and J. Moore. 1990. "Property Rights and the Nature of the Firm." *Journal of Political Economy* 98, no. 6: 1121.

Jensen, M. 1998. *Foundations of Organizational Strategy.* Cambridge, MA: Harvard University Press.

Jones, G.R. 1998. *Organizational Theory: Text and Cases.* 2nd ed. Reading, MA: Addison Wesley.

Milgrom, P., and J. Roberts. 1992. *Economics, Organization, and Management.* Englewood Cliffs, NJ: Prentice Hall.

Moran, P., and S. Ghoshal. 1996. "Theories of Economic Organization: The Case for Realism and Balance." *Academy of Management Review* 21, no. 1: 58–72.

Chapter 14. Knowledge Perspective

Bontis, N., N. Dragonetti, K. Jacobsen, and G. Roos. 1999. "The Knowledge Toolbox: A Review of the Tools Available to Measure and Manage Intangible Resources." *European Management Journal* 17, no. 4: 391–402.

Choo, C.W. 1997. "Managing Knowledge: Perspectives on Cooperation and Competition." *Information Processing and Management* 33, no. 6: 808–811.

"Copyright Law: Overview." 2000. Nolo.com Self-Help Law Center, www. nolo.com (accessed May 20, 2001).

Eisenhardt, K.M., and F.M. Santos. 2002. "Knowledge-Based View: A New Theory of Strategy." In *Handbook of Strategy and Management,* ed. A. Pettigrew, H. Thomas, and R. Whittington, 139–164. London: Sage.

Grant, R.M. 1996. "Toward a Knowledge-Based Theory of the Firm." *Strategic Management Journal* (Winter special issue) 17:109–122.

Kogut, B., and U. Zander. 1992. "Knowledge of the Firm, Combinative Capabilities and the Replication of Technology." *Organization Studies* 3: 383–397.

Liebeskind, J.P. 1996. "Knowledge, Strategy and the Theory of the Firm." *Strategic Management Journal* 17:93–107.

Matusik, S., and C. Hill. 1998. "The Utilization of Contingent Work, Knowledge Creation and Competitive Advantage." *Academy of Management Review* 23, no. 4: 680–698.

"Patent Law: Overview." 2000. Nolo.com Self-Help Law Center, www. nolo.com (accessed May 20, 2001).

Schein, E. 1986. *Organizational Culture and Leadership.* San Francisco: Jossey-Bass.

Spender, J.C., and R.M. Grant. 1996. "Knowledge and the Firm." *Strategic Management Journal* 17:5–9.

"Trade Mark Law: Overview." 2000. Nolo.com Self-Help Law Center, www. nolo.com (accessed May 20, 2001).

"Trade Secret Law: Overview." 2000. Nolo.com Self-Help Law Center, www. nolo.com (accessed May 20, 2001).

Zander, U., and B. Kogut. 1995. "Knowledge and the Speed of the Transfer and Imitation of Organizational Capabilities: An Empirical Test." *Organization Science* 6, no. 1:76–92.

Chapter 15. Evolutionary Perspective

Barnett, W.P., H.R. Greve, and D.Y. Park. 1994. "An Evolutionary Model of Organizational Performance." *Strategic Management Journal* 15:11–28.

Barney, J. 1986. "Types of Competition and the Theory of Strategy: Toward an Integrative Framework." *Academy of Management Review* 11, no. 4: 791–800.

Baum, J.A.C., and J.V. Singh. 1994. "Organizational Hierarchies and Evolutionary Processes: Some Reflections on a Theory of Organizational Evolution." In *Evolutionary Dynamics of Organizations,* ed. J.V. Singh and J.A.C. Baum, 3–19. Oxford: Oxford University Press.

Mahoney, J.T. 1992. "Organizational Economics within the Conversation of Strategic Management." *Advances in Strategic Management* 8:103–155.

Mirowski, P. 1988. *Against Mechanism: Protecting Economics from Science.* Totowa, NJ: Rowman and Littlefield.

Moran, P., and S. Ghoshal. 1996. "Theories of Economic Organization: The Case for Realism and Balance." *Academy of Management Review* 21, no. 1: 58–72.

Nelson, R.R., and S.G. Winter. 1982. *An Evolutionary Theory of Economic Change.* Cambridge, MA: Harvard University Press.

Tsoukas, H., and C. Knudsen. 2002. "The Conduct of Strategy Research." In *Handbook of Strategy and Management,* ed. A. Pettigrew, H. Thomas, and R. Whittington, 411–435. London: Sage.

Williamson, O.E., and S.G. Winter. 1993. *The Nature of the Firm: Origins, Evolution and Development.* New York: Oxford University Press.

Winter, S.G. 1993. "On Coase, Competence, and the Corporation." In *The Nature of the Firm: Origins, Evolution and Development,* ed. O.E. Williamson and S.G. Winter, 179–195. New York: Oxford University Press.

Chapter 16. Natural Environment Perspective

Denton, D.K. 1994. *Enviro-management.* Englewood Cliffs, NJ: Prentice Hall.

Freeman, R. 1984. *Stakeholder Management: A Stakeholder Approach.* Boston: Pitman.

Friedman, F. 1993. *Practical Guide to Environmental Management.* Washington, DC: Environmental Law Institute.

Gladwin, T.N. 1993. "The Meaning of Greening: A Plea for Organizational Theory." In *Environmental Strategies for Industry,* ed. K. Fischer and J. Schot, 37–61. Washington, DC: Island.

Hart, S. 1997. "Beyond Greening: Strategies for a Sustainable World." *Harvard Business Review* (January–February): 66–77.

Klassen, R.D., and D.C. Whybark. 1999. "The Impact of Environmental Technologies on Manufacturing Performance." *Academy of Management Journal* 42, no. 6: 599–615.

Peters, T. 1990. *Lean, Green and Clean: The Profitable Company in the Year 2000.* Palo Alto, CA: Tom Peters Group.

Piasecki, B.W., K.A. Fletcher, and F.J. Mendelson. 1999. *Environmental Management and Business Strategy: Leadership Skills for the Twenty-first Century.* New York: Wiley.

Schmidheiney, S. 1992. *Changing Course: A Global Perspective on Development and the Environment.* Cambridge: MIT Press.

Shelton, R. 1994. "Hitting the Green Wall: Corporate Environmental Strategy." *Journal of Environmental Leadership* 3, no. 2: 10–19.

Part II. Functional Organization Theories

Burrell, G., and G. Morgan. 1979. *Sociological Paradigms and Organisational Analysis: Elements of the Sociology of Corporate Life.* London: Heinemann Educational.

Gioia, D.A., and E. Pitre E. 1990. "Multiparadigm Perspectives on Theory Building." *Academy of Management Review* 15, no. 4: 590.

Grant, R.M. 1996. "Toward a Knowledge-Based Theory of the Firm." *Strategic Management Journal* (Winter special issue) 17:109.

Chapter 17. Bureaucracy Perspective

Bennis, W.G. 1959. "Leadership Theory and Administrative Behavior: The Problem of Authority." *Administrative Science Quarterly* 4:259–301.

Clegg, S., and C. Hardy. 1996. "Representations." In *Handbook of Organization Studies,* ed. S. Clegg, C. Hardy, and W.R. Nord, 676–708. London: Sage.

Daft, R.L. 1983. *Organization Theory and Design.* 2nd ed. St. Paul, MN: West.

Morgan, G. 1986. *Images of Organization.* Beverly Hills, CA: Sage.

Pettigrew, A.M., and E.M. Fenton. 2001. *The Innovating Organization.* London: Sage.

Tawney, R.H. 1958. Foreword to *The Protestant Work Ethic and the Spirit of Capitalism,* by M. Weber, trans. T. Parsons. New York: Scribner's.

Weber, M. 1947. *The Theories of Social and Economic Organizations.* Trans. A.M. Henderson and T. Parsons, 328–334. New York: Free Press.

Wilson, E. 2001. *Organizational Behavior Reassessed: The Impact of Culture.* London: Thousand Oaks.

Chapter 18. Contingency Perspective

Burrell, G., and G. Morgan. 1979. *Sociological Paradigms and Organisational Analysis: Elements of the Sociology of Corporate Life.* London: Heinemann Educational.

Child, J. 1972. "Organization Structure, Environment and Performance: The Role of Strategic Choice." *Sociology* 6:1–22.

Hickson, D.J., C.R. Hinings, C.A. Lee, R.E. Schneck, and J.M. Pennings. 1971. "A Strategic Contingencies Theory of Intra-organizational Power." *Administrative Science Quarterly* 16, no. 2: 216–229.

Jones, G.R. 1995. *Organization Theory: Text and Cases.* Reading, MA: Addison Wesley.

Pettigrew A.M., and E.M. Fenton. 2001. *The Innovating Organization.* London: Sage.

Pfeffer, J. 1982. *Organization and Organization Theory.* Boston: Pitman.

———. 1997. *New Directions for Organization Theory: Problems and Prospects.* New York: Oxford University Press.

Pugh, D.S., D.J. Hickson, C.R. Hinings, and C. Turner. 1969. "The Context of Organization Structures." *Administrative Science Quarterly* 14:91–114.

Robbins, S.P. 1990. *Organization Theory: Structure, Design and Application.* Englewood Cliffs, NJ: Prentice Hall.

Schoonhoven, C.B. 1981. "Problems with Contingency Theory: Testing Assumptions Hidden within the Language of Contingency Theory." *Administrative Science Quarterly* 26:349–377.

Schreyogg, G. 1980. "Contingency and Choice in Organization." *Organization Studies* 4:304–326.

Chapter 19. Strategic Choice Perspective

Barnard, C. 1938. *The Functions of the Executive.* Cambridge, MA: Harvard University Press.

Chandler, A. 1962. *Strategy and Structure.* Cambridge: MIT Press.

Child, J. 1972. "Organization Structure, Environment and Performance: The Role of Strategic Choice." *Sociology* 6:1–22.

Donaldson, L. 1995. *American Anti-management Theories of Organization: A Critique of Paradigm Proliferation.* Cambridge: Cambridge University Press.

———. 2001. *The Contingency Theory of Organizations.* London: Sage.

Dyas, G.P., and H.T. Thanheiser. 1976. *The Emerging European Enterprise. Strategy and Structure in French and German Industry.* London: Macmillan.

Hall, R.H. 1996 *Organizations: Structures, Processes, and Outcomes.* 6th ed. Englewood Cliffs, NJ: Prentice Hall.

Knights, D., and G. Morgan. 1991. "Corporate Strategy, Organizations and Subjectivity: A Critique." *Organizational Studies* 12:251–273.

Palmer, D., R. Friedland, and J.V. Singh. 1986. "The Ties That Bind: Organizational and Class Bases of Stability in a Corporate Interlock Network." *American Sociological Review* 51:781–796.

Selznick, P. 1957. *Leadership in Administration.* New York: Harper and Row.

Spender, J.C. 1990. *Industry Recipes.* Oxford: Basil Blackwell.

Chapter 20. Resource Dependence Perspective

Donaldson, L. 2001. *The Contingency Theory of Organizations.* London: Sage.

Hall, R.H. 1996. *Organizations: Structures, Processes, and Outcomes.* 6th ed. Englewood Cliffs, NJ: Prentice Hall.

Jones, G.R. 1995. *Organizational Theory: Text and Cases.* Reading, MA: Addison Wesley.

Pfeffer, J. 1982. *Organizations and Organization Theory.* Chicago: Pitman.

Pfeffer, J., and G.R. Salancik. 1978. *The External Control of Organizations: A Resource Dependence Perspective.* Chicago: Harper and Row.

Chapter 21. Population Ecology Perspective

Baum, J. 1996. "Organizational Ecology." In *Handbook of Organization Studies,* ed. S. Clegg, C. Hardy, and W.R. Nord, 77–114. London: Sage.

Donaldson, L. 1995. *American Anti-management Theories of Organization: A Critique of Paradigm Proliferation.* Cambridge: Cambridge University Press.

Hannan, M.T., and J.H. Freeman. 1977. "The Population Ecology of Organizations." *American Journal of Sociology* 82:929–964.

———. 1984. "Structural Inertia and Organizational Change." *American Sociological Review* 49:149–164.

Jones, G.R. 1995. *Organizational Theory: Text and Cases.* Reading, MA: Addison Wesley.

Perrow, C. 1986. *Complex Organizations: A Critical Essay.* 3rd ed. New York: Random House.

Pfeffer, J. 1997. *New Directions for Organization Theory: Problems and Prospects.* New York: Oxford University Press.

Ulrich, D., and J.B. Barney. 1985. "Perspectives in Organizations: Resource Dependence, Efficiency, and Population." *Academy of Management Review*: 471–481.

Chapter 22. Institutional Perspective

Daft, R.L. 2001. *Organization Theory and Design.* 7th ed. Cincinnati, OH: South-Western College Publishing.

Dimaggio, P.J., and W.W. Powell. 1983. "The Iron Cage Revisited: Institutional Isomorphism and Collective Rationality in Organizational Fields." *American Sociological Review* 48:147–160.

Donaldson, L. 1995. *American Anti-management Theories of Organization: A Critique of Paradigm Proliferation.* Cambridge: Cambridge University Press.

Hinings, C.R., and R. Greenwood. 1988. *The Dynamics of Strategic Change.* New York: Basil Blackwell.

Nath, Raghu, and V.K. Narayanan. 1993. *Organization Theory: A Strategic Approach.* New York: Richard D. Irwin.

Oliver, C. 1991. "Strategic Responses to Institutional Processes." *Academy of Management Review* 16:145–176.

———. 1997. "Sustainable Competitive Advantage: Combining Institutional and Resource Based Views." *Strategic Management Journal* 18, no. 9: 699.

Pfeffer, J. 1997. *New Directions for Organization Theory: Problems and Prospects.* New York: Oxford University Press.

Robbins, S.R. 1990. *Organization Theory: Structure, Design and Applications.* 3rd ed. Englewood Cliffs, NJ: Prentice Hall.

Scott, W.R. 1987. "The Adolescence of Institutional Theory." *Administrative Science Quarterly* 32:498.

Suchman, M.C. 1995. "Managing Legitimacy: Strategic and Institutional Approaches." *Academy of Management Review* 20, no. 3: 571–610.

Tolbert P.S., and L.G. Zucker. 1996. "The Institutionalization of Institutional Theory." In *Handbook of Organization Studies,* ed. S. Clegg, C. Hardy, and W.R. Nord, 175–190. London: Sage.

Chapter 23. Chaos Perspective

Aihara, K., and R. Katayama. 1995. "Chaos Engineering in Japan." *Communications of the ACM* 38, no. 11: 103–107.

Bercquist, W. 1993. *The Post-modern Organization: Mastering the Art of Irreversible Change.* San Francisco: Jossey-Bass.

Browning, L., J. Beyer, and J.C. Shetler. 1995. "Building Cooperation in a Competitive Industry: SEMATECH and the Semiconductor Industry." *Academy of Management Journal* 38, no. 1: 113–151.

Caulkin, S. 1995. "Chaos Inc." *Across the Board* (July–August): 33–36.

"Chaos under a Cloud." 1996. *The Economist,* 13 January, 69–70.

Ditto, W., and T. Munakata. 1995. "Principles and Applications of Chaotic Systems." *Communications of the ACM* 38, no. 11: 96–102.

Levy, D. 1994. "Chaos Theory and Strategy." *Strategic Management Journal* 15:167–178.

Morgan, G. 1986. *Images of Organization.* Beverly Hills, CA: Sage.
Phelan, S.E. 1995. "From Chaos to Complexity in Strategic Planning." Paper presented to the fifty-fifth annual meeting of the Academy of Management, Vancouver, BC.
Prigogine, I., and I. Stengers. 1994. *Order out of Chaos.* New York: Bantam.
Thietart, R.A., and B. Forgues. 1995. "Chaos Theory and Organization." *Organization Science* 6:19–31.

Part III. Interpretive and Social Constructionist Perspectives

Burrell, G., and G. Morgan. 1979. *Sociological Paradigms and Organisational Analysis: Elements of the Sociology of Corporate Life.* London: Heinemann Educational.
Gioia, D.A., and E. Pitre. 1990. "Multiparadigm Perspectives on Theory Building." *Academy of Management Review* 15, no. 4: 588.

Chapter 24. Symbolic Interactionism Perspective

Berger, P. 1990. *The Sacred Canopy: Elements of a Sociological Theory of Religion.* New York: Anchor.
Berger, P.L., and T. Luckman. 1967. *The Social Construction of Reality.* New York: Anchor.
Daft, R., and K. Weick. 1984. "Towards a Model of Organizations as Interpretive Systems." *Academy of Management Review* 9:1–13.
Glaser, B.G., and A. Strauss. 1967. *The Discovery of Grounded Theory: Strategies for Qualitative Research.* Chicago: Aldine.
Pfeffer, J. 1977. "The Ambiguity of Leadership." *Academy of Management Review* 2:104–112.
Smircich, L., and C. Stubbart. 1985. "Strategic Environment in an Enacted World." *Academy of Management Review* 10:724–736.
Strauss, A.L. 1987. *Qualitative Analysis for Social Sciences.* Cambridge, U.K: Cambridge University Press.
Turner, S. 1986. *The Search for a Methodology of Social Science.* Boston: D. Reidel.

Chapter 25. Dramaturgical Perspective

Abercrombie, N., S. Hill, and B. Turner. 1984. *The Penguin Dictionary of Sociology.* London: Penguin.
Goffman, E. 1959. *The Presentation of Self in Everyday Life.* Garden City, NY: Doubleday.

Kondra, A.Z., and D.C. Hurst. 2003. "A Dramaturgical Perspective on Collective Bargaining Power: An Ethnographic Analysis." Unpublished manuscript, Athabasca University.
Pfeffer, J. 1982. *Organizations and Organization Theory.* Boston: Pitman.

Chapter 26. Metaphorical Perspective

Alvesson, M. 2002. *Understanding Organizational Culture.* London: Sage.
Boje, D. 1991. "The Storytelling Organization: A Study of Story Performance in an Office-Supply Company." *Administrative Science Quarterly* 36: 106–126.
———. 1995. "Stories of the Storytelling Organization: A Postmodern Analysis of Disney as 'Tamara-land.' " *Academy of Management Journal* 38, no. 4: 997–1035.
Burrell, G., and G. Morgan. 1979. *Sociological Paradigms and Organisational Analysis: Elements of the Sociology of Corporate Life.* London: Heinemann Educational.
Crafton, D. 1982. *Before Mickey: The Animated Film, 1898–1928.* Cambridge: MIT Press.
Eliot, M. 1993. *Walt Disney: Hollywood's Dark Prince.* New York: Birch Lane.
Ford, J., and L. Ford. 1995. "The Role of Conversation in Producing Intentional Change in Organizations." *Academy of Management Review* 20: 541–570.
Holliss, R., and B. Sibley. 1988. *The Disney Story.* London: Octopus.
Lackoff, G., and M. Johnson. 1980. *Metaphors We Live By.* Chicago: University of Chicago Press.
Miller, D. 1957. *Disney: The Story of Walt Disney (As Told to Pete Martin).* New York: Dell.
Morgan, G. 1980. "Paradigms, Metaphors and Puzzle Solving in Organizational Theory." *Administrative Science Quarterly* 25:605–622.
———. 1986. *Images of Organization.* Beverly Hills, CA: Sage.
———. 1993. *Imagavization: The Art of Creative Management.* Newbury Park, CA: Sage.
Palmer, I., and R. Dunford. 1996. "Conflicting Use of Metaphors: Reconceptualizing Their Use in the Field of Organizational Change." *Academy of Management Review* 21:691–717.
Pondy, L.R. 1983. "The Role of Metaphors and Myths in Organizations and in the Facilitation of Change." In *Organizational Symbolism,* ed. L.R. Pondy, P.J. Frost, G. Morgan, and T.D. Dandridge, 157–166. Greenwich, CT: JAI Press.
Putnam, L.L., N. Phillips, and P. Chapman. 1996. "Metaphors of Communi-

cation and Organization." In *Handbook of Organization Studies*, ed. S. Clegg, C. Hardy, and W.R. Nord, 375–409. London: Sage.

Thomas, B. 1967. *Walt Disney: An American Original*. New York: Bantam.

Trice, H.M., and J.M. Beyer. 1985. *Six Organizational Rites to Change Culture*. San Francisco: Jossey-Bass.

Chapter 27. Sensemaking Perspective

Calás, M.B., and L. Smircich. 1992. "Re-writing Gender into Organizational Theorizing: Directions from Feminist Perspectives." In *Rethinking Organization: New Directions in Organizational Theory and Analysis*, ed. M. Hughes, 227–254. London: Sage.

Colville, I. 1994. "Review Article: Searching for Karl Weick and Reviewing for the Future." *Organization* 1, no. 1: 218–224.

Colville, I.D., R.H. Waterman et al. 1999. "Organizing and the Search for Excellence: Making Sense of the Times in Theory and Practice." *Organization* 6, no. 1: 129–148.

Ferguson, K. 1994. "On Bringing More Theory, More Voices, and More Politics to the Study of Organization." *Organization* 1, no. 1: 81–99.

Gherardi, S. 1995. *Gender, Symbolism, and Organizational Culture*. London: Sage.

Helms Mills, J.C. 2000. "Making Sense of Organisational Change: A Strategic Use of Weick's Sensemaking Approach to a Case Study of Nova Scotia Power Inc., 1983–1999." *Behavior in Organisations*. Lancaster: University of Lancaster.

Helms Mills, J.C., and A.J. Mills. 2000a. "Rules, Sensemaking, Formative Contexts and Discourse in the Gendering of Organizational Culture." In *Handbook of Organizational Culture and Climate*, ed. M.F. Peterson, 55–70. Thousand Oaks, CA: Sage.

———. 2000b. "Sensemaking and the Gendering of Organizational Culture." In the *Proceedings of the ASAC-IFSAM 2000 Conference*. Montreal.

Laporte, T.R., and P. Consolini. 1991 "Working in Practice But Not in Theory: Theoretical Challenges of High Reliability Organizations." *Journal of Public Administration Research and Theory* 1:19–47.

Nord, W., and S. Fox. 1996. "The Individual in Organizational Studies: The Great Disappearing Act?" In *Handbook of Organizational Studies*, ed. C. Hardy, 148–175. Thousand Oaks, CA: Sage.

Reed, M. 1992. *The Sociology of Organizations: Themes, Perspectives and Prospects*. London: Harvester Wheatsheaf.

Rochlin, G.I., T.R. Laporte, and K.H. Roberts. 1987. "The Self-Designing High Reliability Organization: Aircraft Carrier Flight Operations at Sea." *Naval War College Review* 40, no. 4: 76–90.

Weick, K. 1990. "The Vulnerable System: An Analysis of the Tenerife Air Disaster." *Journal of Management* 16, no. 3: 571–593.

———. 1995. *Sensemaking in Organizations.* London: Sage.

———. 1996. "Drop Your Tools: An Allegory for Organizational Study." *Administrative Science Quarterly* 41:301–313.

Weick, K., and K.H. Roberts. 2001. "Collective Mind in Organizations: Heedful Interrelating on Flight Decks." In *Making Sense of the Organization,* ed. K. Weick, 259–283. Oxford: Blackwell Business.

Chapter 28. Organizational Rules Perspective

Clegg, S., and D. Dunkerley. 1980. *Organization, Class and Control.* London: Routledge and Kegan Paul.

Eldridge, J.E.T., and A.D. Crombie. 1974. *The Sociology of Organisations.* London: Allen and Unwin.

Helms Mills, J.C. 2002. "Employment Practices and the Gendering of Air Canada's Culture during Its Trans-Canada Airlines Days." *Culture and Organization* 8, no. 2: 65.

Helms Mills, J.C., and A.J. Mills. 2000. "Rules, Sensemaking, Formative Contexts and Discourse in the Gendering of Organizational Culture." In *Handbook of Organizational Climate and Culture,* ed. N. Ashkanasy, C. Wilderom, and M. Peterson, 55–70. Thousand Oaks, CA: Sage.

Mills, A.J. 1992. "Organization, Gender and Culture." In *Gendering Organizational Analysis,* ed. A.J. Mills and P. Tancred, 93–111. Newbury Park, CA: Sage.

———. 1997. "Duelling Discourses—Desexulization versus Eroticism in the Corporate Framing of Female Sexuality in the British Airline Industry, 1945–60." In *Managing the Organizational Melting Pot: Dilemmas of Workplace Diversity,* ed. P. Prasad, A.J. Mills, M. Elmes, and A. Prasad, 171–198. Newbury Park, CA: Sage.

Mills, A.J., and S.J. Murgatroyd. 1991. *Organizational Rules: A Framework for Understanding Organizations.* Milton Keynes: Open University Press.

Reed, M. 1992. *The Sociology of Organizations: Themes, Perspectives and Prospects.* London: Harvester Wheatsheaf.

Chapter 29. Culture Perspective

Alvesson, M. 2002. *Understanding Organizational Culture.* London: Sage.

Ashkanasy, N., C. Wilderom, and M. Peterson. 2000. Introduction to *Handbook of Organizational Culture and Climate,* ed. N. Ashkanasy, C. Wilderom, and M. Peterson, 1–18. Thousand Oaks, CA: Sage.

Barney, J. 1996. "Organizational Culture: Can It Be a Source of Competitive Advantage?" *Academy of Management Review* 11, no. 3: 656–665.

Beam, H.B. 1999. "Book Review—The Character of a Corporation: How Your Company's Culture Can Make or Break Your Business." *Academy of Management Executive* (February): 119–120.

Burns, B. 2000. *Managing Change: A Strategic Approach to Organizational Dynamics.* 3rd ed. Harlow, UK: Pearson Education.

Denison, D. 1990. *Corporate Culture and Organizational Effectiveness.* New York: John Wiley.

Feldman, M. 1991. "The Meanings of Ambiguity: Learning from Stories and Metaphors." In *Reframing Organizational Culture,* ed. P. Frost, L. Moore, M. Louis, C. Lundberg, and J. Martin, 145–156. Newbury Park, CA: Sage.

Goffee, R., and G. Jones. 1996. "What Holds the Modern Company Together." *Harvard Business Review* (November–December): 133–148.

Handy, C. 1989. *The Age of Unreason.* London: Arrow.

Helms Mills, J.C. 2002. "Employment Practices and the Gendering of Air Canada's Culture during Its Trans-Canada Airlines Days." *Culture and Organization* 8, no. 2: 117–128.

Martin, J. 2001. *Organizational Culture: Mapping the Terrain.* Newbury Park, CA: Sage.

Martin, J., and P. Frost. 1996. "The Organizational Culture War Games: A Struggle for Intellectual Dominance." In *Handbook of Organizational Studies,* ed. S.R. Clegg, C. Hardy, and W.R. Nord, 599–621. London: Sage.

Meek, V.L. 1988. "Organizational Culture: Origins and Weaknesses." *Organization Studies* 9, no. 4: 453–473.

Meyerson, D. 1991. "Acknowledging and Uncovering Ambiguities in Cultures." In *Reframing Organizational Culture,* ed. P. Frost, L. Moore, M. Louis, C. Lundberg, and J. Martin, 254–270. Newbury Park, CA: Sage.

Mills, A.J., and S.J. Murgatroyd. 1991. *Organizational Rules: A Framework for Understanding Organizations.* Milton Keynes: Open University Press.

Morgan, G. 1993. *Imaginization: The Art of Creative Management.* Newbury Park, CA: Sage.

Pettigrew, A.M. 2000. Foreword to *Handbook of Organizational Culture and Climate,* ed. N. Ashkanasy, C. Wilderom, and M. Peterson, xiii–xv. Thousand Oaks, CA: Sage.

Sathe, V. 1985. *Culture and Related Corporate Realities: Text, Cases and Readings on Organizational Entry, Establishment, and Change.* Homewood, IL: Irwin.

Schein, E. 1985. *Organizational Culture and Leadership.* San Francisco: Jossey Bass.

————. 2000. "Sense and Nonsense about Organizational Culture and Climate." In *Handbook of Organizational Culture and Climate,* ed. N. Ashkanasy, C. Wilderom, and M. Peterson, xxiii–xxx. Thousand Oaks, CA: Sage.

Siehl, C., and J. Martin. 1982. "Learning Organizational Culture." Research Paper No. 654. Graduate School of Business, Stanford University.

Smircich, L. 1983. "Concepts of Culture and Organizational Analysis." *Administrative Science Quarterly* 28:339–358.

Wilderon, C.P.M., U. Glunk, and R. Maslowski. 2000. "Organizational Culture as a Predictor of Performance." In *Handbook of Organizational Culture and Climate,* ed. N. Ashkanasy, C. Wilderom, and M. Peterson, 193–209. Thousand Oaks, CA: Sage.

Wilmott, H. 1993. "Strength Is Ignorance; Slavery Is Freedom: Managing Culture in Modern Organizations." *Journal of Management Studies* 30: 515–552.

————. 2001. "Strength Is Ignorance; Slavery Is Freedom: Managing Culture in Modern Organizations." In *Organization Studies: Critical Perspectives on Business and Management,* ed. Warwick Organizational Behavior Staff, 386–426. London: Routledge.

Part IV. Radical Humanist and Structuralist Perspectives

Burrell, G., and G. Morgan. 1979. *Sociological Paradigms and Organisational Analysis: Elements of the Sociology of Corporate Life.* London: Heinemann Educational.

Gioia, E., and D.A. Pitre. 1990. "Multiparadigm Perspectives on Theory Building." *Academy of Management Review* 15, no. 4: 588–589.

Chapter 30. Configuration Perspective

Abercrombie, N., S. Hill, and B. Turner. 1984. *The Penguin Dictionary of Sociology.* London: Penguin.

Donaldson, L. 2001. *The Contingency Theory of Organizations.* London: Sage.

Giddens, G. 1979. *Central Problems in Social Theory.* London: Macmillan.

Hannan, M.T., and J.H. Freeman. 1977. "The Population Ecology of Organizations." *American Journal of Sociology* 82:929–964.

Hinings, C.R., and R. Greenwood. 1988a. *The Dynamics of Strategic Change.* New York: Basil Blackwell.

———. 1988b. "The Normative Prescription of Organizations." In *Institutional Patterns and Organization,* ed. L. Zucker, 53–70. Chicago: Ballinger.

Meyer, A.D., A.S. Tsui, and C.R. Hinings. 1993. "Configurational Approaches to Organizational Analysis." *Academy of Management Journal* 36, no. 6: 1175–1195.

Miles, R.E., and C.C. Snow. 1978. *Organizational Strategy, Structure and Process.* New York: McGraw Hill.

Miller D. 1986. "Configurations of Strategy and Structure: Towards a Synthesis." *Strategic Management Journal* 7:233–249.

———. 1990. *The Icarus Paradox.* New York: HarperCollins.

Miller, D., and P.H. Friesen. 1978. "Archetypes of Strategy Formulation." *Management Science* 24:921–933.

Mintzberg, H. 1979. *The Structuring of Organizations.* Englewood Cliffs, NJ: Prentice Hall.

Pettigrew, A.M., and E.M. Fenton. 2000. *The Innovating Organization.* London: Sage.

Ranson, S., C.R. Hinings, and R. Greenwood. 1980. "The Structuring of Organizational Structures." *Administrative Science Quarterly* 25:1–17.

Chapter 31. Postmodern Perspective

Adams, M. 1997. *Sex in the Snow: Canadian Social Values and the End of the Millennium.* Toronto, ON: Penguin.

Alvesson, M. 1995. "The Meaning and Meaningless of Postmodernism: Some Ironic Remarks." *Organization Studies* 22, no. 1: 1–24.

Alvesson, M., and S. Deetz. 1996. "Critical Theory and Post-modern Approaches to Organizational Studies." In *Handbook of Organization Studies,* ed. S. Clegg, C. Hardy, and W.R. Nord, 191–217. London: Sage.

Anderson, W.T. 1995. "Postmodernism, Pluralism and the Crisis of Legitimacy." In *Changing Maps: Governing in a World of Rapid Change,* ed. S. Rosell, 8. Ottawa, ON: Carleton University Press.

Bergquist, W. 1993. *The Post-modern Organization: Mastering the Art of Irreversible Change.* San Francisco: Jossey-Bass.

Burns, T., and G.M. Stalker. 1961. *The Management of Innovation.* London: Tavistock.

Burrell, G. 1988. "Modernism, Postmodernism and Organizational Analysis 2: The Contribution of Michel Foucault." *Organization Studies* 92:221–335.

Burrell, G., and G. Morgan. 1979. *Sociological Paradigms and Organisational Analysis: Elements of the Sociology of Corporate Life.* London: Heinemann Educational.

Clegg, S. 1990. *Modern Organizations.* London: Sage.

———. 1992. "Postmodern Management." *Journal of Organizational Change Management* 52:31–49.

Cooper, R. 1988. "Modernism, Postmodernism and Organizational Analysis 3: The Contribution of Jacques Derrida." *Organization Studies* 91:479–502.

Cooper, R., and G. Burrell, 1988. "Modernism, Postmodernism and Organizational Analysis: An Introduction." *Organization Studies* 91:91–112.

Derrida, J. 1973. *Speech and Phenomena.* Evanston, IL: Northwestern University Press.

Feyeraband, P. 1975. *Against Method.* London: New Left.

Gergen, K.J. 1991. "Organization Theory in the Postmodern Era." In *New Directions in Organization Theory and Analysis,* ed. M. Reed, 266–275. London: Sage.

Lyotard, J.F. 1984. *The Post-modern Condition: A Report on Knowledge.* Minneapolis: University of Minnesota Press.

Marsden, R., and B. Townley. 1996. "The Owl of Minerva: Reflections on Theory in Practice." In *Handbook of Organization Studies,* ed. S. Clegg, C. Hardy, and W.R. Nord, 659–675. London: Sage.

Montagna, P. 1992. "Post-modernism and the Management of Large Professional Service Firms." Paper presented at the Conference on Professional Service Firms, University of Alberta, Edmonton, AB, Canada.

Parker, M. 1992. "Post-modern Organization or Post-modern Organization Theory." *Organization Studies* 13, no. 1: 1–17.

Townley, B. 1993. "Foucault, Power/Knowledge, and Its Relevance for Human Resource Management." *Academy of Management Review* 18:518–545.

Chapter 32. Critical Theory Perspective

Abercrombie, N., S. Hill, and B.S. Turner. 1988. *The Penguin Dictionary of Sociology.* London: Penguin.

Alvesson, M. 1985. "A Critical Framework of Organizational Studies." *Organizational Studies* 6, no. 2: 117–138.

Alvesson, M., and S. Deetz. 1996. "Critical Theory and Post-modern Approaches to Organizational Studies." In *Handbook of Organization Studies,* ed. S. Clegg, C. Hardy, and W.R. Nord, 191–217. London: Sage.

Grimes, A.J. 1982. "Critical Theory and Organizational Sciences: A Primer." *Journal of Organizational Change Management* 5, no. 1: 26–30.

Pfeffer, J. 1997. *New Directions for Organization Theory: Problems and Prospects.* New York: Oxford University Press.

Saul, J.R. 1994. *The Doubter's Companion: A Dictionary of Aggressive Common Sense.* Toronto, ON: Viking Penguin.

Chapter 33. Marxist Perspective

Aronowitz, S. 1973. *False Promises: The Shaping of American Working Class Consciousness.* New York: McGraw Hill.
Attewell, P. 1987. "The Deskilling Controversy." *Work and Occupations* 14: 323–346.
Buss, T.F. 1993. "Marxism Is Wrong and Thankfully Dead." *Academy of Management Review* 18, no. 1: 10–11.
Edwards, R. 1979. *Contested Terrain: The Transformation of the Workplace in the Twentieth Century.* London: Heinemann.
Elster, J. 1985. *Making Sense of Marx.* Cambridge: Cambridge University Press.
Gioia, E., and D.A. Pitre. 1990. "Multiparadigm Perspectives on Theory Building." *Academy of Management Review* 15, no. 4: 588–589.
Hall, R.H. 1996. *Organizations: Structures, Processes, and Outcomes.* 6th ed. Englewood Cliffs, NJ: Prentice Hall.
Marx, K. 1859. *Contribution to a Critique of Political Economy.* New York: Signet.
Pfeffer, J. 1982. *Organizations and Organization Theory.* Chicago: Pitman.

Chapter 34. Poststructuralist Feminism Perspective

Calás, M., and L. Smircich. 1990. "Rewriting Gender in Organizational Theorizing: Directions from Feminist Perspectives." In *Re-thinking Organization: New Directions in Organizational Research and Analysis,* ed. M.D. Hughes, 227–253. London: Sage.
———. 1992. "Using the F Word: Feminist Theories and the Social Consequences of Organizational Research." In *Gendering Organizational Analysis,* ed. A.J. Mills and P. Tancred, 222–234. Newbury Park, CA: Sage.
———. 1996. "From the Woman's Point of View: Feminist Approaches to Organization Studies." In *Handbook of Organization Studies,* ed. S. Clegg, C. Hardy, and W.R. Nord, 218–257. London: Sage.
Jaggar, A. 1988. *Feminist Politics and Human Nature.* Sussex: Rowman and Allanheld.
Mills, A.J., and S.J. Murgatroyd. 1991. *Organizational Rules: A Framework for Understanding Organizations.* Milton Keynes: Open University Press.
Mills, A.J., and P. Tancred. 1992. *Gendering Organizational Analysis.* Newbury Park, CA: Sage.

Weedon, C. 1987. *Feminist Practice and Poststructuralist Theory.* Cambridge, MA: Blackwell.

Conclusion

Burrell, G., and G. Morgan. 1979. *Sociological Paradigms and Organisational Analysis: Elements of the Sociology of Corporate Life.* London: Heinemann Educational.

Drucker P. 1997. "Introduction: Toward the New Organization." In *The Organization of the Future,* ed. F. Hesselbein, M. Goldsmith, and R. Beckhardt, 1–8. San Francisco: Jossey-Bass.

Gioia, E., and D.A. Pitre. 1990. "Multiparadigm Perspectives on Theory Building." *Academy of Management Review* 15, no. 4: 588–589.

Recommended Readings

Aldrich, H. 1979. *Organizations and Environments.* Englewood Cliffs, NJ: Prentice Hall.

Alvesson, M., and P.O. Berg. 1992. *Corporate Culture and Organizational Symbolism.* Berlin: de Gruyter.

Ansoff, H.I. 1984. *Implanting Strategic Management.* Englewood Cliffs, NJ: Prentice Hall.

Ashkenas, R., D. Ulrich, T. Jick, and S. Kerr. 1995. *The Boundaryless Organization: Breaking the Chains of Organizational Structure.* San Francisco: Jossey-Bass.

Axelrod, R. 1987. *The Evolution of Cooperation.* New York: Penguin.

Bacharach, S.B. 1989. "Organizational Theories: Some Criteria for Evaluation." *Academy of Management Review* 14, no. 4: 496–515.

Becker, G.S. 1964. *Human Capital.* New York: Columbia University Press.

Calof, J. 1997. "For King and Country and Company." *Business Quarterly* (Spring): 32–37.

Campbell, A., M. Goold, and M. Alexander. 1995. "The Value of the Parent Company." *California Management Review* 38, no. 1: 79–97.

Caves, R. 1982. *Economic Analysis and Multinational Enterprises.* Cambridge: Cambridge University Press.

Clegg, S. 1975. *Power, Rule and Domination.* London: Routledge and Kegan Paul.

Collis, D.J., and C. Montgomery. 1995. "Competing on Resources: Strategy in the 1990's." *Harvard Business Review* (July–August): 118–128.

Commons, J.R. 1950. *The Economics of Collective Action.* New York: Macmillan.

Copeland, T., T. Koller, and J. Murrin. 1990. *Valuation: Measuring and Managing the Value of Companies.* New York: Wiley.

Day, G.S., and D. Reibstein. 1997. *Wharton on Dynamic Competitive Strategy.* New York: Wiley.

Day, G.S., and P. Shoemaker. 2000. *Wharton on Managing Emerging Technologies.* New York: Wiley.

Doty, D.H., W.H. Glick, and G.P. Huber. 1993. "Fit, Equifinality, and Organizational Effectiveness: A Test of Two Configurational Theories." *Academy of Management Journal* 36, no. 6: 1196–1250.

Dunphy, D., and D. Stace. 1994. *Beyond the Boundaries.* Sydney: Wiley.

Euske E.J., and R.S. Player. 1996. "Leveraging Management Improvement Techniques." *Sloan Management Review* (Fall): 69–79.

Fahey, L. 1999. *Competitors.* New York: Wiley.

Fleisher, C.S., and B.E. Bensoussan. 2002. *Strategic and Competitive Analysis.* Upper Saddle River, NJ: Prentice Hall.

Fleisher, C.S., and D.L. Blenkhorn. 2001. *Managing Frontiers in Competitive Intelligence.* Westport, CT: Quorum.

Foucault, M. 1980. *Power/Knowledge.* New York: Pantheon.

Ghemawat, P. 1999. *Strategy and the Business Landscape.* Cambridge, MA: Harvard Business School Publishing.

Ghoshal, S., and C. Bartlett. 1996. "Rebuilding Behavioral Context." *Sloan Management Review* (Winter): 23–36.

Goffee, R., and G. Jones. 1996. "What Holds the Modern Company Together." *Harvard Business Review* (November–December): 133–148.

Grant, R.M. 1991. "The Resource Based Theory of Competitive Advantage." *California Management Review* (Spring): 114–135.

Greenwood, R., C.R. Hinings, and J. Brown. 1990. "The P2 Form of Strategic Management." *Academy of Management Journal* 33, no. 4: 725–755.

Gulati, R. 1995. "Does Familiarity Breed Trust? The Implications of Repeated Ties for Contractual Choice in Alliances." *Academy of Management Journal* 38, no. 2: 85–105.

Hardy, C. 1990. *Retrenchment and Turnaround.* Berlin: de Gruyter.

Harmon, H.H. 1967. *Modern Factor Analysis.* Chicago: University of Chicago Press.

Harrigan, K.R. 1985. *Strategies for Joint Ventures.* Lexington, MA: D.C. Heath.

———. 1988. "Strategic Alliances and Partner Asymmetries." In *Cooperative Strategies in International Business,* ed. F.J. Contractor and P. Lorange. Lexington, MA: Lexington.

Hinings, C.R., and R. Greenwood. 1988. *The Dynamics of Strategic Change.* London: Basil Blackwell.

Jarillo, J.C. 1988. "On Strategic Networks." *Strategic Management Journal* 9, no. 31: 31–41.

Jemison, D.B., and S.B. Sitkin. 1986. "Corporate Acquisitions: A Process Perspective." *Academy of Management Review* 11, no. 1: 145–163.

Kogut, B. 1988. "Joint Ventures: Theoretical and Empirical Perspectives." *Strategic Management Journal* 9: 319–332.

Lorange, P., and J. Roos. 1992. *Strategic Alliances: Formation, Implementation and Evolution.* Cambridge, MA: Blackwell.

Lynch, R.P. 1990. *The Practical Guide to Joint Ventures and Corporate Alliances.* New York: Wiley.

Macaulay, S. 1963. "Non-contractual Relations in Business: A Preliminary Study." *American Sociological Review* 28:55–67.

March, J.G., and H.A. Simon. 1958. *Organizations*. New York: Wiley.

McGonagle, J.J., and C.M. Vella. 1998. *Protecting Your Company against Competitive Intelligence*. Westport, CT: Quorum.

Miles, R.E., H. Coleman Jr., and D. Creed. 1995. "Keys to Success in Corporate Redesign." *California Management Review* (Spring): 128–145.

Miles, R.E., and C.C. Snow. 1986. "Organizations: New Concepts for New Forms." *California Management Review* 34, no. 4: 62–73.

———. 1992. "Causes of Failure in Network Organization." *California Management Review:* 53–72.

Miller, D. 1990. *The Icarus Paradox: How Exceptional Companies Bring about Their Own Downfall*. New York: HarperCollins.

Miller, D., and P.H. Friesen. 1984. *Organizations: A Quantum View*. Englewood Cliffs, NJ: Prentice Hall.

Mintzberg, H. 1998. *Strategy Safari: A Guided Tour through the Wilds of Strategic Management*. New York: Free Press.

Morgan, G. 1986. *Images of Organizations*. Los Angeles: Sage.

Noordhaven, N.G. 1992. "The Problem of Contract Enforcement in Economic Organization Theory." *Organization Studies* 13, no. 2: 229–243.

Nystrom, P.C., and W.H. Starbuck. 1984. "To Avoid Crises, Unlearn." *Organizational Dynamics* 12, no. 4: 53–65.

Pant, P.N., and W.H. Starbuck. 1990. "Innocents in the Forest: Forecasting and Research Methods." *Journal of Management* 16, no 2: 433–460.

Parkhe, A. 1993. "Strategic Alliance Structuring: A Game Theoretic and Transaction Cost Examination of Interfirm Cooperation." *Academy of Management Journal* 36, no. 4: 794–829.

Pearson, C., and I. Mitroff. 1993. "From Crisis Prone to Crisis Prepared: A Framework for Crisis Management." *Academy of Management Executive* 7, no. 1: 48–59.

Perrow, C. 1986. *Complex Organizations: A Critical Essay*. 3rd ed. New York: Random House.

Pettigrew, A.M. 1990. "Longitudinal Field Research on Change: Theory and Practice." *Organizational Science* 1, no. 3: 267–292.

Porter, M.E. 1987. "From Competitive Advantage to Corporate Strategy." *Harvard Business Review* (May–June): 43–59.

———. 1993. "How Competitive Forces Shape Strategy." *Harvard Business Review* (March–April): 137–145.

———. 2001. "Strategy and the Internet." *Harvard Business Review* (March): 63–78.

Powell, W. 1987. "Hybrid Organizational Arrangements: New Forms or Transitional Development." *California Management Review:* 67–87.

———. 1990. "Neither Market nor Hierarchy: Network Forms of Organization." *Research in Organizational Behavior* 12:295–336.

Prahalad, C.K., and G. Hamel. 1990. "The Core Competence of the Corporation." *Harvard Business Review* (May–June): 80–91.

Rousseau, D.M., and J.M. Parks. 1993. "The Contracts of Individuals and Organizations." *Research in Organizational Behavior* 15:1–43.

Saul, J.R. 1994. *The Doubter's Companion. A Dictionary of Aggressive Common Sense.* Toronto, ON: Viking Penguin.

Scherer, F.M. 1980. *Industrial Market Structure and Economic Performance.* Chicago: Rand McNally.

Shoemaker, P. 1995. "Scenario Planning: A Tool for Strategic Thinking." *Sloan Management Review* (Winter): 25–40.

Simon, H.A. 1961. *The New Science of Management Decision.* New York: Harper.

Sitkin, S.B., and A.L. Pablo. 1992. "Reconceptualizing the Determinants of Risk Behavior." *Academy of Management Review* 17, no. 1: 9–38.

Stinchcombe, A.L. 1990. *Information and Organization.* Berkeley: University of California Press.

Stopford, J.M., and L.T. Wells. 1972. *Managing the Multinational Enterprise.* New York: Basic.

Thompson, J.D. 1967. *Organizations in Action.* New York: McGraw Hill.

Tomer, J.F. 1987. *Organizational Capital: The Path to Higher Productivity and Well-Being.* New York: Praeger.

Ulrich, D., and D. Lake. 1990. *Organizational Capability: Competing from the Inside Out.* Toronto, ON: Wiley.

Vibert, C. 2000. *Web-Based Analysis for Competitive Intelligence.* Westport, CT: Quorum.

Weick, K. 1989. "Theory Construction as Discipline Imagination." *Academy of Management Review* 14, no. 4: 516–531.

About the Author and Contributors

About the Principal Author

Conor Vibert, Ph.D., is an associate professor of business strategy at the Fred C. Manning School of Business of Acadia University in Wolf-ville, Nova Scotia, and the author of *Web-Based Analysis for Competitive Intelligence* (2000). At Acadia University, Vibert teaches business strategy and organization theory, while his current research interests focus on the management of higher risk alliance partners and the application of the Internet to contemporary business issues.

About the Contributors

Gregory R. Berry, Ph.D., is an associate professor of management at Texas Wesleyan University in Fort Worth, Texas. He teaches policy, business and society, and strategy courses to both undergraduate and graduate students. His ongoing and funded research is focused on the environmental behavior of chemical firms.

Deborah Hurst, Ph.D., is an associate professor of organizational studies with the Centre for Innovative Management of Athabasca University in Alberta, Canada. Her area of specialization is located within the study of cultural organization change with an interest in knowledge work and development of intellectual capital through ongoing competency development and virtual learning.

Albert J. Mills, Ph.D., is a professor of management at Saint Mary's University, Halifax, Nova Scotia. His research centers on the impact of organizational realities on people, in particular the problem of sex discrimination and employment equity. Much of his research has been devoted to identifying how workplace discrimination develops, is maintained, and can be changed and eradicated.

Jean Helms Mills, Ph.D., is an assistant professor of organizational behavior at Acadia University in Nova Scotia, Canada. Seventeen years with the airline industry has instilled in her the need to make sense of the culture of organizations. Her most recent works include a chapter on rules, sensemaking, and formative contexts in the gendering of organization culture in *The Handbook of Organizational Culture and Climate* (2000).

Index

Vibert, Conor,
Theories of
macro-organizaitonal
behavior : A handbook
of ideas and
explanations

DATE DUE

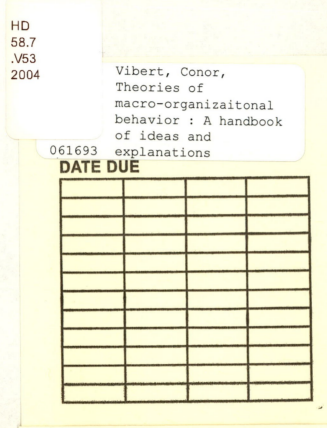